The Most Amazing American:
BENJAMIN FRANKLIN

1706 BENJAMIN FRANKLIN 1790

Mural by Thornton Oakley, in the Lecture Hall of the Franklin Institute, Philadelphia.

2

Colonial Philadelphia, pictured by Norman Rockwell,
was America's busiest and most exciting city during Benjamin Franklin's
residence there. *(Collection of Mrs. Victor H. Neirinck.)*

ERIPUIT CŒLO FULMEN SCEPTRUM QUE TIRANNIS

Au GÉNIE De FRANKLIN

*To the Genius of Franklin, 1778, etching by Honoré Fragonard.
(Philadelphia Museum of Art, gift of Mrs. John D. Rockfeller.)*

The Most
AMAZING AMERICAN
BENJAMIN FRANKLIN

BY THE EDITORS OF COUNTRY BEAUTIFUL

Publisher and Editorial Director: Michael P. Dineen
Executive Editor: Robert L. Polley
Edited by D'Arlyn Marks
Art Direction: Buford Nixon

Country Beautiful

Waukesha, Wisconsin

COUNTRY BEAUTIFUL: *Publisher and Editorial Director:* Michael P. Dineen; *Executive Editor:* Robert L. Polley; *Senior Editors:* Kenneth L. Schmitz, James H. Robb; *Art Director:* Buford Nixon; *Associate Editors:* D'Arlyn Marks, John M. Nuhn; *Editorial Assistants:* Kay Kundinger, Nancy Backes; *Production Manager:* Donna Griesemer; *Editorial Secretary:* Jane Boyd; *Art Assistant:* Tom McCann; *Administration:* Brett E. Gries; *Staff:* Bruce Schneider.

Country Beautiful Corporation is a wholly owned subsidiary of Flick-Reedy Corporation: *President:* Frank Flick; *Vice President and General Manager:* Michael P. Dineen; *Treasurer and Secretary:* August Caamano.

The Franklin text for this book has been excerpted from *The Life and Writings of Benjamin Franklin,* edited by Albert Henry Smyth. Textual reproduction follows the Smyth edition, and spelling, capitalization and punctuation have been unaltered except where the original word might be misunderstood.
"Letter to Mary Stevenson," from volume 15 of *The Papers of Benjamin Franklin,* William B. Willcox, editor, © 1972 by the American Philosophical Society and by Yale University Press. Reprinted by permission of the publishers.

The illustrations painted by Norman Rockwell for *Poor Richard's Almanacks* are copyright © 1964 by The George Macy Companies, Inc.; they are used here by permission of The Heritage Club, Avon, Connecticut.

Introduction 8

CONTENTS

I   Education of a Printer 10

II   Philadelphia Success Story 30

III   America's Foremost Inventor 62

IV   Citizen and Advocate 86

V   Ambassador in Paris
       and Elder Statesman at Home 106

VI   Philosopher, Friend and Humorist 134

Epilogue 154

Chronology 158

(Walters Art Gallery.)

Honoré Balzac, the great nineteenth-century French novelist, epitomized Benjamin Franklin's genius in the epigram: "The hoax is a discovery by Franklin, who invented the lighting rod, the hoax and the republic!" Perhaps his inherent, humorous disposition has been the outstanding legacy for which we know Franklin. As his biographer Carl Van Doren claims, "... wit and grace met in him as if nature had been lavish and happy when he was shaped." Franklin himself felt that "bad humor is an uncleanliness of the soul." Easy-going temperament — a grand spirit of humor — is at the heart of all Franklin's successes as scientist, statesman and writer. He was capable of harmonizing the diverse events of his life to live quite free of discontent, envy or conceit. His contemporaries called this essential quality a philosophic mind. We call this ability taking things in stride. Franklin himself attributed his happiness to the blessings of Divine Providence. Thus endowed, he moved from obscurity to great renown (and accompanying criticism) without losing sight of himself as he had begun — simply Benjamin Franklin, printer.

At an early age Franklin found that a contentious attitude was worthless; only ignorant people resorted to it. He taught himself to write with strength and clarity and considered this ability as a principle means by which he advanced in life. At sixteen years he put his native wit to public use in letters to the editor of the *New England Courant*. His tongue-in-cheek letters

INTRODUCTION

from Silence Dogood, first of many pen names, gained him the respect of Boston's radicals who contributed to the *Courant*. When he was twenty-three, Franklin started his climb to popularity with his *Pennsylvania Gazette*. The paper achieved wide readership principally from the clever news stories, gentle satires and dialogues which filled its pages. His writing was always to a purpose—not the least of which was to entertain, but also to instruct and influence conduct. Franklin's unquenchable wit was two-fold good medicine: well-taken lessons for readers of his *Gazette* and *Poor Richard's Almanack* and much-appreciated income for his pocket.

His experiments in electricity and invention of the lightning rod (1752) were the accomplishments that first drew international attention to Franklin. European scientists considered Franklin the world's expert in this field. Franklin's contribution was scores of original experiments and observations, though he did not have the inclination to coordinate data into wider theory. The practical side of his genius was the first great manifestation of what was to become one of the continuing strengths of this nation. It lead to and was in many ways the model for America's impressive list of firsts — from the telegraph to the phonograph to the landing on the moon — in the fields of applied science and technology.

The wizard of electricity followed this fame with wider popularity for his *Way to Wealth* (1758), a compendium of sayings from *Poor Richard's Almanack* that are the most memorable expressions of the work-and-save ethic that helped build this nation and are now part of common speech: "Early to bed and early to rise, makes a man healthy, wealthy and wise," and if you would be wealthy, "Keep thy shop and thy shop will keep thee," and, "Wish not so much to live long, as to live well," to recall just a few.

Benjamin Franklin was the first American to go beyond national boundaries in the impact of his writing and also in his scientific and political pursuits. His fame as the best-known man in colonial America is unquestionable, and it would be correct to say he was one of the best known people in the eighteenth-century world.

During the long years as Pennsylvania assemblyman and years of negotiations in London (1757-75) and virtually running the U.S. embassy in Paris (1777-85), Franklin, the amiable country sage, was discovered to be a shrewd and bold diplomat. Franklin mixed politics with fearless humor by means of satire.

In London, before the American Revolution, he lobbied for American commercial and civil rights. The political essays written in defense of the colonies contain some of his sharpest wit and are quite bold in criticizing what he saw as injustice or pettiness of the King or Parliament. We are indebted to Franklin for his daring humor used in support of America.

Of Franklin's many gifts, his genius as a calm,
knowledgeable elder statesman greatly benefitted the young nation.
In this Currier and Ives print, 1876, he stands with the drafters
of the Declaration of Independence (left to right):
Thomas Jefferson, Roger Sherman, Franklin,
Robert R. Livingston and John Adams.
(Library of Congress.)

Though discontent and revolt in the 1770's seemed inevitable, Franklin did
much in writing and in person to maintain congenial ties with sympathetic
Englishmen. Accumulation of untreated grievances radicalized him by 1775,
and, back in America, he was a militant supporter of revolution. For his
work in Paris which followed, he is given principal credit for securing
money and supplies, without which the Revolution's success is doubtful.

The wizard-sage-diplomat gained lasting literary fame for his lively
Autobiography of life from poverty to splendor, circulated and translated
soon after he died in 1790. Franklin's life story has world-wide appeal and
now has been translated into all European languages. It is one of the first
literary masterpieces to come from America. This robust but carefully
chosen language set an early high standard for prose writers, though
Franklin's purpose was to influence conduct rather than literary style. In
sum, as America's first cosmopolitan, he symbolized the ideal of the new
concept in government — republicanism. Franklin's personal attributes —
grand serenity, humor and generosity, ingenuity and bold ambition —
perhaps became the characteristics that both Europeans and Americans
themselves hoped to find in the new nation.

A good example is the best sermon, as Poor Richard says. The best
sermon on Franklin's genius is his own writing. This anthology of his
writings is offered as an introduction to America's most agreeable genius.
The biography of his life that emerges from the following excerpts of
Franklin's writings may be astonishing when one considers the multitude of
enterprises Franklin engaged in. The most amazing thing is that Franklin the
man transcended them all. His genius lies in his happy balance of talents.

The childhood and early years of Benjamin Franklin are better known to readers around the world than the young life of any other of our Founding Fathers. Mark Twain complained that Franklin's example of early and sober industry has been a burden to altogether too many young boys in America. On the other hand, Franklin's early religious and sexual *errata* (as he called them) have been denounced as too tarnished a picture to pass for a good example. Whatever the judgments, everyone has heard that Franklin grew up as poor as a Boston church mouse, ran off to Philadelphia at seventeen with no more than a Dutch dollar in his pocket, soon became one of that city's leading businessmen and scientists, and remained at the center of social and political affairs in America for three-quarters of a century.

We know so much about Franklin from his *Autobiography*, the most famous work of its kind in the English language. Franklin first set out to record his life in 1771, while resting at the English country estate in Hampshire of his friend, Jonathan Shipley, Bishop of Asaph. Here he wrote his history from 1706 to 1730 in the form of a letter to his son, William Franklin. The excerpts in this chapter come from this section of the *Autobiography*, which was continued with sections written at three later times, relating his life through 1757.

I EDUCATION OF A PRINTER

Franklin's style is easy and intimate, that of a poised old man, well-aware of and pleased with his world reputation, yet with a clear memory of his poor and obscure beginnings. Perhaps age tempered his recollection of his mistakes, but he had a firm wish that his memoirs might instruct "the effects of prudent and imprudent conduct in the commencement of a life of business." His sprightly sense of humor is everywhere, beginning with his frank confession that he wrote his *Autobiography* in part to indulge his old man's vanity and talkativeness. We find his story much more than a mere how-to-succeed-in-business book. Franklin shows himself cheerful and eager, someone so approachable and whose successes seem they could be easily ours, if only we could learn his knack — genius.

Franklin found it helpful to know who his ancestors were and how they lived. He found the Franklins of Ecton, Northamptonshire, had been sturdy farmers and blacksmiths, modest but free. Franklin's description of his parents, included here, indicates they were a good and stimulating influence. His formal schooling was brief — less than two years. The skills he became most talented in, masterful and persuasive writing and speech, were ones he taught himself. His accounts included in this chapter show how he learned careful but vivid language, to which he attributed much of his success in carrying out public services and personal ambitions.

At sixteen, after sensibly abandoning attempts at poetry, Franklin humorously began his literary career with his letters from Silence Dogood, fourteen in all, and published anonymously in his half-brother James's *New England Courant*. In addition to the satires on university education and defense of women's education in this chapter, Franklin poked fun at women's fashions, New England poetry, courtship, the clergy and politicians and proposed insurance for widows and for aging virgins who honestly tried to get married.

By this time Benjamin had learned much of printing and publishing, particularly while James was imprisoned for the persistent political satires and impiety in the *Courant*. For several months, before he ran away, Benjamin was listed as the paper's sole publisher to protect James. However, the brothers were not compatible, James being domineering and Benjamin defiant. Benjamin had received full discharge from his first indentures but still chaffed under his brother's rule. James, knowing he would leave if he could, insured that no other printer in Boston would give him work. Consequently, Benjamin decided to leave secretly so his family could not stop him. His trip to Philadelphia included a near-shipwreck off Long Island, a fifty-mile walk across new Jersey and about a ten-mile rowboat ride in October weather from Burlington, New Jersey, to Philadelphia.

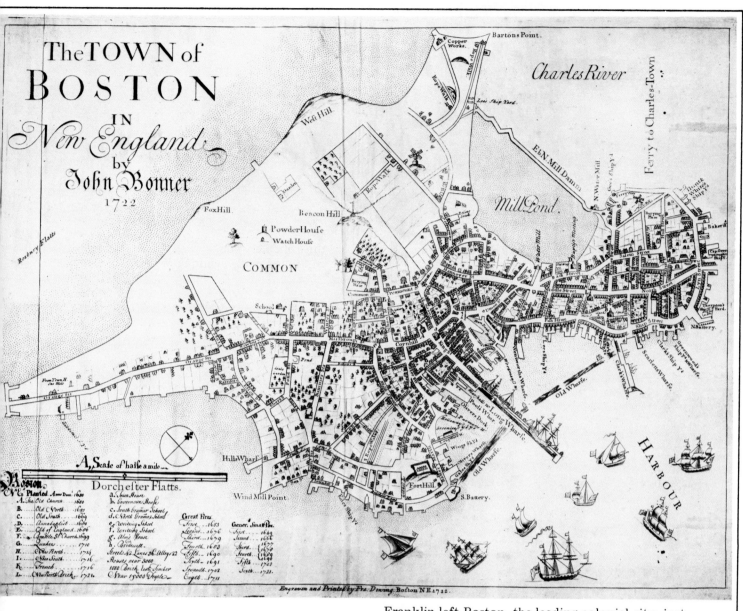

The TOWN of
BOSTON
IN
New England
by
John Bonner
1722

Charles River

Ferry to Charles-Town

Mill Pond.

COMMON

PowderHouse
WatchHouse

FoxHill

Beacon Hill

West Hill

HARBOUR

A Scale of half a mile

Boston
Planted Anno Dom. 1630

A....The Old Church....1680
B....Old C North....1650
C....Old South....1669
D....Anabaptist....1680
E....Ch. of England....1686
F....Brattle St Church 1699
G....Quakers....1710
H....C New North....1714
I....C New South....1716
K....French....1716
L....C New North Brick 1721

Dorchefter Flatts.

a...Town House
b...Governour's House
c...South Gramar School
d...C North Gramar School
e...Writing School
f...Writing School
g...Alms House
h...Bridewell

Streets 42 Lanes 36 Alleys 22
Houses near 3000
1000 Brick rest Timber
Near 15000 People

Great Fires
First....1653
Second....1676
Third....1679
Fourth....1683
Fifth....1690
Sixth....1691
Seventh....1702
Eighth....1711

Gener. Small Pox.
First....1649
Second....1666
Third....1677
Fourth....1689
Fifth....1702
Sixth....1721

Wind Mill Point

Hills Wharf

Fort Hill

S. Battery.

Engraven and Printed by Fra. Dewing. Boston NE. 1722.

Franklin left Boston, the leading colonial city, just
a year after John Bonner drew this map, the earliest plan
of Boston, showing the major wharves and public buildings.
*(I. N. Phelps Stokes Collection, Prints Division,
New York Public Library, Astor, Lenox and Tilden Foundations.)*

Franklin in 1758 visited this small stone house in Ecton, England, which had been the ancestral home for centuries. *(American Philosophical Society.)*

Autobiography

Twyford, at the Bishop of St. Asaph's, 1771.
. . . Having emerged from the poverty and obscurity in which I was born and bred, to a state of affluence and some degree of reputation in the world, and having gone so far through life with a considerable share of felicity, the conducing means I made use of, which with the blessing of God so well succeeded, my posterity may like to know, as they may find some of them suitable to their own situations, and therefore fit to be imitated.

Autobiography

Twyford, at the Bishop of St. Asaph's, 1771.
Hereby, too, I shall indulge the inclination so natural in old men, to be talking of themselves and their own past actions; and I shall indulge it without being tiresome to others, who, through respect to age, might conceive themselves obliged to give me a hearing, since this may be read or not as any one pleases. And, lastly (I may as well confess it, since my denial of it will be believed by nobody), perhaps I shall a good deal gratify my own *vanity.* Indeed, I scarce ever heard or saw the introductory words, *"Without vanity I may say,"* etc., but some vain thing immediately followed. Most people dislike vanity in others, whatever share they have of it themselves; but I give it fair quarter wherever I meet with it, being persuaded that it is often productive of good to the possessor, and to others that are within his sphere of action; and therefore, in many cases, it would not be altogether absurd if a man were to thank God for his vanity among the other comforts of life.

Autobiography

Twyford, at the Bishop of Asaph's, 1771.
The notes of one of my uncles (who had the same kind of curiosity in collecting family anecdotes) once put into my hands, furnished me with several particulars relating to our ancestors. From these notes I learned that the family had lived in the same village, Ecton, in Northamptonshire, for three hundred years . . . on a freehold of about thirty acres, aided by the smith's business, which had continued in the family till his time, the eldest son being always bred to that business; a custom which he and my father followed as to their eldest sons. When I searched the registers at Ecton . . . I perceived that I was the youngest son of the youngest son for five generations back. . . .

Josiah, my father, married young, and carried his wife with three children into New England, about 1682. . . . By the same wife he had four children more born there, and by a second wife ten more, in all seventeen; of which I remember thirteen sitting at one time at his table, who all grew up

(continued on p. 16)

An original printing press used by Franklin in Philadelphia, much like the one he learned on in his half-brother's shop in Boston, is on display at the Franklin Institute, Philadelphia.

What is serving God? 'Tis doing good to Man.
— Poor Richard's Almanack.

Penn's Treaty with the Indians, by Benjamin West (above), depicts the Great Treaty of peace in 1683 between the Quaker colonist William Penn and the Indians, which the philosopher Voltaire called "the only treaty not sworn to and never broken." Franklin found the same atmosphere of friendliness when he later entered Penn's colony. *(Pennsylvania Academy of the Fine Arts, Philadelphia, Joseph and Sarah Harrison Collection.)*

A View of Philadelphia, ca. 1718, by Peter Cooper, details the flurry of activity in the prospering port city that shortly would be Franklin's beloved home for the rest of his life. *(Collection of the Library Company of Philadelphia.)*

Home for Christmas, by J. G. L. Ferris.
This scene of colonial Philadelphia shows the wealth and charm the city
emanated as the second largest in the British Empire in Franklin's time.
*(Collection of William E. Ryder. Photo courtesy of
Historical Times Incorporated, The Stackpole Company.)*

Franklin's birthplace on Milk Street in Boston is depicted in a nineteenth-century etching. *(The Bostonian Society, Old State House.)*

to be men and women, and married; I was the youngest son, and the youngest child but two, and was born in Boston, New England. My mother, the second wife, was Abiah Folger, daughter of Peter Folger, one of the first settlers of New England.

Autobiography

Twyford, at the Bishop of Asaph's, 1771.

I think you may like to know something of his [Josiah Franklin's] person and character. He had an excellent constitution of body, was of middle stature, but well set, and very strong; he was ingenious, could draw prettily, was skilled a little in music, and had a clear pleasing voice, so that when he played psalm tunes on his violin and sung withal, as he sometimes did in an evening after the business of the day was over, it was extremely agreeable to hear. He had a mechanical genius too, and, on occasion, was very handy in the use of other tradesmen's tools; but his great excellence lay in a sound understanding and solid judgment in prudential matters, both in private and public affairs. . . . I remember well his being frequently visited by leading people, who consulted him for his opinion in affairs of the town or of the church he belonged to, and showed a good deal of respect for his judgment and advice; he was also much consulted by private persons about their affairs when any difficulty occurred, and frequently chosen an arbitrator between contending parties. At his table he liked to have, as often as he could, some sensible friend or neighbour to converse with, and always took care to start some ingenious or useful topic for discourse, which might tend to improve the minds of his children. By this means he turned our attention to what was good, just, and prudent in the conduct of life.

Autobiography

Twyford, at the Bishop of Asaph's, 1771.

My mother had likewise an excellent constitution: she suckled all her ten children. I never knew either my father or mother to have any sickness but that of which they dy'd, he at 89, and she at 85 years of age. They lie buried together at Boston, where I some years since placed a marble over their grave, with this inscription:

JOSIAH FRANKLIN
And
ABIAH his wife,
Lie here interred.
They lived lovingly together in wedlock
Fifty-five years.
Without an estate, or any gainful employment,
By constant labor and industry,
With God's blessing,
They maintained a large family
Comfortably,
And brought up thirteen children
And seven grandchildren
Reputably.
From this instance, reader,
Be encouraged to diligence in thy calling,
And distrust not Providence.
He was a pious and prudent man;
She, a discreet and virtuous woman.
Their youngest son,
In filial regard to their memory,
Places this stone.
J. F. born 1655, died 1744, AEtat 89.
A. J. born 1667, died 1752, ————85.

Autobiography

Twyford, at the Bishop of Asaph's, 1771.

. . . I was put to the grammar-school at eight years of age, my father intending to devote me, as the tithe of his sons, to the service of the Church. My early readiness in learning to read, which must have been very early, as I do not remember when I could not read, and the opinion of all his friends, that I should certainly make a good scholar, encouraged him in this purpose of his. . . . I continued, however, at the grammar-school not quite one year, though in that time I had risen gradually from the middle of the class of that year to be the head of it, and farther was removed into the next class above it, in order to go with that into the third at the end of the year. But my father, in the meantime, from a view of the expense of a college education . . . altered his first intention, took me from the grammar-school, and sent me to a school for writing and arithmetic, kept by a then famous man, Mr. George Brownell, very successful in his profession generally, and that by mild, encouraging methods. Under him I acquired fair writing pretty soon, but I failed in the arithmetic, and made no progress in it. At ten years old I was taken home to assist my father in his business, which was that of a tallow-chandler and sope-boiler. . . . Accordingly, I was employed in cutting wick for the candles, filling the dipping mold and the molds for cast candles, attending the shop, going of errands, etc.

I disliked the trade, and had a strong inclination for the sea, but my father declared against it; however, living near the water, I was much in and about it, learnt early to swim well, and to manage boats; and when in a boat or canoe with other boys, I was commonly allowed to govern, especially in any case of difficulty; and upon other occasions I was generally a leader among the boys, and sometimes led them into scrapes, of which I will mention one instance, as it shows an early projecting public spirit, tho' not then justly conducted.

There was a salt marsh that bounded part of a mill-pond, on the edge of which, at high water, we used to stand to fish for minnows. By much trampling, we had made it a mere quagmire. My proposal was to build a wharff there fit for us to stand upon, and I showed my comrades a large heap of stones, which were intended for a new house near the marsh, and which would very well suit our purpose. Accordingly, in the evening, when the workmen were gone, I assembled a number of my play-fellows, and working with them diligently like so many emmets [ants], sometimes two or three to a stone, we brought them all away and built our little wharff. The next morning the workmen were surprised at missing the stones, which were found in our wharff. Inquiry was made after the removers; we were discovered and complained of; several of us were corrected by our fathers; and, though I pleaded the usefulness of the work, mine convinced me that nothing was useful which was not honest.

Autobiography

Twyford, at the Bishop of Asaph's, 1771.

. . . I continued thus employed in my father's business for two years, that is, till I was twelve years old. . . . But my dislike to the trade continuing, my father was under apprehensions that if he did not find one for me more agreeable, I should break away and get to sea, as his son Josiah had done, to his great vexation. He therefore sometimes took me to walk with him, and see joiners, bricklayers, turners, braziers, etc., at their work, that he might observe my incli-

nation, and endeavour to fix it on some trade or other on land. It has ever since been a pleasure to me to see good workmen handle their tools; and it has been useful to me, having learnt so much by it as to be able to do little jobs myself in my house when a workman could not readily be got, and to construct little machines for my experiments.

Autobiography

Twyford, at the Bishop of Asaph's, 1771.

From a child I was fond of reading, and all the little money that came into my hands was ever laid out in books. Pleased with the *Pilgrim's Progress*, my first collection was of John Bunyan's works in separate little volumes. I after-

Franklin's travel or lap desk, used on his widespread journeys. *(Franklin Institute, Philadelphia.)*

A printer's ink roller from Franklin's shop. *(The Franklin Institute.)*

ward sold them to enable me to buy R. Burton's *Historical Collections*. . . . My father's little library consisted chiefly of books in polemic divinity, most of which I read and have since often regretted that, at a time when I had such a thirst for knowledge, more proper books had not fallen in my way, since it was now resolved I should not be a clergyman. Plutarch's *Lives* there was in which I read abundantly, and I still think that time spent to great advantage. There was also a book of DeFoe's, called an *Essay on Projects*, and another of Dr. Mather's, called *Essays to do Good*, which

Franklin borrowed books on writing and debate, read them overnight, if necessary, and returned them before his next day's work. *(American Philosophical Society.)*

perhaps gave me a turn of thinking that had an influence on some of the principal future events of my life.

This bookish inclination at length determined my father to make me a printer, though he had already one son (James) of that profession. In 1717 my brother James returned from England with a press and letters to set up his business in Boston. I liked it much better than that of my father, but still had a hankering for the sea. To prevent the apprehended effect of such an inclination, my father was impatient to have me bound to my brother. I stood out some time, but at last was persuaded, and signed the indentures when I was yet but twelve years old. I was to serve as an apprentice till I was twenty-one years of age, only I was to be allowed journeyman's wages during the last year. In a little time I made great proficiency in the business, and became a useful hand to my brother.

Autobiography

Twyford, at the Bishop of Asaph's, 1771.

And after some time an ingenious tradesman, Mr. Matthew Adams, who had a pretty collection of books, and who frequented our printing-house, took notice of me, invited me to his library, and very kindly lent me such books as I chose to read. I now took a fancy to poetry, and made some little pieces. . . . One [ballad] was called *The Lighthouse Tragedy*, and contained an account of the drowning of Captain Worthilake, with his two daughters: the other was a sailor's song, on the taking of *Teach* (or Blackbeard) the pirate. They were wretched stuff, in the Grub street

ballad style; and when they were printed he sent me about the town to sell them. The first sold wonderfully, the event being recent, having made a great noise. This flattered my vanity; but my father discouraged me by ridiculing my performances, and telling me verse-makers were generally beggars. So I escaped being a poet, most probably a very bad one. . . .

Autobiography

Twyford, at the Bishop of Asaph's, 1771.

About this time I met with an odd volume of the *Spectator*. It was the third. . . . I bought it, read it over and over, and was much delighted with it. I thought the writing excellent, and wished, if possible, to imitate it. With this view I took some of the papers, and, making short hints of the sentiment in each sentence, laid them by a few days, and then, without looking at the book, try'd to compleat the papers again, by expressing each hinted sentiment at length, and as fully as it had been expressed before, in any suitable words that should come to hand. Then I compared my *Spectator* with the original, discovered some of my faults, and corrected them. But I found I wanted a stock of words, or a readiness in recollecting and using them, which I thought I should have acquired before that time if I had gone on making verses. . . . Therefore I took some of the tales and turned them into verse; and, after a time, when I had pretty well forgotten the prose, turned them back again. I also sometimes jumbled my collections of hints into confusion, and after some weeks endeavoured to reduce them into the best order. . . . This was to teach me method in the arrangement of thoughts. By comparing my work afterwards with the original, I discovered many faults and amended them; but I sometimes had the pleasure of fancying that, in certain particulars of small import, I had been lucky enough to improve the method or the language, and this encouraged me to think I might possibly in time come to be a tolerable English writer, of which I was extreamly ambitious.

Autobiography

Twyford, at the Bishop of Asaph's, 1771.
When about 16 years of age I happened to meet with a book, written by one Tryon, recommending a vegetable diet. I determined to go into it. . . . I made myself acquainted with Tryon's manner of preparing some of his dishes, such as boiling potatoes or rice, making hasty pudding, and a few others, and then proposed to my brother, that if he would give me, weekly, half the money he paid for my board, I would board myself. He instantly agreed to it, and I presently found that I could save half what he paid me. This was an additional fund for buying books. But I had another advantage in it. My brother and the rest going from the printing-house to their meals, I remained there alone, and, despatching presently my light repast, which often was no more than a bisket or a slice of bread, a handful of raisins or a tart from the pastry-cook's, and a glass of water, had the rest of the time till their return for study, in which I made the greater progress, from that greater clearness of head and quicker apprehension which usually attend temperance in eating and drinking.

Autobiography

Twyford, at the Bishop of Asaph's, 1771.
. . . Hitherto I had stuck to my resolution of not eating animal food, and on this occasion I consider'd, with my master Tryon, the taking every fish as a kind of unprovoked murder, since none of them had, or ever could do us any injury that might justify the slaughter. All this seemed very reasonable. But I had formerly been a great lover of fish, and, when this came hot out of the frying-pan, it smelt admirably well. I balanc'd some time between principle and inclination, till I recollected that, when the fish were opened, I saw smaller fish taken out of their stomachs; then thought I, "If you eat one another, I don't see why we mayn't eat you." So I dined upon cod very heartily, and continued to eat with other people, returning only now and then occasionally to a vegetable diet. So convenient a thing it is to be a *reasonable creature*, since it enables one to find or make a reason for every thing one has a mind to do.

Autobiography

Twyford, at the Bishop of Asaph's, 1771.
I procur'd Xenophon's *Memorable Things of Socrates*, wherein there are many instances of the same method [of rhetoric and logic]. I was charm'd with it, adopted it, dropt my abrupt contradiction and positive argumentation, and put on the humble inquirer and doubter. . . . I found this method safest for myself and very embarassing to those against whom I used it; therefore I took a delight in it,

practis'd it continually, and grew very artful and expert in drawing people, even of superior knowledge, into concessions, the consequences of which they did not foresee, entangling them in difficulties out of which they could not extricate themselves, and so obtaining victories that neither myself nor my cause always deserved. I continu'd this method some few years, but gradually left it, retaining only the habit of expressing myself in terms of modest diffidence; never using, when I advanced anything that may possibly be disputed, the words *certainly, undoubtedly*, or any others that give the air of positiveness to an opinion; but rather say, I conceive or apprehend a thing to be so and so; it appears to me, or *I should think it so or so*, for such and such reasons; or *I imagine it to be so*; or *it is so, if I am not mistaken*. This habit, I believe, has been of great advantage to me when I have had occasion to inculcate my opinions, and persuade men into measures that I have been from time to time engaged in promoting; and, as the chief ends of conversation are to *inform* or to be *informed*, to *please* or to *persuade*, I wish well-meaning, sensible men would not lessen their power of doing good by a positive, assuming manner, that seldom fails to disgust, tends to create opposition, and to defeat everyone of those purposes for which speech was given to us, to wit, giving or receiving information or pleasure. For, if you would inform, a positive and dogmatical manner in advancing your sentiments may provoke contradiction and prevent a candid attention. If you wish information and improvement from the knowledge of others, and yet at the same time express yourself as firmly fix'd in your present opinions, modest, sensible men, who do not love disputation, will probably leave you undisturbed in the possession of your error. And by such a manner, you can seldom hope to recommend yourself in pleasing your hearers, or to persuade those whose concurrence you desire. Pope says, judiciously:

"Men should be taught as if you taught them not,
And things unknown propos'd as things forgot."

Autobiography

Twyford, at the Bishop of Asaph's, 1771.
My brother had, in 1720 or 1721, begun to print a newspaper. It was . . . called the *New England Courant*. . . .
He had some ingenious men among his friends, who amus'd themselves by writing little pieces for this paper, which gain'd it credit and made it more in demand, and these gentlemen often visited us. Hearing their conversations, and their accounts of the approbation their papers were received with, I was excited to try my hand among them; but, being still a boy, and suspecting that my brother would object to printing anything of mine in his paper if he knew it to be mine, I contrived to disguise my hand, and, writing an anonymous paper, I put it in at night under the door of the printing-house. It was found in the morning, and communicated to his writing friends when they call'd in as usual. They read it, commented on it in my hearing, and I had the exquisite pleasure of finding it met with their approbation, and that, in their different guesses at the author, none were named but men of some character

Humorous letters from "Silence Dogood" to the *New England Courant*, penned anonymously by Frankli arrived at the print shop while the young author overheard the approving comments.
(Historical Pictures Service, Chicago.)

among us for learning and ingenuity. I suppose now that I was rather lucky in my judges, and that perhaps they were not really so very good ones as I then esteem'd them.

Encourag'd, however, by this, I wrote and convey'd in the same way to the press several more papers which were equally approv'd; and I kept my secret till my small fund of sense for such performances was pretty well exhausted. . . .

[*The papers Franklin refers to are the Dogood Papers, a sampling of which follows, beginning with "Silence Dogood's" self-description. —Ed.*]

From the DOGOOD PAPERS

The New-England Courant, Monday April 9 to Monday April 16, 1722.

To the Author of the New-England Courant

. . .Know then, That I am an Enemy to Vice, and a Friend to Vertue. I am one of extensive Charity, and a great Forgiver of *private* Injuries: A hearty Lover of the Clergy and all good Men, and a mortal Enemy to arbitrary Government & unlimited Power. I am naturally very jealous for the Rights and Liberties of my Country: & the least appearance of an Incroachment on those invaluable Priviledges, is apt to make my Blood boil exceedingly. I have likewise a natural Inclination to observe and reprove the Faults of others, at which I have an excellent Faculty. I speak this by Way of Warning to all such whose offences shall come under my Cognizance, for I never intend to wrap my Talent in a Napkin. To be brief; I am courteous and affable, good-humor'd (unless I am first provok'd,) and handsome, and sometimes witty, but always, Sir,

Your Friend, and
Humble Servant,

Silence Dogood.

The New-England Courant, Monday May 7 to Monday May 14, 1722.

To the Author of the New-England Courant.

Sir,

Discoursing the other Day at Dinner with my Reverend Boarder, formerly mention'd, (whom for Distinction sake we will call by the Name of *Clericus*), concerning the Education of Children, I ask'd his Advice about my young Son *William*, whether or no I had best bestow upon him Academical Learning, or (as our Phrase is) *bring him up at our College*: He persuaded me to do it by all Means, using many weighty arguments with me, and answering all the Objections that I could form against it; telling me withal, that he did not doubt but that the Lad would take his Learning very well, and not idle away his Time as too many there now-a-days do. These words of *Clericus* gave me a Curiosity to inquire a little more strictly into the present Circumstances of that famous Seminary of Learning; but the Information which he gave me, was neither pleasant, nor such as I expected.

As soon as Dinner was over, I took a solitary Walk into my Orchard, still ruminating on *Clericus's* Discourse with much Consideration, until I came to my usual Place of Retirement under the *Great Apple-Tree*; where having seated my self, and carelesly laid my Head on a verdant Bank, I fell by Degrees into a soft and undisturbed Slumber. My waking Thoughts remained with me in my Sleep, and before I awak'd again, I dreamt the following *Dream*.

I fancy'd I was travelling over pleasant and delightful Fields and Meadows, and thro' many small Country Towns and Villages; and as I pass'd along, all Places resounded with the Fame of the Temple of *Learning*: Every Peasant, who had wherewithal, was preparing to send one of his Children at least to this famous Place; and in this Case most of them consulted their own Purses instead of their Childrens Capacities: So that I observed, a great many, yea, the most part of those who were travelling thither, were little better than Dunces and Blockheads. Alas! Alas!

At length I entered upon a spacious Plain, in the Midst of which was erected a large and stately Edifice: It was to this that a great Company of Youths from all Parts of the Country were going; so stepping in among the Crowd, I passed on with them, and presently arrived at the Gate.

The Passage was Kept by two sturdy Porters named *Riches* and *Poverty*, and the latter obstinately refused to give Entrance to any who had not first gain'd the Favour of the former; so that I observed, many who came even to the very Gate, were obliged to travel back again as ignorant as they came, for want of this necessary Qualification. However, as a Spectator I gain'd Admittance, and with the rest entered directly into the Temple.

In the Middle of the great Hall stood a stately and magnificent Throne, which was ascended to by two high and difficult Steps. On the Top of it sat *Learning* in awful State; she was apparelled wholly in Black, and surrounded almost on every side with innumerable Volumes in all Languages. She seem'd very busily employ'd in writing something on half a Sheet of Paper, and upon Enquiry, I understood she was preparing a Paper, call'd, *The New England Courant*. On her Right Hand sat *English*, with a pleasant smiling Countenance, and handsomely attired; and on her left were seated several *Antique Figures* with their Faces vail'd. I was considerably puzzl'd to guess who they were, until one informed me, (who stood beside me,) that those Figures on her left Hand were *Latin, Greek, Hebrew*, &c. and that they were very much reserv'd, and seldom or never unvail'd their Faces here, and then to few or none, tho' most of those who have in this Place acquir'd so much Learning as to distinguish them from *English*, pretended to an intimate Acquaintance with them. I then enquir'd of him, what could be the Reason why they continued vail'd, in this Place especially: He pointed to the Foot of the Throne, where I saw *Idleness*, attended with *Ignorance*, and these (he informed me) were they, who first vail'd them, and still kept them so.

Now I observed, that the whole Tribe who entered into the Temple with me, began to climb the Throne; but the Work proving troublesome and difficult to most of them, they withdrew their Hands from the Plow, and contented themselves to sit at the Foot, with Madam *Idleness* and her Maid *Ignorance*, until those who were assisted by Diligence and a docible Temper, had well nigh got up the first Step: But the Time drawing nigh in which they could no way avoid ascending, they were fain to crave the Assistance of those who had got up before them, and who, for the Reward perhaps of a *Pint of Milk*, or a *Piece of Plumb-Cake*, lent the Lubbers a helping Hand, and sat them in the Eye of the World, upon a Level with themselves.

The other Step being in the same Manner ascended, and the usual Ceremonies at an End, every Beetle-Scull seem'd well satisfy'd with his own Portion of Learning, tho' perhaps he was *e'en just* as ignorant as ever. And now the Time of their Departure being come, they march'd out of Doors to make Room for another Company, who waited for Entrance: And I, having seen all that was to be seen, quitted

THE
New-England Courant.

From MONDAY December 11. to MONDAY December 18. 1721.

To the Author of the New-England Courant

SIR,

Dec. 8. 1721.

SINCE in your laſt Courant you was pleaſed to ſay, *That both Anti-Inoculators and Inoculators ſhould be welcome to ſpeak their Minds in your Paper,* I ſend the following Reaſons againſt inoculating the Small Pox, which I hope in purſuance of your Promiſe, you will inſert in your next, if you have Room.

The Firſt Reaſon then is, That this Operation being perform'd upon none but ſuch as are in perfect Health, and who, for any thing the Doctor or Patients know, may be ſuch who may never have that Diſtemper in their Lives, or if they have, not to that Degree as to make it mortal to them : and then ſurely it muſt be needleſs to the laſt Degree, for any Man to have himſelf made ſick in order to prevent that which for any thing he knows, he is in no Danger of.

But in the Second Place, much more ſo, when the Perſons that are for that Operation, cannot anſwer this Small Queſtion to the Satisfaction of any rational Creature, viz. *Whether this Operation is Infallible, ſo that hitherto there is not any Body has periſhed, that has had the Small Pox produced by it.* I ſay, this is a Point the World will find them for ever tender upon: And altho' they would fain inſinuate that it is infallible, yet they will never give you a direct Anſwer, but will put you off with this, *That there is nothing infallible in Phyſick ; for that they have known Perſons dye by a Vomit, and others by Bleeding,* &c. But allowing what they ſay to be true, for once ; theſe Gentlemen never diſtinguiſh betwixt making a *well Man ſick,* and endeavouring to make a *ſick Man well* ; for certainly, there is not any thing will defend any Man's bringing a Sickneſs on himſelf, unleſs he is ſure that he cannot die of that Illneſs he does ſo bring upon him ; for we are obliged to preſerve the Health we have, as much as we are obliged to preſerve our Lives : Whereas on the other Hand, in giving of *Vomits,* &c. it is never done by wiſe Phyſicians, but to Perſons who have *really loſt their Healths,* and of Courſe it is allowable to run a little Riſque to recover that Health which it has pleaſed God to take from him. But let theſe Gentlemen talk as they will about ſuch things, I dare ſay that every reaſonable Man will think it very ridiculous, to compare Inoculating the Small Pox to *Bleeding* or *Vomiting,* &c. when the one is done to none but ſuch as are in perfect Health, and the other to Perſons that are ſick. Beſides, I have ſeen Phyſick practiſed by ſome of the ableſt Phyſicians that ever the World ſaw, and have been practiſing of it my ſelf this twenty Years paſt. But I muſt ſay, I never ſaw any Man die by *Bleeding* or *Bliſtering,* or by *Vomiting* or *Purging,* provided they were given in proper Doſes. But if ignorant People, who neither underſtand Phy-

ſick not the Doſes of Medicines, will be doing what they ſhould not do, no Wonder if we ſee Inſtances of theſe innocent Things proving Mortal : But then the Fault is to be put to the Account of the *Perſons who gave the things ignorantly,* and not to the *things themſelves.* But it is quite otherwiſe with *Inoculation* ; for there is not any Body that I know that can tell the Doſe of that Juice ſo as to make it infallible. But he muſt be a very poor & heedleſs Phyſician indeed, that cannot prevent the aforeſaid *Bleeding,* &c. from being hurtful to any Body.

And the third Reaſon is, that if they ſhould ſay, *Inoculating the Small Pox is an infallible way to preſerve Life.* I ſay, if they ſhould ſay ſo, yet it is falſe in Fact ; For Dr. *Emanuel Timonius* in his Letter to the Royal Society, owns, that he ſaw Two die that were Inoculated ; but at the ſame Time would fain inſinuate, that they died of ſome other Diſtemper, which is the very Error his Diſciples on this ſide the Great *Atlantick* fall into ; for when they are ask'd, *If it be Infallible, how came Mrs.* D——l *and ſeveral others to die of it ?* They anſwer, She and they did not die of the *Small Pox,* but of ſome *other Diſtemper,* or elſe had received the Infection the Common Way firſt ; which is certainly very ridiculous if one conſiders the following things.

Every Body knows that it's the Nature of *Hellebore* to purge ; and of Courſe too great a Doſe of it taken will kill any Man : And for any Body to ſay, that had given an exceſſive Doſe of it to a Patient, and that Patient had purged to Death by it ; I ſay, to ſay that that Patient died of ſome other Diſtemper, would certainly be very ridiculous ; and ſo is it every whit as ridiculous to ſay, that a Perſon that is in perfect Health, and is inoculated, and has the Effects of that Operation the ſame way as others have that have taken the utmoſt Precaution, viz. the *ſame Fever,* the *ſame Puſtules,* only the Fever *more violent,* and a *greater Quantity* of Puſtules, and at laſt *Death.* I ſay, It would be very ridiculous for any to ſay, that ſuch Perſons did not dy of the *Inoculated Small Pox* ; when, as I ſaid before, they had the Small Pox after that Operation, and were in perfect Health before it was performed upon them ; which is the very Caſe of Mrs. D——l, and the reſt of them that have dyed by it, ſo far as I can learn. As to Mrs. D——l, this I know, that they boaſted much of having made ſuch a Convert, and owned publickly that ſhe had got the Small Pox by Inoculation. But when it pleaſed God to ſhew them that ſhe muſt depart this Life, notwithſtanding their Infallible Remedy ; Oh! then they turn their Tones, and ſay truly, ſhe dyed of *Hyſterick* ; which by the way, are the worſt Fits they could have pitch'd upon ; for of all Fits they prove the ſeldomeſt Mortal : And it it is as certain as the Sun ſhines at Noon in a clear Day, that ſhe died of the Small Pox, which ſhe received by Inoculation ; and Mr. B——n himſelf muſt have thought ſo too, otherwiſe he was a very ſilly Man to inoculate her, when he had reaſon to ſuſpect ſhe had received the Infection the Common Way firſt, which probably might ſpoil the Reputation of his infallible Remedy.

Mr

the Hall likewise, and went to make my Observations on those who were just gone out before me.

Some I perceiv'd took to Merchandizing, others to Travelling, some to one Thing, some to another, and some to Nothing; and many of them from henceforth, for want of Patrimony, liv'd as poor as church Mice, being unable to dig, and asham'd to beg, and to live by their Wits it was impossible. But the most Part of the Crowd went along a large beaten Path, which led to a Temple at the further End of the Plain, call'd, *The Temple of Theology*. The Business of those who were employ'd in this Temple being laborious and painful, I wonder'd exceedingly to see so many go towards it; but while I was pondering this Matter in my Mind, I spy'd *Pecunia* [personification of money] behind a Curtain, beckoning to them with her Hand, which Sight immediately satisfy'd me for whose Sake it was, that a great Part of them (I will not say all) travel'd that Road. In this Temple I saw nothing worth mentioning, except the ambitious and fraudulent Contrivances of *Plagius*, who (notwithstanding he had been severely reprehended for such Practices before) was diligently transcribing some eloquent Paragraphs out of *Tillotson's Works*, &c. to embellish his own.

Now I bethought myself in my Sleep, that it was Time to be at Home, and as I fancy'd I was travelling back thither, I reflected in my Mind on the extream Folly of those Parents, who, blind to their Childrens Dulness, and insensible of the Solidity of their Skulls, because they think their Purses can afford it, will needs send them to the Temple of Learning, where for want of a suitable Genius, they learn little more than how to carry themselves handsomely, and enter a Room genteely, (which might as well be acquir'd at a Dancing-School,) and from whence they return, after Abundance of Trouble and Charge, as great Blockheads as ever, only more proud and self-conceited.

While I was in the midst of these unpleasant Reflections, *Clericus* (who with a Book in his Hand was walking under the Trees) accidentally awak'd me; to him I related my Dream with all its Particulars, and he, without much Study, presently interpreted it, assuring me, *That it was a lively Representation of Harvard College, Etcetera. I remain, Sir,*

Your Humble Servant,
Silence Dogood.

The New-England Courant, Monday May 21, to Monday May 28, 1722.

To the Author of the New-England Courant.

Sir,

I Shall here present your Readers with a Letter from one, who informs me that I have begun at the wrong End of my Business, and that I ought to begin at Home, and censure the Vices and Follies of my own Sex, before I venture to meddle with your's. . . .

To Mrs. Dogood
Madam,

My Design in troubling you with this Letter is, to desire you would begin with your own Sex first: Let the first Volley of your Resentments be directed against *Female* Vice; let Female Idleness, Ignorance and Folly, (which are Vices more peculiar to your Sex than to our's,) be the Subject of your Satyrs, but more especially Female Pride, which I think is intolerable. Here is a large Field that wants Cultivation, and which I believe you are able (if willing) to im-

prove with Advantage; and when you have once reformed the Women, you will find it a much easier Task to reform the Men, because Women are the prime Causes of a great many Male Enormities. This is all at present from

Your Friendly Wellwisher,
Ephraim Censorious.

After Thanks to my Correspondent for his Kindness in cutting out Work for me, I must assure him, that I find it a very difficult Matter to reprove Women separate from the Men; for what Vice is there in which the Men have not as great a Share as the Women? and in some have they not a far greater as in Drunkenness, Swearing, &c? And if they have, then it follows, that when a Vice is to be reproved, Men, who are most culpable, deserve the most Reprehension, and certainly therefore, ought to have it. But we will wave this point . . . and proceed to a particular Consideration of what my Correspondent calls *Female Vice*.

As for Idleness, if I should *Quaere* [query], Where are the greatest Number of its Votaries to be found, with us or the Men? it might I believe be easily and truly answer'd,

Benjamin learned to compose type and print off sheets on the hand press in his brother's shop. *(Bettmann Archives)*

With the latter. For notwithstanding the Men are commonly complaining how hard they are forc'd to labour, only to maintain their Wives in Pomp and Idleness, yet if you go among the Women, you will learn, *that they have always more Work upon their Hands than they are able to do*, and that *a Woman's Work is never done*, &c. But however, Suppose we should grant for once, that we are generally more idle than the Men, (without making any Allowance for the *Weakness of the Sex*,) I desire to know whose Fault it is? Are not the Men to blame for their Folly in maintaining us in Idleness? Who is there that can be handsomely supported in Affluence, Ease and Pleasure by another, that will choose rather to earn his Bread by the Sweat of his

(continued on p. 29)

Above: The successes of his early writings multiplied
when Franklin set up his own newspaper in Philadelphia.
Artist Norman Rockwell painted him dashing off a piece for
his *Gazette* or perhaps *Poor Richard's Almanack*.
(Collection of Mr. Joseph Hennage.)

Though pictured together in a late eighteenth-century print of France's favorite writers, Franklin was yet a boy in Boston while his fellow philosopher Voltaire (left) was already hailed a modern rival of Sophocles. Rousseau (center) was more nearly Franklin's contemporary. *(Metropolitan Museum of Art, gift of William H. Huntington.)*

America's first native sculptor, William Rush, also a Phildelphian, carved this wooden portrait bust of Franklin. *(Index of American Design and Decorative Arts.)*

Leonard Rhodes - - Cyr Agency.

Elfreth's Alley, Phildelphia, preserved much as
it was in Franklin's time, was an area he probably
saw when he entered the city as a very young man,
though the cobblestones and street lamps were
installed later as a result of his formative influence.

The Old Massachusetts Statehouse in Boston,
now the oldest standing capitol building in America,
was built during Franklin's childhood in that city.

own Brows? And if a Man will be so fond and foolish, as to labour hard himself for a Livelihood, and suffer his Wife in the mean Time to sit in Ease and Idleness, let him not blame her if she does so, for it is in a great Measure his own Fault.

And now for the Ignorance and Folly which he reproaches us with, let us see (if we are Fools and Ignoramus's) whose is the Fault, the Men's or our's. An ingenious Writer, having this Subject in Hand, has the following Words, wherein he lays the Fault wholly on the Men, for not allowing Women the Advantages of Education.

"I have (says he) often thought of it as one of the most barbarous Customs in the World, considering us as civiliz'd and Christian Country, that we deny the Advantages of Learning to Women. We reproach the Sex every Day with Folly and Impertinence, while I am confident, had they the Advantages of Education equal to us, they would be guilty of less than ourselves. One would wonder indeed how it should happen that Women are conversible at all, since they are only beholding to natural Parts for all their Knowledge. Their Youth is spent to teach them to stitch and sow, or make Baubles. They are taught to read indeed, and perhaps to write their Names, or so; and that is the Heigth of a Womans Education. And I would but ask any who slight the Sex for their Understanding, What is a Man (a Gentleman, I mean) good for that is taught no more? If Knowledge and Understanding had been useless Additions to the Sex, God Almighty would never have given them Capacities, for he made nothing Needless. What has the Woman done to forfeit the Priviledge of being taught? Does she plague us with her Pride and Impertinence? Why did we not let her learn, that she might have had more Wit? Shall we upraid Women with Folly, when 'tis only the Error of this inhumance Custom that hindered them being made wiser."

So much for Female Ignorance and Folly; and now let us a little consider the Pride which my Correspondent thinks is *intolerable*. By this Expression of his, one would think he is some dejected Swain, tyranniz'd over by some cruel haughty Nymph, who (perhaps he thinks) has no more Reason to be proud than himself. *Alas-a-day!* What shall we say in this Case! Why truly, if Women are proud, it is certainly owing to the Men still; for if they will be such *Simpletons* as to humble themselves at their Feet, and fill their credulous Ears with extravagant Praises of their Wit, Beauty and other Accomplishments (perhaps where there are none too,) and when Women are by this Means persuaded that they are Something more than humane, what Wonder is it, if they carry themselves haughtily, and live extravagantly. Notwithstanding, I believe there are more Instances of extravagant Pride to be found among Men than among Women, and this Fault is certainly more heinous in the former than in the latter.

Upon the whole, I conclude, that it will be impossible to lash any Vice, of which the Men, are not equally guilty with the Women, and consequently, deserve an equal (if not a greater,) Share in the Censure. However, I exhort both to amend, where both are culpable, otherwise they may expect to be severely handled by Sir,

Your Humble Servant,
Silence Dogood.

A caliper from Franklin's shop.
(Franklin Institute, Philadelphia.)

[*When Benjamin Franklin was about 17, his brother James was censured by the Massachusetts Assembly, imprisoned for a month and ordered to no longer print the* New-England Courant, *in punishment for a political point made in the paper. It was decided in secret that Benjamin should be called the printer, that he should receive new and more liberal indentures from his brother, and the paper would go on. –Ed.*]

Autobiography

Twyford, at the Bishop of Asaph's, 1771.

At length, a fresh difference arising between my brother and me, I took upon me to assert my freedom, presuming that he would not venture to produce the new indentures. It was not fair in me to take this advantage, and this I therefore reckon one of the first errata of my life; but the unfairness of it weighed little with me, when under the impressions of resentment for the blows his passion too often urged him to bestow upon me, though he was otherwise not an ill-natur'd man; perhaps I was too saucy and provoking.

When he found I would leave him, he took care to prevent my getting employment in any other printing-house of the town.... I was rather inclin'd to leave Boston when I reflected that I had already made myself a little obnoxious to the governing party, and, from the arbitrary proceedings of the Assembly in my brother's case, it was likely I might, if I stay'd, soon bring myself into scrapes; and farther, that my indiscrete disputations about religion began to make me pointed at with horror by good people as an infidel or atheist. I determin'd on the point, but my father now siding with my brother, I was sensible that, if I attempted to go openly, means would be used to prevent me. My friend Collins, therefore, undertook to manage a little for me.

29

Industry and frugality: perhaps Franklin overused these words — for he continued to remind people of them, even as a wealthy old man who no longer needed to practice them — and they tend to leave us with a distorted image of a penny-pinching workmonger. The fact was he retired handsomely after twenty-five years in printing and publishing, the last ten years of which he mostly managed and invested. Moreover he *lived* his *Poor Richard* maxim, "Wealth is not his that has it, but his that enjoys it." Franklin cared for wealth only as a means to secure leisure for scientific experiments and for public service, which he considered his duty.

When Franklin entered Philadelphia in 1723, however, industry and frugality, and a large measure of genius and common sense, were his only means to independence. He found a job with Samuel Keimer, printer, and began saving for his own shop. Governor Sir William Keith, a well-intentioned but inept ruler, patronized Franklin and assured him support in his venture of becoming independent. Young Franklin believed his offers, and as his *Autobiography* accounts, set off for England with promises of letters of credit and reference from Keith to follow. Franklin found himself in London, deceived, without money or friends. He found a printing job, but spent his money on plays, amusements and "foolish intrigues with low women." He forgot his promises to Deborah Reed of Philadelphia, "attempted familiarities" with a Mrs. T—, "which she repulsed with a proper resentment," and lived from hand to mouth at times.

II PHILADELPHIA SUCCESS STORY

After eighteen months he returned to Philadelphia. The city in 1726 was on the verge of becoming the principal colonial city. It was ideally located for shipping and already prospered from its busy harbor. William Penn's Quaker beliefs had given it a character of tolerance and piety. By mid-century, Philadelphia would be the colonies' largest city and the second largest in the Empire. Shaped by Franklin and other leading citizens — Robert Morris, financier; Dr. Benjamin Rush; John Bartram, naturalist; David Rittenhouse, astronomer; Charles Willson Peale, artist — Philadelphia became the focus of artistic, intellectual, political, scientific and social activity.

Franklin started as a clerk then signed again with Keimer until a co-worker's father agreed to set up his son and Franklin in printing. Franklin kept accounts meticulously, shrewdly cultivated acquaintances with those who might give them business and by 1729 began his *Pennsylvania Gazette.* At this time Franklin's partner sold out to become a farmer. Franklin prospered, gaining more subscribers to his witty *Gazette* with his satires printed under pseudonyms such as Anthony Afterwit, Celia Single and Alice Addertongue and his more serious essays on politics, morals and customs. He received government print orders, opened a stationers shop and began paying off debts.

In 1730 he married, without ceremony, Deborah Reed Rogers, who was technically married to but deserted by another man. She was thrifty and devoted, and together they thrived. Franklin's son, William (age six months to a year), became part of the household several months later. Franklin kept his own council, and no one has ever ascertained whether William's mother was Deborah or another. Deborah bore a son, Francis Folger, and a daughter, Sarah.

Printing, apparently, was not sufficient to occupy Franklin's mind, and in 1727 he formed the Junto Club of young, ambitious men who emphasized self-improvement. They started the first circulating library in the colonies (the Library Company of Philadelphia) and discussed the pros and cons of political issues in Pennsylvania.

Nothing less than moral perfection became Franklin's next undertaking. It is related at length in this chapter. With the modern tendency to disbelieve in absolutes, it is awesome to see the plan of someone who sincerely believed he could approach perfection. Franklin, relating this plan about forty years after in the *Autobiography,* gives the endeavor a perspective of humor and temperance, the first virtue for which Franklin aimed.

About this time, Franklin's wit found another outlet in the popular *Poor Richard's Almanack,* begun in 1732 and continued to 1757. *Father Abraham's Speech,* a brilliant harangue constructed of twenty-five years' maxims, is included in this chapter. It later became internationally known as *The Way to Wealth* and had over 1,300 editions. Richard Saunders' almanac from the

A happy result of Franklin's frugal, industrious years in Philadelphia
was the success of his *The Way to Wealth*, or the preface to *Poor Richard's Almanack* of 1758, which was
reprinted extensively. Many of his humorous hints for those who would be rich are contained
in this 1859 engraving "Poor Richard Illustrated." *(Library of Congress.)*

beginning outsold its competitors, and in fifteen years was a Pennsylvania institution, selling 10,000 copies a year and renamed *Poor Richard Improved*. To gain such popularity, Franklin had drawn on the wisdom and wit of past sages and cultures. Under his scrutiny, the old lines were "pointed up," as he called it, sharpened and shortened, dramatized.

By 1736 Franklin had secured enough leisure from printing to enter more fully into Pennsylvania affairs. He was elected clerk of the General Assembly; became deputy postmaster at Philadelphia; proposed a fire company; inspected every postoffice but one in the colonies; supported the Pennsylvania Assembly in its struggle over taxation with the proprietary party (descendents of William Penn and their beneficiaries); assisted British General Braddock in a military expedition; wrote the proposal which organized The American Philosophical Society; proposed a plan of curriculum, faculty and physical plant which became the Pennsylvania Academy and later the University of Pennsylvania; wrote *Plain Truth*, a pamphlet advocating a milita for defense, which paper rallied the quarreling Pennsylvania factions; supported Dr. Thomas Bond's work in building the Philadelphia Hospital; and at fifty, traveled to the Pennsylvanian frontier to supervise building forts against French and Indian attacks. He was also on the Governor's commission of the peace, the city common council, was an alderman and burgess in the Pennsylvania Assembly, and Grand Master of the Masonic Lodge in Pennsylvania.

ENGINE SIDE OF THE FRANKLIN ENGINE COMPANY
FOUNDED JANUARY 17, 1792
(PAINTED BY DAVID RENT ETTER ABOUT 1830)

Observe all men, thyself the most.
— Poor Richard's Almanack.

Autobiography

Twyford, at the Bishop of Asaph's, 1771.

I have been the more particular in this description of my journey, and shall be so of my first entry into that city, that you may in your mind compare such unlikely beginnings with the figure I have since made there. I was in my working dress, my best clothes being to come round by sea. I was dirty from my journey; my pockets were stuff'd out with shirts and stockings, and I knew no soul nor where to look for lodging. I was fatigued with travelling, rowing, and want of rest, I was very hungry; and my whole stock of cash consisted of a Dutch dollar, and about a shilling in copper. . . .

Then I walked up the street, gazing about till near the market-house I met a boy with bread. I had made many a meal on bread, and, inquiring where he got it, I went immediately to the baker's he directed me to, in Second-street, and ask'd for bisket, intending such as we had in Boston; but they, it seems, were not made in Philadelphia. Then I asked for a three-penny loaf, and was told they had none such. So not considering or knowing the difference of money, and the greater cheapness nor the names of his bread, I bad him give me three-penny worth of any sort. He gave me, accordingly, three great puffy rolls. I was surpriz'd at the quantity, but took it, and, having no room in my pockets, walk'd off with a roll under each arm, and eating the other. Thus I went up Market-street as far as Fourth-street, passing by the door of Mr. Read, my future wife's father; when she, standing at the door, saw me, and thought I made, as I certainly did, a most awkward, ridiculous appearance. Then I turned and went down Chestnut-street and part of Walnut-street, eating my roll all the way, and, coming round, found myself again at Market-street wharf, near the boat I came in, to which I went for a draught of the river water; and, being filled with one of my rolls, gave the other two to a woman and her child that came down the river in the boat with us, and were waiting to go farther. Thus refreshed, I walked again up the street, which by this time had many clean-dressed people in it, who were all walking the same way. I joined them, and thereby was led into the great meeting-house of the Quakers near the market. I sat down among them, and, after looking round awhile and hearing nothing said, being very drowsy thro' labour and want of rest the preceding night, I fell fast asleep, and continu'd so till the meeting broke up, when one was kind enough to rouse me. This was, therefore, the first house I was in, or slept in, in Philadelphia.

Left: Franklin's amusing appearance as he entered Philadelphia was painted by David Rent Etter on the decorative side panel of a fire engine, as was the style for such machines. *(Insurance Company of North America.)* Right: A hand printing press from Franklin's period. *(Bettmann Archive.)*

Autobiography

Twyford, at the Bishop of Asaph's, 1771.

I had hitherto kept the proposition of my setting up, a secret in Philadelphia, and I still kept it. Had it been known that I depended on the governor [Sir William Keith], probably some friend, that knew him better, would have advis'd me not to rely on him, as I afterwards heard it as his known character to be liberal of promises which he never meant to keep. Yet, unsolicited as he was by me, how could I think his generous offers insincere? I believ'd him one of the best men in the world.

I presented him an inventory of a little print'g-house, amounting by my computation to about one hundred pounds sterling. He lik'd it, but ask'd me if my being on the spot in England to choose the types, and see that every thing was good of the kind, might not be of some advantage. "Then," says he, "when there, you may make acquaintances, and establish correspondences in the book-selling and stationery way." I agreed that this might be advantageous. "Then," says he, "get yourself ready to go with Annis;" which was the annual ship, and the only one at that time usually passing between London and Philadelphia.

[On arriving in England, Franklin found that the promised letters of recommendation and credit from Governor Keith were non-existent and that he was without work in a strange city. He soon found work, however, at Palmer's printing house and within a year moved to the prospering Watts printing house where he made a reputation for himself. –Ed.]

Autobiography

Twyford, at the Bishop of Asaph's, 1771.

At my first admission into this printing-house [Watts] I took to working at press, imagining I felt a want of the bodily exercise I had been us'd to in America, where press-work is mix'd with composing. I drank only water; the other workmen, near fifty in number, were great guzzlers of beer. On occasion, I carried up and down stairs a large form of types in each hand, when others carried but one in both hands. They wondered to see, from this and several instances, that the *Water-American*, as they called me, was *stronger* than themselves, who drank *strong* beer! We had an alehouse boy who attended always in the house to supply the workmen. My companion at the press drank every day a pint before breakfast, a pint at breakfast with his bread and cheese, a pint between breakfast and dinner, a

pint at dinner, a pint in the afternoon about six o'clock, and another when he had done his day's work. I thought it a detestable custom; but it was necessary, he suppos'd, to drink *strong* beer, that he might be *strong* to labour. I endeavoured to convince him that the bodily strength afforded by beer could only be in proportion to the grain or flour of the barley dissolved in the water of which it was made; that there was more flour in a pennyworth of bread; and therefore, if he would eat that with a pint of water, it would give him more strength than a quart of beer. . . .

I was now on a fair footing with them, and soon acquir'd considerable influence. I propos'd some reasonable alterations in their chappel laws, and carried them against all opposition. From my example, a great part of them left their muddling breakfast of beer, and bread, and cheese,

[*Back in Philadelphia in 1727, Franklin closed a contract to work again with his former employer, Samuel Keimer, planning secretly to save and set up his own print shop in competition. While with Keimer, he trained several unlearned men to become fair or good printers, put the printing house in order, cast his own type, learned to engrave, make ink and act as warehouseman. He called himself "quite a fac-totum." –Ed.*]

Autobiography

Twyford, at the Bishop of Asaph's, 1771.

I should have mentioned before, that, in the autumn of the preceding year, I had form'd most of my ingenious acquaintance into a club of mutual improvement, which we called the JUNTO; we met on Friday evenings. The rules

Franklin was quick at composing type, and the work he performed in London printing houses was like the activity in this composing room from Diderot's 18th-century *Encyclopedia.* Figure 1 (left) composes type; figure 2 places the letters in a galley tray, and figure 3 arranges pages in sequence. *(Historical Pictures Service, Chicago.)*

finding they could with me be supply'd from a neighbouring house with a large porringer of hot water-gruel, sprinkled with pepper, crumb'd with bread, and a bit of butter in it, for the price of a pint of beer, viz., three half-pence. This was a more comfortable as well as cheaper breakfast, and kept their heads clearer. Those who continued sotting with beer all day, were often, by not paying, out of credit at the alehouse, and us'd to make interest with me to get beer; their *light*, as they phrased it, *being out*. I watch'd the pay-table on Saturday night, and collected what I stood engaged for them, having to pay sometimes near thirty shillings a week on their accounts. This, and my being esteem'd a pretty good *riggite*, that is, a jocular verbal satirist, supported my consequence in the society. My constant attendance (I never making a St. Monday) recommended me to the master; and my uncommon quickness at composing occasioned my being put upon all work of dispatch, which was generally better paid. So I went on now very agreeably.

that I drew up required that every member, in his turn, should produce one or more queries on any point of Morals, Politics, or Natural Philosophy, to be discuss'd by the company; and once in three months produce and read an essay of his own writing, on any subject he pleased. Our debates were to be under the direction of a president, and to be conducted in the sincere spirit of inquiry after truth, without fondness for dispute, or desire of victory; and, to prevent warmth, all expressions of positiveness in opinions, or direct contradiction, were after some time made contraband, and prohibited under small pecuniary penalties. . . .

A Monday Morning View of

FRIENDS MEETING HOUSE and ACADEMY, PHILAD⁴

Forty years ago.

But my giving this account of it here is to show something of the interest I had, every one of these exerting themselves in recommending business to us. [Joseph] Breintnal particularly procur'd us from the Quakers the printing forty sheets of their history, the rest being to be done by Keimer; and upon this we work'd exceedingly hard, for the price was low. It was a folio, pro patria size, in pica, with long primer notes. I compos'd of it a sheet a day, and Meredith worked it off at press; it was often eleven at night, and sometimes later, before I had finished my distribution for the next day's work, for the little jobbs sent in by our other friends now and then put us back. But so determin'd I was to continue doing a sheet a day of the folio, that one night, when, having impos'd my forms, I thought my day's work over, one of them by accident was broken, and two pages reduced to pi, I immediately distributed and compos'd it over again before I went to bed; and this industry, visible to our neighbors, began to give us character and credit; particularly, I was told, that mention being made of the new printing-office at the merchants' Every-night club, the general opinion was that it must fail, there being already two printers in the place, Keimer and Bradford; but Dr. Baird (whom you and I saw many years after at his native place, St. Andrew's in Scotland) gave a

The numerous Quakers had several meeting-houses in Philadelphia, in addition to the one Franklin mentions sleeping in when he first arrived, and these large buildings at 4th and Chestnut, built in 1763, served for their meetings and classes. *(The Quaker Collection, Haverford College Library.)*

contrary opinion: "For the industry of that Franklin," says he, "is superior to any thing I ever saw of the kind; I see him still at work when I go home from club, and he is at work again before his neighbors are out of bed." This struck the rest, and we soon after had offers from one of them to supply us with stationery; but as yet we did not choose to engage in shop business.

I mention this industry the more particularly and the more freely, tho' it seems to be talking in my own praise, that those of my posterity, who shall read it, may know the use of that virtue, when they see its effects in my favour throughout this relation.

Autobiography

Twyford, at the Bishop of Asaph's, 1771.

. . . In order to secure my credit and character as a tradesman, I took care not only to be in *reality* industrious

(continued on p. 41)

Franklin made a point of looking the industrious
tradesman when he opened his own printing shop
in 1728 in Philadelphia at the young age of 22.
(Historical Pictures Service, Chicago.)

HIGH STREET, From the Country Market-place PHILADELPHIA.

High Street, Philadelphia, was the area in which
Franklin settled, upon his return to the city in
1726. His business and home were built along
this street. *(Historical Society of Pennsylvania.)*

A maxim from "Poor Richard Illustrated":
Creditors have better memories than debtors.
(Library of Congress.)

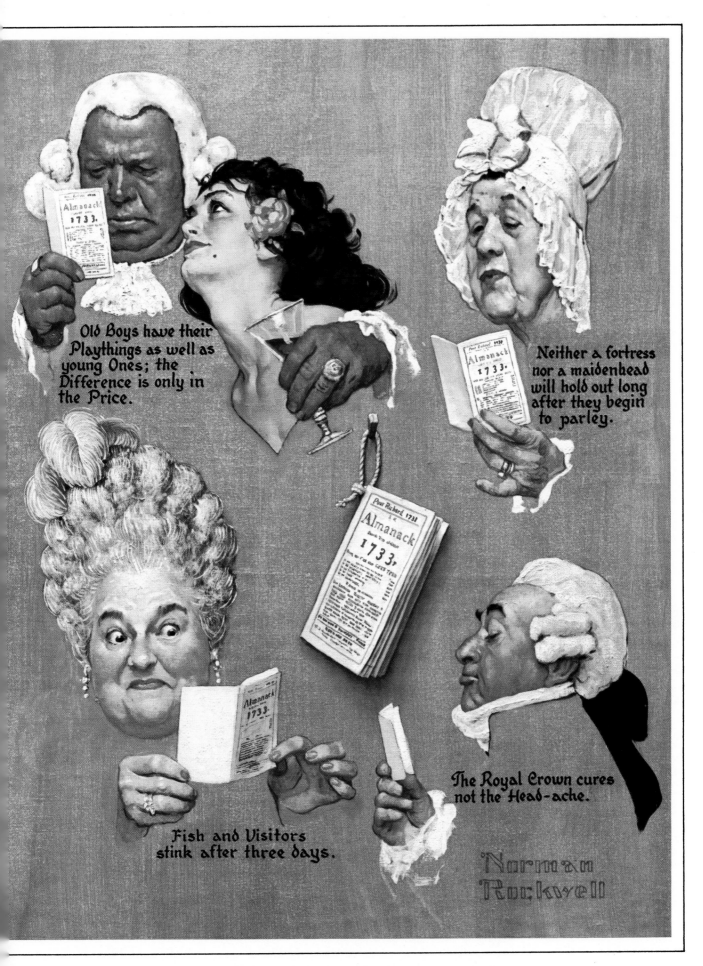

Old Boys have their Playthings as well as young Ones; the Difference is only in the Price.

Neither a fortress nor a maidenhead will hold out long after they begin to parley.

Fish and Visitors stink after three days.

The Royal Crown cures not the Head-ache.

Norman Rockwell

The year 1733 saw the first of the incomparable *Poor Richard's Almanacks*, which, over the 25 years of their publication, became a Pennsylvania institution that farmers, businessmen, matrons, lovers and politicians alike looked forward to. *(Norman Rockwell painting from the collection of Mr. Joseph Hennage.)*

A good Wife and Health, is a Man's best Wealth. — Poor Richard's Almanack.

Deborah Reed became Franklin's wife in September 1730, a marriage
that lasted 44 companionable years. Because of his absences in London
over the course of 15 years, Franklin commissioned Benjamin Wilson to
paint this portrait of Deborah and one of himself to be hung together in
their Philadelphia home. *(American Philosophical Society.)*

A son, Francis Folger, lived only 4 years and died of small-pox, which Franklin bitterly regretted, for he speculated that this boy might have grown to be the best of his three children. *(Attributed to Samuel Johnson, Frick Art Reference Library.)*

places; but soon found that, the business of a printer being generally thought a poor one, I was not to expect money with a wife, unless with such a one as I should not otherwise think agreeable. In the mean time, that hard-to-be-governed passion of youth hurried me frequently into intrigues with low women that fell in my way, which were attended with some expense and great inconvenience, besides a continual risque to my health by a distemper which of all things I dreaded, though by great good luck I escaped it. A friendly correspondence as neighbours and old acquaintances had continued between me and Mrs. Read's family, who all had a regard for me from the time of my first lodging in their house. I was often invited there and consulted in their affairs, wherein I sometimes was of service. I piti'd poor Miss Read's unfortunate situation, who was generally dejected, seldom chearful, and avoided company. I considered my giddiness and inconstancy when in London as in a great degree the cause of her unhappiness, tho' the mother was good enough to think the fault more her own than mine, as she had prevented our marrying before I went thither, and persuaded the other match in my absence. Our mutual affection was revived, but there were now great objections to our union. The match was indeed looked upon as invalid, a preceding wife [of Deborah

and frugal, but to avoid all appearances to the contrary. I drest plainly; I was seen at no places of idle diversion. I never went out a fishing or shooting; a book, indeed, sometimes debauch'd me from my work, but that was seldom, snug, and gave no scandal; and, to show that I was not above my business, I sometimes brought home the paper I purchas'd at the stores thro' the streets on a wheelbarrow. Thus being esteem'd an industrious, thriving young man, and paying duly for what I bought, the merchants who imported stationery solicited my custom; others proposed supplying me with books, and I went on swimmingly. In the mean time, Keimer's credit and business declining daily, he was at last forc'd to sell his printing-house to satisfy his creditors. He went to Barbadoes, and there lived some years in very poor circumstances. . . .

There remained now no competitor with me at Philadelphia but the old one, Bradford; who was rich and easy, did a little printing now and then by straggling hands, but was not very anxious about the business. However, as he kept the post-office, it was imagined he had better opportunities of obtaining news; his paper was thought a better distributer of advertisements than mine, and therefore had many more, which was a profitable thing to him, and a disadvantage to me; for, tho' I did indeed receive and send papers by the post, yet the publick opinion was otherwise, for what I did send was by bribing the riders, who took them privately, Bradford being unkind enough to forbid it, which occasion'd some resentment on my part; and I thought so meanly of him for it, that, when I afterward came into his situation, I took care never to imitate it.

Autobiography

Twyford, at the Bishop of Asaph's, 1771.
. . . Having turned my thoughts to marriage, I look'd round me and made overtures of acquaintance in other

Franklin said of his wife, Deborah, shown here stitching pamphlets: "Frugality is an enriching Virtue; A Virtue I never could acquire in myself; but I was once lucky enough to find it in a Wife, who thereby became a Fortune to me."
(Yale University Library.)

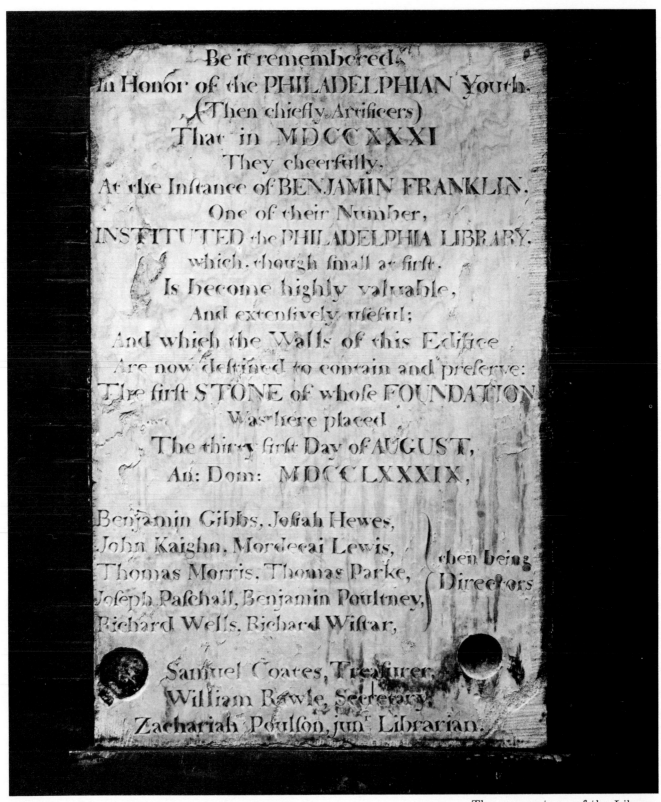

The cornerstone of the Library Company of Philadelphia with a tribute to Franklin, who initiated the plan for its founding. *(Library Company of Philadelphia.)*

Read's first husband, who deserted her in 1727 or 1728] being said to be living in England; but this could not easily be prov'd, because of the distance; and, tho' there was a report of his death, it was not certain. Then, tho' it should be true, he had left many debts, which his successor might be call'd upon to pay. We ventured, however, over all these difficulties, and I took her to wife, September 1st, 1730. None of the inconveniences happened that we had apprehended; she proved a good and faithful helpmate, assisted me much by attending the shop; we throve together, and have ever mutually endeavour'd to make each other happy. Thus I corrected that great *erratum* as well as I could.

Autobiography

Passy, near Paris, 1784.

We have an English proverb that says, "*He that would thrive, must ask his wife.*" It was lucky for me that I had one as much dispos'd to industry and frugality as myself. She assisted me chearfully in my business, folding and stitching pamphlets, tending shop, purchasing old linen rags for the paper-makers, etc., etc. We kept no idle servants,

Franklin at a desk, by David Rent Etter,
from the side panel of a hand pump engine.
(Insurance Company of North America.)

our table was plain and simple, our furniture of the cheapest. For instance, my breakfast was a long time bread and milk (no tea), and I ate it out of a twopenny earthen porringer, with a pewter spoon. But mark how luxury will enter families, and make a progress, in spite of principle: being call'd one morning to breakfast, I found it in a China bowl, with a spoon of silver! They had been bought for me without my knowledge by my wife, and had cost her the enormous sum of three-and-twenty shillings, for which she had no other excuse or apology to make, but that she thought *her* husband deserv'd a silver spoon and China bowl as well as any of his neighbors. This was the first appearance of plate and China in our house, which afterward, in a course of years, as our wealth increas'd, augmented gradually to several hundred pounds in value.

Autobiography

Twyford, at the Bishop of Asaph's, 1771.
And now I set on foot my first project of a public nature, that for a subscription library. I drew up the proposals, got them put into form by our great scrivener, Brockden, and, by the help of my friends in the Junto, procured fifty subscribers of forty shillings each to begin with, and ten shillings a year for fifty years, the term our company was to continue. We afterwards obtain'd a charter, the company being increased to one hundred: this was the mother of all the North American subscription libraries, now so numerous. It is become a great thing itself, and continually increasing. These libraries have improved the general conversation of the Americans, made the common tradesmen and farmers as intelligent as most gentlemen from other countries, and perhaps have contributed in some degree to the stand so generally made throughout the colonies in defence of their privileges.

Autobiography

Passy, near Paris, 1784.
It was about this time I conceiv'd the bold and arduous project of arriving at moral perfection. I wish'd to live with-

out committing any fault at any time; I would conquer all that either natural inclination, custom, or company might lead me into. As I knew, or thought I knew, what was right and wrong, I did not see why I might not always do the one and avoid the other. But I soon found I had undertaken a task of more difficulty than I had imagined. While my care was employ'd in guarding against one fault, I was often surprised by another; habit took the advantage of inattention; inclination was sometimes too strong for reason. I concluded, at length, that the mere speculative conviction that it was our interest to be completely virtuous, was not sufficient to prevent our slipping; and that the contrary habits must be broken, and good ones acquired and established, before we can have any dependence on a steady, uniform rectitude of conduct. For this purpose I therefore contrived the following method.

In the various enumerations of the moral virtues I had met with in my reading, I found the catalogue more or less numerous. . . . I propos'd to myself, for the sake of clearness, to use rather more names, with fewer ideas annex'd to each, than a few names with more ideas; and I included under thirteen names of virtues all that at that time occurr'd to me as necessary or desirable, and annexed to each a short precept, which fully express'd the extent I gave to its meaning.

These names of virtues, with their precepts, were:

1. Temperance.
Eat not to dullness; drink not to elevation.
2. Silence.
Speak not but what may benefit others or yourself; avoid trifling conversation.

The Philadelphia artist Charles Wilson Peale, also a many-talented genius, painted Franklin's portrait about 1785, capturing the aura of benevolence and tranquility for which Franklin aimed in his plan for moral perfection. *(Pennsylvania Academy of the Fine Arts, Joseph and Sarah Harrison Collection.)*

3. Order.

Let all your things have their places; let each part of your business have its time.

4. Resolution.

Resolve to perform what you ought; perform without fail what you resolve.

5. Frugality.

Make no expense but to do good to others or yourself; *i.e.*, waste nothing.

6. Industry.

Lose no time; be always employ'd in something useful; cut off all unnecessary actions.

7. Sincerity.

Use no hurtful deceit; think innocently and justly, and, if you speak, speak accordingly.

8. Justice.

Wrong none by doing injuries, or omitting the benefits that are your duty.

9. Moderation.

Avoid extreams; forbear resenting injuries so much as you think they deserve.

10. Cleanliness.

Tolerate no uncleanliness in body, clothes, or habitation.

11. Tranquillity.

Be not disturbed at trifles, or at accidents common or unavoidable.

12. Chastity.

Rarely use venery but for health or offspring, never to dullness, weakness, or the injury of your own or another's peace or reputation.

13. Humility.

Imitate Jesus and Socrates.

My intention being to acquire the *habitude* of all these virtues, I judg'd it would be well not to distract my attention by attempting the whole at once, but to fix it on one of them at a time; and, when I should be master of that, then to proceed to another, and so on, till I should have gone thro' the thirteen; and, as the previous acquisition of some might facilitate the acquisition of certain others, I arrang'd them with that view, as they stand above. . . .

I made a little book, in which I allotted a page for each of the virtues. I rul'd each page with red ink, so as to have seven columns, one for each day of the week, marking each column with a letter for the day. I cross'd these columns with thirteen red lines, marking the beginning of each line with the first letter of one of the virtues, on which line, and in its proper column, I might mark, by a little black spot, every fault I found upon examination to have been committed respecting that virtue upon that day. . . .

I determined to give a week's strict attention to each of the virtues necessary. . . . Thus, if in the first week I could keep my first line, marked T, clear of spots, I suppos'd the habit of that virtue so much strengthen'd, and its opposite weaken'd, that I might venture extending my attention to include the next, and for the following week keep both lines clear of spots. Proceeding thus to the last, I could go thro' a course compleat in thirteen weeks, and four courses in a year. And like him who, having a garden to weed, does not attempt to eradicate all the bad herbs at once, which would exceed his reach and his strength, but works on one of the beds at a time, and, having accomplish'd the first, proceeds to a second, so I should have, I hoped, the encouraging pleasure of seeing on my pages the progress I made in virtue, by clearing successively my lines of their

spots, till in the end, by a number of courses, I should be happy in viewing a clean book, after a thirteen weeks' daily examination. . . .

The precept of *Order* requiring that *every part of my business should have its allotted time*, one page in my little book contain'd the following scheme of employment for the twenty-four hours of a natural day.

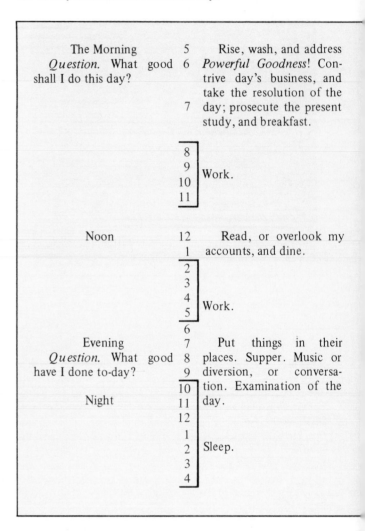

The Morning	5	Rise, wash, and address
Question. What good	6	*Powerful Goodness!* Contrive day's business, and take the resolution of the
shall I do this day?	7	day; prosecute the present study, and breakfast.
	8	
	9	Work.
	10	
	11	
Noon	12	Read, or overlook my
	1	accounts, and dine.
	2	
	3	
	4	Work.
	5	
	6	
Evening	7	Put things in their
Question. What good	8	places. Supper. Music or
have I done to-day?	9	diversion, or conversation. Examination of the
	10	tion. Examination of the
Night	11	day.
	12	
	1	
	2	Sleep.
	3	
	4	

I enter'd upon the execution of this plan for self-examination, and continu'd it with occasional intermissions for some time. I was surpris'd to find myself so much fuller of faults than I had imagined; but I had the satisfaction of seeing them diminish. . . . After a while I went thro' one course only in a year, and afterward only one in several years, till at length I omitted them entirely, being employ'd in voyages and business abroad, with a multiplicity of affairs that interfered; but I always carried my little book with me.

My scheme of Order gave me the most trouble; and I found that, tho' it might be practicable where a man's business was such as to leave him the disposition of his time, that of a journeyman printer, for instance, it was not possible to be exactly observed by a master, who must mix with the world, and often receive people of business at their own hours. *Order*, too, with regard to places for things, papers, etc., I found extreamly difficult to acquire. I had not been early accustomed to it, and, having an exceeding good memory, I was not so sensible of the inconvenience attending want of method. This article, therefore, cost me so much painful attention, and my faults in it vexed me so much, and I made so little progress in amendment, and had such frequent relapses, that I was almost ready to give up the attempt, and content myself with a faulty character in that respect.... For something ... that pretended to be reason, was every now and then suggesting to me that such extream nicety as I exacted of myself might be a kind of foppery in morals, which, if it were known, would make me ridiculous; that a perfect character might be attended with the inconvenience of being envied and hated; and that a benevolent man should allow a few faults in himself, to keep his friends in countenance.

Autobiography

Passy, near Paris, 1784.

My list of virtues contain'd at first but twelve; but a Quaker friend having kindly informed me that I was generally thought proud; that my pride show'd itself frequently in conversation; that I was not content with being in the right when discussing any point, but was overbearing, and rather insolent, of which he convinc'd me by mentioning several instances; I determined endeavouring to cure myself, if I could, of this vice or folly among the rest, and I added *Humility* to my list, giving an extensive meaning to the word.

I cannot boast of much success in acquiring the *reality* of this virtue, but I had a good deal with regard to the *appearance* of it. I made it a rule to forbear all direct contradiction to the sentiments of others, and all positive assertion of my own. . . .

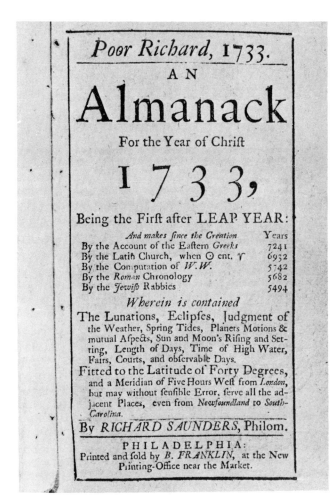

The title page of Franklin's first *Poor Richard's Almanack.* (Philip H. and A.S.W. Rosenbach Foundation, Philadelphia.)

Form of the pages.

Temperance.						
Eat Not To Dulness. Drink Not To Elevation.						
	S.	M.	T.	W.	T.	F.	S.
T.							
S.	*	*		*		*	
O.	* *	*	*		*	*	*
R.			*			*	
F.		*		*			
I.		*					
S.							
J.							
M.							
C.							
T.							
C.							
H.							

Franklin's "little book" for daily examination of virtues maintained and errors committed.

And this mode, which I at first put on with some violence to natural inclination, became at length so easy, and so habitual to me, that perhaps for these fifty years past no one has ever heard a dogmatical expression escape me. And to this habit (after my character of integrity) I think it principally owing that I had early so much weight with my fellow-citizens when I proposed new institutions, or alterations in the old, and so much influence in public councils when I became a member; for I was but a bad speaker, never eloquent, subject to much hesitation in my choice of words, hardly correct in language, and yet I generally carried my points.

In reality, there is, perhaps, no one of our natural passions so hard to subdue as *pride*. Disguise it, struggle with it, beat it down, stifle it, mortify it as much as one pleases, it is still alive, and will every now and then peep out and show itself; you will see it, perhaps, often in this history; for, even if I could conceive that I had compleatly overcome it, I should probably be proud of my humility.

Autobiography

Philadelphia, August, 1788.

In 1732 I first publish'd my Almanack, under the name of *Richard Saunders*; it was continu'd by me about twenty-five years, commonly call'd *Poor Richard's Almanack*. I endeavour'd to make it both entertaining and useful, and it accordingly came to be in such demand, that I reap'd considerable profit from it, vending annually near ten thousand. And observing that it was generally read, scarce any neighborhood in the province being without it, I consider'd

it as a proper vehicle for conveying instruction among the common people, who bought scarcely any other books; I therefore filled all the little spaces that occurr'd between the remarkable days in the calendar with proverbial sentences, chiefly such as inculcated industry and frugality, as the means of procuring wealth, and thereby securing virtue; it being more difficult for a man in want, to act always honestly, as, to use here one of those proverbs, *it is hard for an empty sack to stand upright.*

These proverbs, which contained the wisdom of many ages and nations, I assembled and form'd into a connected discourse prefix'd to the Almanack of 1757, as the harangue of a wise old man to the people attending an auction. The bringing all these scatter'd counsels thus into a focus enabled them to make greater impression.

From the *Preface to* **Poor Richard's Almanack**, 1733

Courteous Reader,

I might in this place attempt to gain thy Favour, by declaring that I write Almanacks with no other View than that of the publick Good; but in this I should not be sincere; and Men are now adays too wise to be deceiv'd by Pretences how specious soever. The Plain Truth of the Matter is, I am excessive poor, and my Wife, good Woman, is, I tell her, excessive proud; she cannot bear, she says, to sit spinning in her Shift of Tow, while I do nothing but gaze at the Stars; and has threatned more than once to burn all my Books and Rattling-Traps (as she calls my Instruments) if I do not make some profitable Use of them for the Good of

my Family. The Printer has offer'd me some considerable share of the Profits, and I have thus begun to comply with my Dame's Desire.

THE WAY TO WEALTH
From the *Preface to* **Poor Richard Improved**: 1758
FATHER ABRAHAM'S SPEECH

... I stopped my Horse lately where a great Number of People were collected at a Vendue of Merchant Goods. The Hour of Sale not being come, they were conversing on the Badness of the Times and one of the Company call'd to a plain clean old Man, with white Locks, "Pray, Father Abraham, what think you of the Times? Won't these heavy Taxes quite ruin the Country? How shall we be ever able to pay them? What would you advise us to?" Father *Abraham* stood up, and reply'd, "If you'd have my Advice, I'll give it you in short, for *A Word to the Wise is enough*, and *many Words won't fill a Bushel*, as *Poor Richard* says." They join'd in desiring him to speak his Mind, and gathering round him, he proceeded as follows;

"Friends," says he, and Neighbours, "the Taxes are indeed very heavy, and if those laid on by the Government were the only Ones we had to pay, we might more easily discharge them; but we have many others, and much more grievous to some of us. We are taxed twice as much by our *Idleness*, three times as much by our *Pride*, and four times as much by our *Folly*; and from these Taxes the Commissioners cannot ease or deliver us by allowing an Abatement. However let us hearken to good Advice, and something may be done for us; *God helps them that help themselves*, as *Poor Richard* says, in his Almanack of 1733.

It would be thought a hard Government that should tax its People one-tenth Part of their *Time*, to be employed in its Service. But *Idleness* taxes many of us much more, if we reckon all that is spent in absolute *Sloth*, or doing of nothing, with that which is spent in idle Employments or Amusements, that amount to nothing. *Sloth*, by bringing on Diseases, absolutely shortens Life. . . . *But dost thou love Life, then do not squander Time, for that's the stuff Life is made of*, as *Poor Richard* says. How much more than is necessary do we spend in sleep, forgetting that *The sleeping Fox catches no Poultry*, and that *There will be sleeping enough in the Grave*, as *Poor Richard* says.

If Time be of all Things the most precious, wasting Time must be, as *Poor Richard* says, *the greatest Prodigality*; since, as he elsewhere tells us, *Lost Time is never found again; and what we call Time enough, always proves little enough*; Let us then up and be doing, and doing to the Purpose; so by Diligence shall we do more with less Perplexity. *Sloth makes all Things difficult, but Industry all easy*, as *Poor Richard* says; and *He that riseth late must trot all Day, and shall scarce overtake his Business at Night*; while *Laziness travels so slowly, that Poverty soon overtakes him*, as we read in *Poor Richard*, who adds, *Drive thy Business, let not that drive thee*; and *Early to Bed, and early to rise, makes a Man healthy, wealthy, and wise*.

So what signifies *wishing* and *hoping* for better Times. We may make these Times better, if we bestir ourselves. *Industry need not wish*, as *Poor Richard* says, *and he that lives upon Hope will die fasting*. . . . And, as *Poor Richard* likewise observes, *He that hath a Trade hath an Estate; and he that hath a Calling, hath an Office of Profit and Honour*. . . . Work while it is called To-day, for you know not how much you may be hindered To-morrow, which makes *Poor Richard* say, *One to-day is worth two To-morrows*, and farther, *Have you somewhat to do To-morrow, do it To-day*. If you were a Servant, would you not be ashamed that a good Master should catch you idle? Are you then your own Master, *be ashamed to catch yourself idle*, as *Poor Dick* says. When there is so much to be

Below: ' He that hath a trade hath an estate," an maxim from "Poor Richard Illustrated." *(Yale University Library.)*

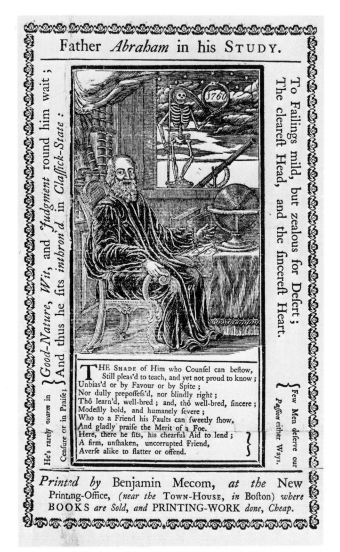

"Father Abraham in his study" is depicted on this 1760 edition of *The Way to Wealth*. *(Rare Book Division, New York Public Library.)*

done for yourself, your Family, your Country, and your gracious King, be up by Peep of Day; *Let not the Sun look down and say, Inglorious here he lies*. Handle your Tools without Mittens; remember that *The Cat in Gloves catches no Mice*, as *Poor Richard* says. 'Tis true there is much to be done, and perhaps you are weak-handed, but stick to it steadily; and you will see great Effects, for *Constant Dropping wears away Stones*, and by *Diligence and Patience the Mouse ate in two the Cable*; and *Little Strokes fell great Oaks*, as *Poor Richard* says in his Almanack, the Year I cannot just now remember.

Methinks I hear some of you say, *Must a Man afford himself no Leisure?* I will tell thee, my friend, what *Poor Richard* says, *Employ thy Time well, if thou meanest to gain Leisure; and, since thou art not sure of a Minute, throw not away an Hour*. Leisure, is Time for doing something useful; this Leisure the diligent Man will obtain, but the lazy Man never; so that, as *Poor Richard* says *A Life of Leisure and a Life of Laziness are two Things*. . . .

But with our Industry, we must likewise be *steady, settled*, and *careful*, and oversee our own Affairs *with our own Eyes*, and not trust too much to others; for, as *Poor Richard* says

I never saw an oft-removed Tree,
Nor yet an oft-removed Family,
That throve so well as those that settled be.

And again, *Three Removes is as bad as a Fire*; and again, *Keep thy Shop, and thy Shop will keep thee....* And again, *The Eye of a Master will do more Work than both his Hands*; and, again, *Want of Care does us more Damage than Want of Knowledge*; and again, *Not to oversee Workmen, is to leave them your Purse open.* Trusting too much to others' Care is the Ruin of many; for, as the Almanack says, *In the Affairs of this World, Men are saved, not by Faith, but by the Want of it....* And again, he adviseth to Circumspection and Care, even in the smallest Matters, because

Gleanings from the 1753 *Almanack* went into "Father Abraham's Speech," the long-winded harangue which was also published as *The Way to Wealth.* (*Franklin Institute, Philadelphia.*)

sometimes *A little Neglect may breed great Mischief*; adding, *for want of a Nail the Shoe was lost; for want of a Shoe the Horse was lost; and for want of a Horse the Rider was lost, being overtaken and slain by the Enemy; all for want of Care about a Horse-shoe Nail.*

So much for Industry, my Friends, and Attention to one's own Business; but to these we must add *Frugality*, if we would make our *Industry* more certainly successful. A

Man may, if he knows not how to save as he gets, *keep his Nose all his Life to the Grindstone*, and die not worth a *Groat* at last. *A fat Kitchen makes a lean Will....* And farther, *What maintains one Vice, would bring up two Children.* You may think perhaps, that a *little* Tea or a *little* Punch now and then, Diet a *little* more costly, Clothes a *little* finer, and a *little* Entertainment now and then, can be no *great* Matter; but remember what *Poor Richard* says, *Many a Little makes a Mickle*; and farther, Beware of *little Expences*; a *Small Leak will sink a great Ship*; and again, *Who Dainties love, shall Beggars prove*; and moreover, *Fools make Feasts, and wise Men eat them.*

Here you are all got together at this Vendue of *Fineries* and *Knicknacks.* You call them *Goods*; but if you do not take Care, they will prove *Evils* to some of you.... Remember what *Poor Richard* says; *Buy what thou hast no Need of, and ere long thou shalt sell thy Necessaries....* Many a one, for the Sake of Finery on the Back, have gone with a hungry Belly, and half-starved their Families. *Silks and Sattins, Scarlet and Velvets*, as *Poor Richard* says, *put out the Kitchen Fire.*

These are not the *Necessaries* of Life; they can scarcely be called the *Conveniences*; and yet only because they look pretty, how *many* want to *have* them! The *artificial* Wants of Mankind thus become more numerous than the *Natural....* But who through Industry and Frugality have maintained their Standing; in which Case it appears plainly, that *A Ploughman on his Legs is higher than a Gentleman on his Knees*, as *Poor Richard* says. Perhaps they have had a small Estate left them, which they knew not the Getting of; they think, *'tis Day, and will never be Night*; that a little to be spent out of *so much*, is not worth minding; *a Child and a Fool*, as *Poor Richard* says, *imagine Twenty shillings and Twenty Years can never be spent* but, *always taking out of the Meal-tub, and never putting in, soon comes to the Bottom*; as *Poor Dick* says, *When the Well's dry, they know the Worth of Water.* But this they might have known before, if they had taken his Advice; *If you would know the Value of Money, go and try to borrow some; for, he that goes a borrowing goes a sorrowing....* And again, *Pride is as loud a Beggar as Want, and a great deal more saucy....* And 'tis as truly Folly for the Poor to ape the Rich, as for the Frog to swell, in order to equal the ox.

> *Great Estates may venture more,*
> *But little Boats should keep near Shore.*

'Tis, however, a Folly soon punished; for *Pride that dines on Vanity, sups on Contempt*, as *Poor Richard* says. And in another Place, *Pride breakfasted with Plenty, dined with Poverty, and supped with Infamy....*

...But, ah, think what you do when you run in Debt; *you give to another Power over your Liberty.* If you cannot pay at the Time, you will be ashamed to see your Creditor; you will be in Fear when you speak to him; you will make poor pitiful sneaking Excuses, and by Degrees come to lose your Veracity, and sink into base downright lying.... But Poverty often deprives a Man of all Spirit and Virtue: *'Tis hard for an empty Bag to stand upright*, as *Poor Richard* truly says.

...And yet you are about to put yourself under that Tyranny, when you run in Debt for such Dress!... When you have got your Bargain, you may, perhaps, think little of Payment; but *Creditors, Poor Richard* tells us, *have better Memories than Debtors....* Then since, as he says, *The Borrower is a Slave to the Lender, and the Debtor to the Creditor*, disdain the Chain, preserve your Freedom; and maintain your Independency: Be *industrious* and *free*; be

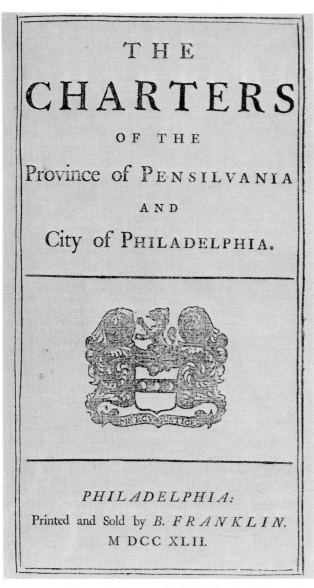

THE

CHARTERS

OF THE

Province of PENSILVANIA

AND

City of PHILADELPHIA.

PHILADELPHIA:
Printed and Sold by *B. FRANKLIN.*
M DCC XLII.

Two of the profitable jobs that Franklin secured from his contacts in the Assembly were printing the colonial charters (above) and paper currency, for which he contrived a detailed pattern which would be difficult to counterfeit — if the threat of death to counterfeiters was not enough. *(Insurance Company of North America* and *American Philosophical Society.)*

frugal and *free.* At present, perhaps you may think yourself in thriving Circumstances, and that you can bear a little Extravagance without Injury; but,

For Age and Want, save while you may;
No Morning Sun lasts a whole Day,

as *Poor Richard* says. Gain may be temporary and uncertain, but ever while you live, Expence is constant and certain; and *'tis easier to build two Chimnies, than to keep one in Fuel,* as *Poor Richard* says. So, *Rather go to Bed supperless than rise in Debt. . . .*

This Doctrine, my Friends, is *Reason* and *Wisdom;* but after all, do not depend too much upon your own *Industry,* and *Frugality,* and *Prudence,* though excellent Things, for they may all be blasted without the Blessing of Heaven; and therefore, ask that Blessing humbly, and be not uncharitable to those that at present seem to want it, but comfort and help them. Remember, *Job* suffered, and was afterwards prosperous.

And now to conclude, *Experience keeps a dear School, but Fools will learn in no other, and scarce in that;* for it is true, *we may give Advice, but we cannot give Conduct,* as *Poor Richard* says: However, remember this, *They that won't be counselled, can't be helped,* as *Poor Richard* says: and farther, That, *if you will not hear Reason, she'll surely rap your Knuckles."*

Thus the old Gentleman ended his Harangue. The People heard it, and approved the Doctrine, and immediately practised the contrary, just as if it had been a common Sermon; for the Vendue opened, and they began to buy extravagantly, notwithstanding, his Cautions and their own Fear of Taxes. . . . The frequent Mention he made of me must have tired any one else, but my Vanity was wonderfully delighted with it, though I was conscious that not a tenth Part of the Wisdom was my own, which he ascribed to me, but rather the *Gleanings* I had made of the Sense of all Ages and Nations. However, I resolved to be the better for the Echo of it; and though I had at first determined to buy Stuff for a new Coat, I went away resolved to wear my old One a little longer. *Reader,* if thou wilt do the same, thy Profit will be as great as mine. *I am, as ever, thine to serve thee,*

Richard Saunders.
July 7, 1757

Autobiography

Philadelphia, August, 1788.

My first promotion was my being chosen, in 1736, clerk of the General Assembly. The choice was made that year without opposition; but the year following, when I was again propos'd (the choice, like that of the members, being annual), a new member made a long speech against me, in order to favour some other candidate. I was, however, chosen, which was the more agreeable to me, as, besides the pay for the immediate service as clerk, the place gave me a better opportunity of keeping up an interest among the members, which secur'd to me the business of printing the votes, laws, paper money, and other occasional jobbs for the public, that, on the whole, were very profitable.

A 1792 hand pump engine owned by the
Franklin Company of firefighters in Philadelphia.
(Insurance Company of North America.)

This colonial postrider looks like a
caricature of Franklin, not an unlikely
association, since as a widely-traveled
Postmaster General, he must have been
synonymous with the office throughout the
colonies. *(American Antiquarian Society.)*

Autobiography

Philadelphia, August, 1788.

In 1737, Colonel Spotswood, late governor of Virginia, and then postmaster-general, being dissatisfied with the conduct of his deputy at Philadelphia, respecting some negligence in rendering, and inexactitude of his accounts, took from him the commission and offered it to me. I accepted it readily, and found it of great advantage; for tho' the salary was small, it facilitated the correspondence that improv'd my newspaper, increas'd the number demanded, as well as the advertisements to be inserted, so that it came to afford me a considerable income. My old competitor's newspaper declin'd proportionably, and I was satisfy'd without retaliating his refusal, while postmaster, to permit my papers being carried by the riders. Thus he suffer'd greatly from his neglect in due accounting; and I mention it as a lesson to those young men who may be employ'd in managing affairs for others, that they should always render accounts, and make remittances, with great clearness and punctuality. The character of observing such a conduct is the most powerful of all recommendations to new employments and increase of business.

Autobiography

Philadelphia, August, 1788.

About this time I wrote a paper (first to be read in Junto, but it was afterward publish'd) on the different accidents and carelessnesses by which houses were set on fire, with cautions against them, and means proposed of avoiding them. This was much spoken of as a useful piece, and gave rise to a project, which soon followed it, of forming a company for the more ready extinguishing of fires, and mutual assistance in removing and securing of goods when in danger. Associates in this scheme were presently found, amounting to thirty. Our articles of agreement oblig'd every member to keep always in good order, and fit for use, a certain number of leather buckets, with strong bags and baskets (for packing and transporting of goods), which were to be brought to every fire; and we agreed to meet once a month and spend a social evening together, in discoursing and communicating such ideas as occurred to us upon the subject of fires, as might be useful in our conduct on such occasions.

The utility of this institution soon appeared, and many more desiring to be admitted than we thought convenient for one company, they were advised to form another, which was accordingly done; and this went on, one new company being formed after another, till they became so numerous as to include most of the inhabitants who were men of property; and now, at the time of my writing this, tho' upward of fifty years since its establishment, that which I first formed, called the Union Fire Company, still subsists and flourishes.

From A PROPOSAL FOR PROMOTING USEFUL KNOWLEDGE AMONG THE BRITISH PLANTATIONS IN AMERICA

Philadelphia, May 14, 1743.

... The first drudgery of settling new colonies, which confines the attention of people to mere necessaries, is now pretty well over; and there are many in every province in circumstances that set them at ease, and afford leisure to cultivate the finer arts and improve the common stock of knowledge. To such of these who are men of speculation, many hints must from time to time arise, many observations occur, which if well examined, pursued, and improved, might produce discoveries to the advantage of some or all of the British plantations, or to the benefit of man-kind in general.

But as from the extent of the country such persons are widely separated, and seldom can see and converse or be acquainted with each other, so that many useful particulars remain uncommunicated, die with the discoverers, and are lost to mankind; it is, to remedy this inconvenience for the future, proposed.

That one society be formed of *virtuosi* or ingenious men, residing in the several colonies, to be called *The American Philosophical Society*, who are to maintain a constant correspondence.

Franklin joined in fighting fires, probably with the Union Fire Company which he formed in 1736. *(Insurance Company of North America.)* Metal badges like this eagle were called "fire marks" and identified houses of those insured with the Insurance Company of North America. *(Index of American Design and Decorative Arts.)*

That Philadelphia, being the city nearest the centre of the continent colonies . . . and having the advantage of a good growing library, be the centre of the Society.

That at Philadelphia there be always at least seven members, viz. a physician, a botanist, a mathematician, a chemist, mechanician, a geographer, and a general natural philosopher, besides a president, treasurer, and secretary.

That these members meet once a month, or oftener, at their own expense, to communicate to each other their observations and experiments, to receive, read, and consider such letters, communications, or queries as shall be sent from distant members; to direct the dispersing of copies of such communications as are valuable, to other distant members, in order to procure their sentiments thereupon.

That the subjects of the correspondence be: all new-discovered plants, herbs, trees, roots, their virtues, uses, &c.; methods of propagating them, and making such as are useful, but particular to some plantations, more general; improvements of vegetable juices, as ciders, wines, &c.; new methods of curing or preventing diseases; all new-discovered fossils in different countries, as mines, minerals, and quarries; new and useful improvements in any branch of mathematics; new discoveries in chemistry, such as improvements in distillation, brewing, and assaying of ores; new mechanical inventions for saving labour, as mills and carriages, and for raising and conveying of water, draining of meadows, &c.; all new arts, trades, and manufactures, that may be proposed or thought of; surveys, maps, and charts of particular parts of the sea-coasts or inland countries; course and junction of rivers and great roads, situation of lakes and mountains, nature of the soil and productions; new methods of improving the breed of useful animals; introducing other sorts from foreign countries; new improvements in planting, gardening, and clearing land; and all philosophical experiments that let light into the nature of things, tend to increase the power of man over matter, and multiply the conveniences or pleasures of life.

Autobiography

Philadelphia, August, 1788.

I had, on the whole, abundant reason to be satisfied with my being established in Pennsylvania. There were, however, two things that I regretted, there being no provision for defense, nor for a compleat education of youth; no militia, nor any college.

[*With respect to the first, Franklin began organizing support for a voluntary militia in order to have a defense against possible attacks on the western frontier from the French and Indians. He began with a pamphlet, PLAIN TRUTH, in which he "stated our defenceless situation in strong lights, with the necessity of union and descipline." The essay shamed the various contending factions of Quakers, proprietaries (the Penns), wealthy merchants or ordinary laborers into organizing for the public good. A militia was formed and armed and Franklin took his turn of duty as a common soldier. —Ed.*]

Autobiography

Philadelphia, August, 1788.

Peace being concluded, and the association business therefore at an end, I turn'd my thoughts again to the affair of establishing an academy. The first step I took was to associate in the design a number of active friends, of whom the Junto furnished a good part; the next was to write and publish a pamphlet, entitled *Proposals Relating to the Education of Youth in Pennsylvania*. This I distributed among the principal inhabitants gratis; and as soon as I could sup-

pose their minds a little prepared by the perusal of it, I set on foot a subscription for opening and supporting an academy; it was to be paid in quotas yearly for five years; by so dividing it, I judg'd the subscription might be larger, and I believe it was so, amounting to no less, if I remember right, than five thousand pounds. . . .

The subscribers, to carry the project into immediate execution, chose out of their number twenty-four trustees, and appointed Mr. Francis, then attorney general, and myself to draw up constitutions for the government of the academy; which being done and signed, a house was hired, masters engag'd, and the schools opened, I think, in the same year, 1749. . . .

The trustees of the academy, after a while, were incorporated by a charter from the governor; their funds were increas'd by contributions in Britain and grants of land from the proprietaries, to which the Assembly has since made considerable addition; and thus was established the present University of Philadelphia.

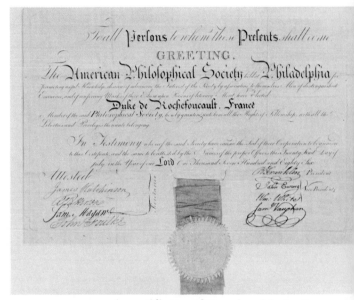

A certificate of membership in the American Philosophical Society, with Benjamin Franklin's signature as president. *(Insurance Company of North America.)*

From PROPOSALS RELATING TO THE EDUCATION OF YOUTH IN PENNSYLVANIA

[1749]

That we may obtain the Advantages arising from an Increase of Knowledge, and prevent as much as may be the mischievous Consequences that would attend a general Ignorance among us, the following Hints are offered towards forming a Plan for the Education of the Youth of *Pennsylvania*, viz.

It is propos'd,

That some Persons of Leisure and publick Spirit apply for a Charter, by which they may be incorporated, with Power to erect an Academy for the Education of Youth, to govern the same, provide Masters, make Rules, receive Donations, purchase Lands, etc., and to add to their Number, from Time to Time such other Persons as they shall judge suitable. . . .

That the Rector be a Man of good Understanding, good Morals, diligent and patient, learn'd in the Languages and Sciences, and a correct pure Speaker and Writer of the *English* Tongue; to have such Tutors under him as shall be necessary.

That the boarding Scholars diet together, plainly, temperately, and frugally.

That, to keep them in Health, and to strengthen and render active their Bodies, they be frequently exercis'd in Running, Leaping, Wrestling, and Swimming, &c. . . .

That they have peculiar Habits to distinguish them from other Youth, if the Academy be in or near the Town; for this, among other Reasons, that their Behaviour may be the better observed.

As to their Studies, it would be well if they could be taught every Thing that is useful, and every Thing that is ornamental: But Art is long, and their Time is short. It is therefore propos'd that they learn those Things that are likely to be *most useful* and *most ornamental*. Regard being had to the several Professions for which they are intended.

All should be taught to write a *fair Hand*, and swift, as that is useful to All. And with it may be learnt something

Non Votis, &c.

Franklin's 1747 pamphlet *Plain Truth*, advocating a militia to defend Pennsylvania frontiers, was printed with "The Waggoneer and Hercules," perhaps the first political cartoon in America. Hercules tells the farmer to prepare himself rather than to pray. *(American Philosophical Society.)*

of *Drawing*, by Imitation of Prints, and some of the first Principles of Perspective.

Arithmetick, Accounts, and some of the first Principles of *Geometry* and *Astronomy*.

The *English* Language might be taught by Grammar; in which some of our best Writers, as *Tillotson, Addison, Pope, Algernoon Sidney, Cato's Letters*, &c., should be Classicks: the Styles principally to be cultivated, being the clear and the concise. Reading should also be taught, and pronouncing, properly, distinctly, emphatically; not with an even Tone, which *under-does*, nor a theatrical, which *over-does* Nature. . . .

But if History be made a constant Part of their Reading, such as the Translations of the Greek and Roman Historians, and the modern Histories of ancient *Greece* and *Rome*, &c. may not almost all Kinds of useful Knowledge be that Way introduc'd to Advantage, and with Pleasure to the Student? As

Geography, by reading with Maps, and being required to point out the Places *where* the greatest Actions were done, to give their old and new Names, with the Bounds, Situation, Extent of the Countries concern'd, &c.

Chronology, by the Help of *Helvicus* or some other Writer of the Kind, who will enable them to tell *when* those Events happened. . . .

Antient Customs, religious and civil, being frequently mentioned in History, will give Occasion for explaining them; in which the Prints of Medals, Basso-Relievos, and antient Monuments will greatly assist.

Morality, by descanting and making continual Observations on the Causes of the Rise or Fall of any Man's Character, Fortune, Power &c. mention'd in History; the Advantages of Temperance, Order, Frugality, Industry, Perseverance &c. &c. Indeed the general natural Tendency of Reading good History must be, to fix in the Minds of Youth deep Impressions of the Beauty and Usefulness of Virtue of all Kinds, Publick Spirit, Fortitude, &c.

History will show the wonderful Effects of Oratory, in governing, turning and leading great Bodies of Mankind, Armies, Cities, Nations. When the Minds of Youth are struck with Admiration at this, then is the Time to give them the Principles of that Art, which they will study with Taste and Application. . . .

History will also afford frequent Opportunities of showing the Necessity of a *Publick Religion*, from its Usefulness to the Publick; the Advantage of a Religious Character among private Persons; the Mischiefs of Superstition, &c. and the Excellency of the Christian Religion above all others antient or modern.

History will also give Occasion to expatiate on the Advantage of Civil Orders and Constitutions; how Men and their Properties are protected by joining in Societies and establishing Government; their Industry encouraged and rewarded, Arts invented, and Life made more comfortable: The Advantages of *Liberty*, Mischiefs of *Licentiousness*, Benefits arising from good Laws and a due Execution of Justice, &c. Thus may the first Principles of sound *Politicks* be fix'd in the Minds of Youth. . . .

With the History of Men, Times, and Nations, should be read at proper Hours or Days, some of the best *Histories of Nature*, which would not only be delightful to Youth, and furnish them with Matter for their Letters, &c. as well as other History; but afterwards of great Use to them, whether they are Merchants, Handicrafts, or Divines; enabling the first the better to understand many Commodities, Drugs, &c.; the second to improve his Trade or Handicraft by new Mixtures, Materials, &c., and the last to adorn his Discourses by beautiful Comparisons, and strengthen them by new Proofs of Divine Providence. . . . *Natural History* will also afford Opportunities of introducing many Observations, relating to the Preservation of Health, which may be afterwards of great Use. . . .

While they are reading Natural History, might not a little *Gardening, Planting, Grafting, Inoculating*, etc., be taught and practised; and now and then Excursions made to the neighbouring Plantations of the best Farmers, their Methods observ'd and reason'd upon for the Information of Youth? The Improvement of Agriculture being useful to all, and Skill in it no Disparagement to any.

The History of *Commerce*, of the Invention of Arts, Rise of Manufactures, Progress of Trade, Change of its Seats, with the Reasons, Causes, &c., may also be made entertaining to Youth, and will be useful to all. And this, with the Accounts in other History of the prodigious Force and Effect of Engines and Machines used in War, will naturally

A View of the House of Employment, Alms house, Pensylvania Hospital, & part of the City of Philadelph

introduce a Desire to be instructed in *Mechanicks*, and to be inform'd of the Principles of that Art by which weak Men perform such Wonders, Labour is sav'd, Manufactures expedited, &c. . . .

With the whole should be constantly inculcated and cultivated, that *Benignity of Mind*, which shows itself in *searching for* and *seizing* every Opportunity to *serve* and *to oblige*; and is the Foundation of what is called Good Breeding: highly useful to the Possessor, and most agreeable to all.

The Idea of what is *true Merit* should also be often presented to Youth, explain'd and impress'd on their Minds, as consisting in an *Inclination* join'd with an *Ability* to serve Mankind, one's Country, Friends and Family; which *Ability* is (with the Blessing of God) to be acquir'd or greatly encreas'd by *true Learning*; and should indeed be the great *Aim* and *End* of all Learning.

Autobiography

Philadelphia, August, 1788.

In 1751, Dr. Thomas Bond, a particular friend of mine, conceived the idea of establishing a hospital in Philadelphia (a very beneficent design, which has been ascrib'd to me, but was originally his), for the reception and cure of poor sick persons, whether inhabitants of the province or strangers. He was zealous and active in endeavouring to procure subscriptions for it, but the proposal being a novelty in America, and at first not well understood, he met with but small success.

At length he came to me with the compliment that he found there was no such thing as carrying a public-spirited project through without my being concern'd in it. "For," says he, "I am often ask'd by those to whom I propose subscribing, Have you consulted Franklin upon this business? And what does he think of it? And when I tell them that I have not (supposing it rather out of your line), they do not subscribe, but say they will consider of it." I enquired into the nature and probable utility of his scheme, and receiving from him a very satisfactory explanation, I not only subscrib'd to it myself, but engag'd heartily in the design of procuring subscriptions from others. Previously, however, to the solicitation, I endeavoured to prepare the minds of the people by writing on the subject in the newspapers, which was my usual custom in such cases, but which he had omitted.

One of the earliest portraits of Franklin, painted
between 1738-46 and attributed to Robert Feke,
shows him about the time he invented his famous
stove and began experimenting with electricity.
(Fogg Art Museum, Harvard University.)

Franklin directed his regiment in building a stockade fort on the Pennsylvania frontier in 1756. *(Bettmann Archive.)*

The subscriptions afterwards were more free and generous; but, beginning to flag, I saw they would be insufficient without some assistance from the Assembly, and therefore propos'd to petition for it, which was done. . . .

[*Franklin's bill proposed to the Assembly that it would not have to give from its treasury until the populace at large raised a certain large sum. The Assembly agreed. To its surprise, a large public contribution was raised, the Assembly paid its pledge, and the hospital was built. —Ed.*]

Autobiography

Philadelphia, August, 1788.

[*French and Indian attacks had continued on the western frontier of Pennsylvania, and a well publicized attack was the burning and massacre of the Moravian village of Gnadenhut. In 1756, when Franklin was fifty years old, the governor asked him to lead a troop of men there to build a line of forts. He soon raised 560 volunteers and set out with his son William, an officer. —Ed.*]

It was the beginning of January when we set out upon this business of building forts. . . . We continu'd our march, and arriv'd at the desolated Gnadenhut. There was a saw-mill near, round which were left several piles of boards, with which we soon hutted ourselves; an operation the more necessary at that inclement season, as we had no tents. Our first work was to bury more effectually the dead we found there, who had been half interr'd by the country people.

The next morning our fort was plann'd and mark'd out, the circumference measuring four hundred and fifty-five feet, which would require as many palisades to be made of trees, one with another, of a foot diameter each. Our axes, of which we had seventy, were immediately set to work to cut down trees, and, our men being dextrous in the use of them, great despatch was made. . . . While these were preparing, our other men dug a trench all round, of three feet

(continued on p. 61)

Likenesses of Franklin were widely reproduced during his life and posthumously on snuffboxes, bottles, mugs, miniature busts and even wooden hats. (*Index of American Design and Decorative Arts.*)

Drawn, Engraved, & Published by W. Birch & Son.

ARCH STREET FERR

Sold by R. Campbell & Cº Nº 50 Chesnut Street Philadª 1800

PHILADELPHIA.

Above: It is unlikely that Franklin ever donned such a hat and coat as the painter Charles Wright imagined, but the portrait is evidence of the adaptability of Franklin's image to suit the needs of those organizations he supported. *(Insurance Company of North America.)*

By the second half of the eighteenth century, Philadelphia was America's biggest and busiest city. The engraver Thomas Birch caught some of this activity at the Arch Street Ferry in an etching, ca. 1800. *(Historical Society of Pennsylvania.)*

The Green Tree fire mark, 1784, identified homes insured against
fires by the Mutual Assurance Company. In the early days of fire fighting,
if the company that first arrived on the scene of a fire was not the one with
which the house was insured, the firemen let it burn. By the
1760's in Philadelphia, however, companies cooperated.
(Index of American Design and Decorative Arts.)

The officers of Franklin's regiment surprised and embarrassed him once by escorting him for a short distance while mounted, in uniform and with swords drawn. Print from Holley's *The Life of Benjamin Franklin, 1848. (Benjamin Franklin Collection, Yale University Library.)*

deep, in which the palisades were to be planted; and, our waggons, the bodys being taken off, and the fore and hind wheels separated by taking out the pin which united the two parts of the perch, we had ten carriages, with two horses each, to bring the palisades from the woods to the spot. When they were set up, our carpenters built a stage of boards all round within, about six feet high, for the men to stand on when to fire thro' the loopholes. We had one swivel gun, which we mounted on one of the angles, and fir'd it as soon as fix'd, to let the Indians know, if any were within hearing, that we had such pieces; and thus our fort, if such a magnificent name may be given to so miserable a stockade, was finish'd in a week, though it rain'd so hard every other day that the men could not work. . . .

This kind of fort, however contemptible, is a sufficient defense against Indians, who have no cannon.

Finding ourselves now posted securely, and having a place to retreat to on occasion, we ventur'd out in parties to scour the adjacent country. We met with no Indians, but we found the places on the neighbouring hills where they had lain to watch our proceedings. There was an art in their contrivance of those places that seems worth mention. It being winter, a fire was necessary for them; but a common fire on the surface of the ground would by its light have discover'd their position at a distance. They had therefore dug holes in the ground about three feet diameter, and somewhat deeper; we saw where they had with their hatchets cut off the charcoal from the sides of burnt logs lying in the woods. With these coals they had made small fires in the bottom of the holes, and we observ'd among the weeds and grass the prints of their bodies, made by their laying all round, with their legs hanging down in the holes to keep their feet warm, which, with them, is an essential point. This kind of fire, so manag'd, could not discover them, either by its light, flame, sparks, or even smoke.

"For my own Part, when I am employed in serving others, I do not look upon myself as conferring Favours, but as paying Debts. In my Travels, and since my Settlement, I have received much Kindness from Men, to whom I shall never have any Opportunity of making the least direct Return . . . I can therefore only Return on their Fellow Men; and I can only show my Gratitude for these mercies from God, by a readiness to help his other Children and my Brethren."

Franklin's words to a friend in Pennsylvania, Joseph Huey, best explain his attitude not only toward what he considered his civic duties, but also his investigations as scientist, or philosopher, as the term was used in the eighteenth century. During the time he reserved for study, he made some of the most famous and certainly most practical discoveries of his time.

Nearly every American gradeschooler learns of his famous experiments with the kite and electricity. Even in his time he was famous among scientists as the world's foremost expert on electricity. To summarize briefly his discoveries in this field: The most important concepts were the existence of *postive* and *negative* electricity, the fluidity of electricized particles and the identity of lightning and electricity — the last proved by the kite experiment related in this chapter. Franklin also invented and named the battery from his experiments with the Leyden jar, and his electrical experiments were performed and confirmed all over the world scientific community. His suggestion and practical device for protecting houses from lightning was another first. For his work, he was elected to the English Royal Academy of Sciences in 1756.

"What signifies Philosophy that does not apply to some Use?"This line summarizes his attitude towards his inventions. He never claimed a patent for any of his devices and always related his observations to the practical

III AMERICA'S FOREMOST INVENTOR

experiences of people. Significantly, his scientific writing is clear, unstrained and logical. His Pennsylvania Fireplace, the Franklin stove, for example, was highly efficient and available to anyone who cared to construct it. His pamphlet on this invention, though long, gives detailed and clear "how-to" directions, with explanation of scientific basis and functioning parts. The stove became widely used, but Franklin never collected a penny from it.

Other practical inventions were the lightning rod, 'bifocals, a flexible catheter, an armchair that converted to library stepladder and a device for removing books from high shelves, all of which came about as solutions to ordinary needs. His insatiable curiosity about everyday phenomena ranged in wider directions. Letters to fellow scientists include observations on the effect of oil on water, the cause of the aurora borealis (northern lights), water-spouts, whirlwinds and thunderstorms, the direction of rivers and tides, salt and seawater, sunspots, heat absorption by the color of an object, magnetism and the theory of the earth, earthquakes, sound traveling in fluidlike waves, prehistoric fossils, causes of colds, the tonic effects of cold air and ventilation, cooling by evaporation, sources of lead poisoning, causes and cures of smoky chimneys, the relationship of tobacco to hand tremors, effects of diet and activity on general health, depth of water and speed of boats, the course of the Gulf Stream and its effects on shipping, the southwest origin of our northeast storms and more! He bought a farm and experimented with grass culture; he advised the cultivation of native Indian corn and silkworms and introduced rhubarb to the colonies. In sum, his curiosity touched on nearly every part of eighteenth-century intellectual pursuit.

Among personal accomplishments, he designed (based on previous plans), built and played the harmonica described in this chapter and also played the harp, guitar and violin. His interest in music and love for Scottish tunes lead to his composing several short pieces and writing original opinions on harmony and melody. He taught himself a reading knowledge of French, Italian, Spanish, German and Latin. His lifelong interest in medicine and health was acknowledged in his election to the Royal Medical Society of Paris and honorary membership in the Medical Society of London. In his business of printing, of course, he was expert in knowledge of ink, typefaces and paper and kept close business and personal relations with the King's printer, William Strahan. In his own words, Benjamin Franklin was "quite a factotum" — with a charge of genius.

Benjamin Franklin of Philadelphia, 1761,
mezzotint by James McArdell. Franklin the
scientist stands surrounded by symbols of his
work: a book marked *Elecric Exp*., a static
electricity machine with glass globe (right) and
lightning in the background. *(New York Public Library.)*

WATER SPOUT.

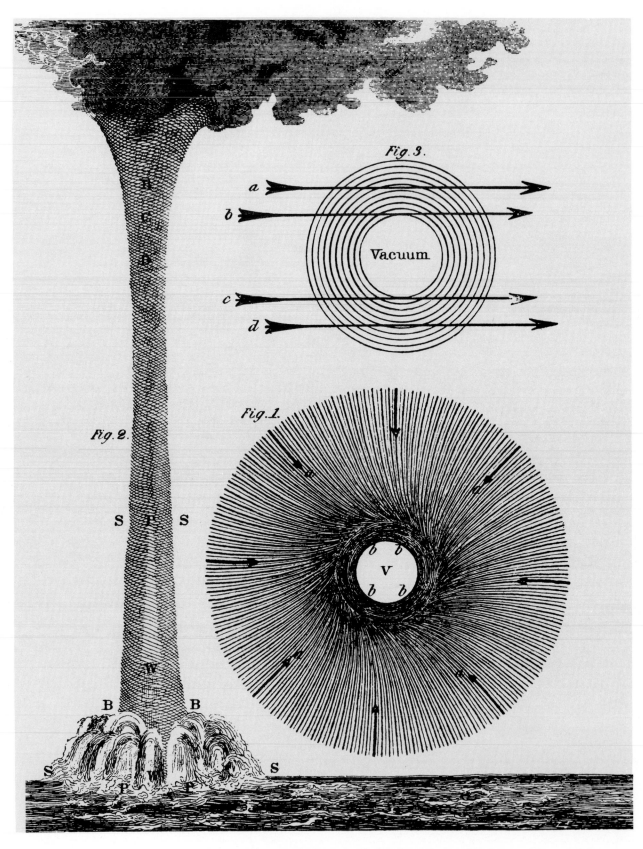

Among his scores of scientific observations, Franklin analyzed the forces that cause whirlwinds and waterspouts (fig. 2), diagramming two cross-sections (figs. 1 and 3) of a central vacuum (V), surrounded by swift, dense, warm air which rises to form a whirlwind.

Plate XII.

Boston, Published by Hilliard, Gray & Co.

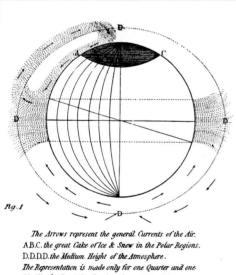

Fig.1

The Arrows represent the general Currents of the Air.
A.B.C. the great Cake of Ice & Snow in the Polar Regions.
D.D.D.D. the Medium Height of the Atmosphere.
The Representation is made only for one Quarter and one
Meridian of the Globe; but is to be understood the same
for all the rest.

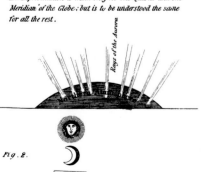

Fig.2

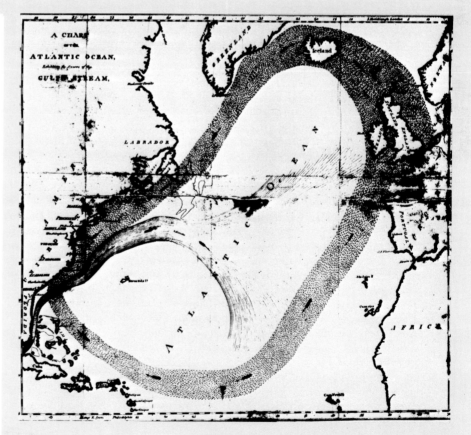

A CHART OF THE ATLANTIC OCEAN, Exhibiting the Course of the GULF STREAM,

Top: Franklin's *Maritime Observations*, a long letter of 1785, included
ideas gathered during his eight Atlantic crossings. His drawing shows sea
anchors, double hulls, suggestions for ballast, ship design and means
of propulsion. Above: Franklin's map of the Gulf Stream. Left: Franklin
conjectured that the aurora borealis (northern lights) was electrified
air carried from the tropics to the north pole in moist clouds; the
electricity became visible as light in the vacuum above the pole.

65

A Franklin stove of cast iron, ca. 1795.
(The Metropolitan Museum of Art, Rogers Fund.)

Autobiography

Philadelphia, August, 1788

In order of time, I should have mentioned before, that having, in 1742, invented an open stove for the better warming of rooms, and at the same time saving fuel, as the fresh air admitted was warmed in entering, I made a present of the model to Mr. Robert Grace, one of my early friends, who, having an iron-furnace, found the casting of the plates for these stoves a profitable thing, as they were growing in demand. To promote that demand, I wrote and published a pamphlet, entitled *"An Account of the new-invented Pennsylvania Fireplaces; wherein their Construction and Manner of Operation is particularly explained; their Advantages above every other Method of warming Rooms demonstrated; and all Objections that have been raised against the Use of them answered and obviated. [With direction for putting them up, and for using them to the best advantage. And a copper-plate in which the several parts of the machine are exactly laid down, from a scale of equal parts.]"* This pamphlet had a good effect. Gov'r. Thomas was so pleas'd with the construction of this stove, as described in it, that he offered to give me a patent for the sole vending of them for a term of years; but I declin'd it from a principle which has ever weighed with me on such occasions, viz., *That, as we enjoy great advantages from the inventions of others, we should be glad of an opportunity to serve others by any invention of ours; and this we should do freely and generously.*

From AN ACCOUNT OF THE NEW-INVENTED PENNSYLVANIA FIREPLACES

Philadelphia, 1744

The Fire being made at *A*, the Flame and Smoke will ascend and strike the Top, *which will thereby receive a considerable Heat. The Smoke, finding no Passage upwards,* turns over the Top of the Air-box, and descends between it and the Back Plate to the Holes in the Bottom Plate, heating, as it passes, both Plates of the Air-box, and the said Back Plate; the Front Plate, Bottom and Side Plates are also all heated at the same Time. The Smoke proceeds in the Passage that leads it under and behind the false Back, and so rises into the Chimney. The Air of the Room, warm'd behind the Back Plate, and by the Sides, Front, and Top Plates, becoming specifically lighter than the other Air in the Room, is oblig'd to rise; but the Closure over the Fireplace hindering it from going up the Chimney, it is forc'd out into the Room, rises by the Mantle-piece to the Ceiling, and spreads all over the Top of the Room, whence being crowded down gradually by the Stream of newly-warm'd Air that follows and rises above it, the whole Room becomes in a short time equally warmed.

At the same Time the Air, warmed under the Bottom Plate and in the Air-Box, rises, and comes out of the Holes in the Side Plates, very swiftly if the Door of the Room be shut, and joins its Current with the Stream before mentioned, rising from the Side, Back, and Top Plates.

66

What signifies Philosophy [science] that does not apply to some Use?
— Letter to Mary (Polly) Stevenson.

The Air that enters the Room thro' the Air-box is fresh, tho' warm; and computing the Swiftness of its Motion with the Areas of the Holes, 'tis found that near 10 Barrels of fresh Air are hourly introduc'd by the Air-Box; and by this Means the Air in the Room is continually changed, and kept at the same Time sweet and warm. . . .

The Advantages of this Fire-place
Its Advantages above the common Fire-places are,

That your whole Room is equally warmed; so that People need not croud so close round the Fire, but may sit near the Window, and have the Benefit of the Light for Reading, Writing, Needlework, &c. They may sit with Comfort in any Part of the Room, which is a very considerable Advan-tage in a large Family, where there must often be two Fires kept, because all cannot conveniently come at one.

If you sit near the Fire, you have not that cold Draught of uncomfortable Air nipping your Back and Heels, as when before common Fires, by which many catch Cold, being scorched before, and, as it were, froze behind.

If you sit against a Crevice, there is not that sharp Draught of cold Air playing on you, as in Rooms where there are Fires in the common way; by which many catch Cold, whence proceed Coughs, Catarrhs, Tooth-achs, Fevers, Pleurisies, and many other Diseases.

In Case of Sickness, they make most excellent Nursing-Rooms; as they constantly supply a Sufficiency of fresh Air, so warmed at the same time as to be no way inconvenient or dangerous. . . .

In common Chimneys, the strongest Heat from the Fire, which is upwards, goes directly up the Chimney, and is lost; and there is such a strong Draught into the Chimney, that not only the upright Heat, but also the back, sides, and downward Heats are carried up the Chimney by that Draught of Air; and the Warmth given before the Fire, by the Rays that strike out towards the Room, is continually

The parts of Franklin's stove, the Pennsylvanian Fireplace, are these: **M**, mantlepiece of chimney; **C**, funnel; **B**, false back and closing; **E**, true back; **T**, top of fireplace; **F**, front of fireplace; **A**, place where fire is made; **D**, air box; **K**, hole in side plate through which warm air leaves air box into room; **H**, hollow filled with fresh air, entering at passage **I**, and ascending into air box through the hole in bottom plate near **G**, the partition to keep air and smoke apart; **P**, passage under false back for smoke; ✝ course of the smoke.

PROFILE OF THE PENNSYLVANIA CHIMNEY AND FIRE-PLACE

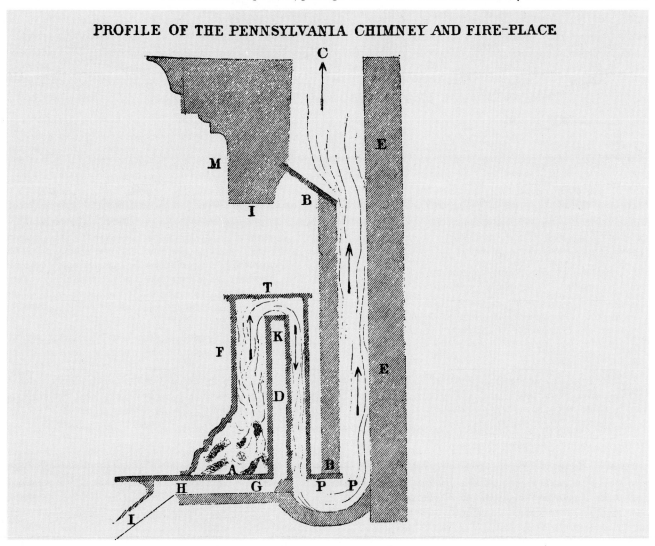

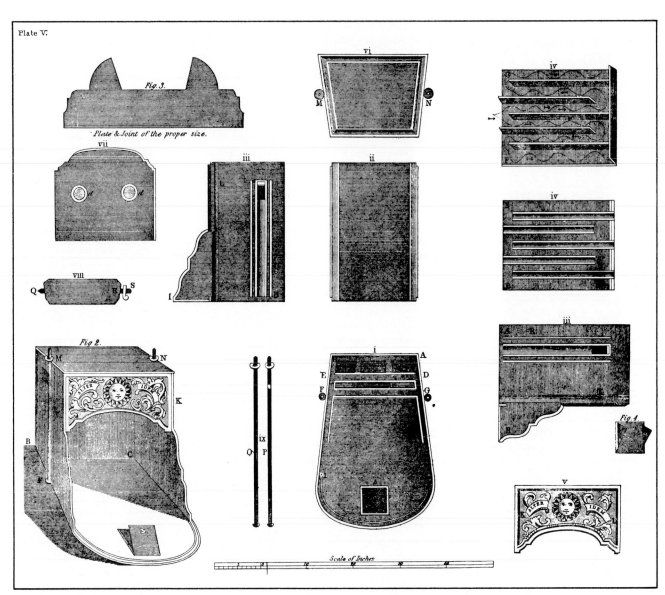

Plate V.

Fig. 3.

Plate & Joint of the proper size.

vi

iv

vii

iii

ii

iv

viii

Q R S

I H

iii

Fig 2.

M N

ALTER IDEM

K

B

C

ix

Q P

i

A

E D

F G

B

Fig. 4

v

ALTER IDEM

Scale of Inches

The iron parts of Franklin's stove include *(i)*, a bottom plate; *(ii)*, a back plate; *(iii, iii)*, two side plates; *(iv, iv)*, two middle plates; *(v)*, a front plate; *(vi)*, a top plate; *(vii)*, shutter; *(viii)*, register; and screw rods *O,P*. Figure 2 shows the device assembled.

driven back, crowded into the Chimney, and carried up, by the same Draught of Air. But here the upright Heat strikes and heats the Top Plate, which warms the Air above it, and that comes into the Room. The heat likewise, which the Fire communicates to the Sides, Back Bottom and Air-Box, is all brought into the Room; for you will find a constant Current of warm Air coming out of the Chimney-Corner into the Room. . . .

Thus, as very little of the Heat is lost, when this Fire-Place is us'd, *much less Wood*[1] will serve you, which is a considerable Advantage where Wood is dear. . . .

This Fire-place cures most smoky chimneys, and thereby preserves both the Eyes and Furniture.

It prevents the Fouling of Chimneys; much of the Lint and Dust that contributes to foul a Chimney, being by the low Arch oblig'd to pass thro' the Flame, where 'tis consum'd. Then, less Wood being burnt, there is less Smoke made. . . .

A Fire may be soon extinguished by closing it with the Shutter before, and turning the Register behind, which will stifle it, and the Brands will remain ready to rekindle.

The Room being once warm, the Warmth may be retain'd in it all Night.

And lastly, the Fire is so secur'd at Night, that not one Spark can fly out into the Room to do Damage.

With all these Conveniences, you do not lose the pleasing Sight nor Use of the Fire, as in the Dutch Stoves, but may boil the Tea-Kettle, warm the Flat-Irons, heat Heaters, keep warm a Dish of Victuals by setting it on the Top, &c. &c. . . .

[1]People, who have us'd these Fire-places, differ much in their Accounts of the Wood saved by them. Some say five-sixths, others three-fourths, and others much less. . . . I suppose, taking a Number of Families together, that two thirds, or half the Wood, at least, is saved. My common Room, I know, is made twice as warm as it used to be, with a quarter of the Wood I formerly consum'd there. —[Franklin]

68

The Old Academy buildings of the University of Pennsylvania (above)
opened in 1751 largely as a result of Franklin's proposal on education. Charles M. Lefferts
made this watercolor sketch in 1913 based on an earlier print. *(The Edgar Fahs Smith Memorial Collection,*
University of Pennsylvania.) Below: Another public building in Franklin's time was the Friends'
(Quakers) Almshouse, built in 1729. *(The Quaker Collection, Haverford College Library.)*

A South-East Prospect of the Pensylvania

This Building, by the Bounty of the Government, And of many private

Montgomery and Winter Del.   Printed and Sold by Rich.ᵈ Kennedy Philad.ᵃ   Built A Do

Hoſpital, with the Elevation of the intended Plan *Perſons, Was Piouſly founded, for the Relief of the Sick and Miſerable* *55. from Nº 1 to 2* *J Steeper & HCDawkins Sculp*

A South-East Prospect of the Pennsylvania Hospital with the Elevation of the Intended Plan, engraved by H. Dawkins. Dr. Thomas Bond with Franklin's help began the Pennsylvania Hospital in 1751. (Courtesy, Henry Francis du Pont Winterthur Museum, Joseph Downs Manuscript Collection, No. 62 x 33.)

*Human felicity is produced
not so much by great pieces
of good fortune that seldom happen,
as by little advantages
that occur every day. — Autobiography.*

Drawn Engraved & Published by W. Birch & Son   Sold by R. Campbell &C.° N.° 30 Chesnut Street Philad.° 1

BACK of the STATE HOUSE, PHILADELPHIA.

The American Philosophical Society, another of
Franklin's proposals, is housed in the building seen
through the trees in this engraving, ca. 1779, by William
Birch and Son. *(Historical Society of Pennsylvania.)*

From **Experiments and Observations on Electricity**
To Peter Collinson

Sir,   Philadelphia, March 28, 1747.

Your kind present of an electric tube, with directions for using it, has put several of us on making electrical experiments, in which we have observed some particular phaenomena, that we look upon to be new. . . . For my own part, I never was before engaged in any study that so totally engrossed my attention and my time as this has lately done; for what with making experiments when I can be alone, and repeating them to my Friends and Acquaintance, who, from the novelty of the thing, come continually in crowds to see them, I have, during some months past, had little leisure for any thing else. I am, &c.

B. Franklin

To Peter Collinson

Sir, ,   Philadelphia, July 11, 1747.

In my last I informed you that in pursuing our electrical enquiries, we had observed some particular phaenomena, which we looked upon to be new, and of which I promised to give you some account. . . .

The first is the wonderful effect of pointed bodies, both in *drawing off* and *throwing off* the electrical fire. For example,

Place an iron shot of three or four inches diameter on the mouth of a clean dry glass bottle. By a fine silken thread from the ceiling, right over the mouth of the bottle, suspend a small cork ball, about the bigness of a marble; the thread of such a length, as that the cork ball may rest against the side of the shot. Electrify the shot, and the ball will be repelled to the distance of four or five inches, more or less, according to the quantity of Electricity. When in this state, if you present to the shot the point of a long slender sharp bodkin, at six or eight inches distance, the repellency is instantly destroy'd, and the cork flies to the shot. A blunt body must be brought within an inch, and draw a spark, to produce the same effect. . . . If you present the point [of a knife] in the dark, you will see, sometimes at a foot distance, and more, a light gather upon it, like that of a fire-fly, or glow-worm; the less sharp the point, the nearer you must bring it to observe the light; and, at whatever distance you see the light, you may draw off the electrical fire, and destroy the repellency. . . .

To show that points will *throw off* as well as *draw off* the electrical fire; lay a long sharp needle upon the shot, and you cannot electrise the shot so as to make it repel the rock ball. Or fix a needle to the end of a suspended gun-barrel, or iron rod, so as to point beyond it like a little bayonet; and while it remains there, the gun-barrel, or rod, cannot by applying the tube to the other end be electrised so as to give a spark, the fire continually running out silently at the point. In the dark you may see it make the same appearance as it does in the case before mentioned. . . .

These appearances we attempt to account for thus: We suppose, as aforesaid, that electrical fire is a common element, of which every one . . . has his equal share, before any operation is begun with the tube. *A*, who stands on wax and rubs the tube, collects the electrical fire from himself into the glass; and his communication with the common stock being cut off by the wax, his body is not again immediately supply'd. *B*, (who stands on wax likewise) passing his knuckle along near the tube, receives the fire which was collected by the glass from *A*; and his communication with the common stock being likewise cut off, he

retains the additional quantity received. To *C* standing on the floor, both appear to be electrised: for he having only the middle quantity of electrical fire, receives a spark upon approaching *B*, who has an over quantity; but gives one to *A*, who has an under quantity. If *A* and *B* approach to touch each other, the spark is stronger, because the difference between them is greater: After such touch there is no spark between either of them and *C*, because the electrical fire in all is reduced to the original equality. If they touch while electrising, the equality is never destroy'd, the fire only circulating. Hence have arisen some new terms among us: we say, *B*, (and bodies like circumstanced) is electrised *positively*; *A*, *negatively*. Or rather, *B* is electrised *plus*; *A*, *minus*. And we daily in our experiments electrise bodies *plus* or *minus*, as we think proper. . . .

Franklin, with his son William, carried on the famous kite experiment in 1752 which equated lightning with electricity. (Engine side, *Insurance Company of North America.)*

From **Experiments and Observation on Electricity**
To Peter Collinson

Electrical Kite

[Philadelphia] Oct. 19, 1752.

Sir,

As frequent mention is made in public papers from *Europe* of the success of the *Philadelphia* experiment for drawing the electric fire from clouds by means of pointed rods of iron erected on high buildings, &c., it may be agreeable to the curious to be informed, that the same experiment has succeeded in *Philadelphia,* though made in a different and more easy manner, which is as follows:

Make a small cross of two light strips of cedar, the arms so long as to reach to the four corners of a large thin silk handkerchief when extended; tie the corners of the handkerchief to the extremities of the cross, so you have the body of a kite; which being properly accommodated with a tail, loop. and string, will rise in the air, like those made of paper; but this being of silk, is fitter to bear the wet and wind of a thunder-gust without tearing. To the top of the upright stick of the cross is to be fixed a very sharp-pointed wire, rising a foot or more above the wood. To the end of the twine, next the hand, is to be tied a silk ribbon, and where the silk and twine join, a key may be fastened. This kite is to be raised when a thunder-gust appears to be coming on, and the person who holds the string must stand within a door or window, or under some cover, so that the silk ribbon may not be wet; and care must be taken that the twine does not touch the frame of the door or window. As soon as any of the thunder-clouds come over the kite, the pointed wire will draw the electric fire from them, and the kite, with all the twine, will be electrified, and the loose filaments of the twine will stand out every way, and be attracted by an approaching finger. And when the rain has wet the kite and twine, so that it can conduct the electric fire freely, you will find it stream out plentifully from the key on the approach of your knuckle. At this key the phial may be charged; and from electric fire thus obtained, spirits may be kindled, and all the other electric experiments be performed, which are usually done by the help of a rubbed glass globe or tube, and thereby the sameness of the electric matter with that of lightning completely demonstrated.

B. Franklin

From **Experiments and Observations on Electricity**
From a letter to John Pringle

Craven-Street, Jan. 6, 1758.

Sir,

I return Mr. Mitchell's paper on the strata of the earth with thanks. The reading of it, and perusal of the draft that accompanies it, have reconciled me to those convulsions which all naturalists agree this globe has suffered. Had the different strata of clay, gravel, marble, coals, limestone, sand, minerals, &c., continued to lie level, one under the other, as they may be supposed to have done before those

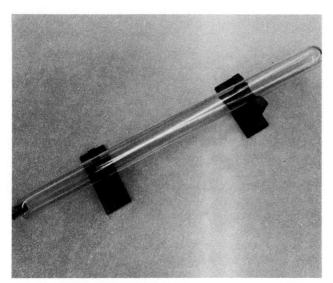

This glass tube was Peter Collinson's gift to Franklin, who used it frequently in his early electrical experiments to store or give charges. *(Franklin Institute, Philadelphia.)*

convulsions, we should have had the use only of a few of the uppermost of the strata, the others lying too deep and too difficult to be come at; but the shell of the earth being broke, and the fragments thrown into this oblique position, the disjointed ends of a great number of strata of different kinds are brought up to day, and a great variety of useful materials put into our power, which would otherwise have remained eternally concealed from us. So that what has been usually looked upon as a *ruin* suffered by this part of the universe, was, in reality, only a preparation, or means of rendering the earth more fit for use, more capable of being to mankind a convenient and comfortable habitation.

I am, Sir, with great esteem, yours, &c.

B. F[ranklin.]

[*Franklin wrote David Hume, the British philosopher, a detailed letter on the construction of lightning rods, which Hume read to the English Royal Society. This practical device was acclaimed there, and Franklin's description was published with the Society's endorsement. Hume replied the following. —Ed.*]

From David Hume to B. Franklin
Edinburgh, May 10, 1762.

Dear Sir,

I have a great many thanks to give you for your goodness in remembering my request, and for the exact description which you sent me of your method of preserving houses from thunder. I communicated it to our Philosophical Society, as you gave me permission, and they desire to tell you, that they claim it as their own, and intend to enrich with it the first collection, which they may publish. The established rule of our Society is, that, after a paper is read to them, it is delivered by them to some member, who is obliged, in a subsequent meeting, to read some paper of remarks upon it. . . .

I am very sorry, that you intend soon to leave our hemisphere. America has sent us many good things, gold, silver, sugar, tobacco, indigo, &c.; but you are the first philosopher, and indeed the first great man of letters for whom we are beholden to her. It is our own fault, that we have not kept him; whence it appears, that we do not agree with

Solomon, that wisdom is above gold; for we take care never to send back an ounce of the latter, which we once lay our fingers upon.

I saw yesterday our friend Sir Alexander Dick, who desired to present his compliments to you. We are all very unwilling to think of your settling in America, and that there is some chance of our never seeing you again; but no one regrets it more than does, Dear Sir,

Your most affectionate humble servant,
David Hume.

From a letter to Cadwallader Colden
Philadelphia, April 23, 1752

May not all the Phaenomena of Light be more conveniently solved, by supposing universal Space filled with a subtle elastic Fluid, which, when at rest, is not visible, but whose Vibrations affect that fine Sense the Eye, as those of Air do the grosser Organs of the Ear? We do not, in the Case of Sound, imagine that any sonorous Particles are thrown off from a Bell, for Instance, and fly in straight Lines to the Ear; why must we believe that luminous Particles leave the Sun and proceed to the Eye? Some Diamonds, if rubbed, shine in the Dark, without losing any Part of their matter. . . . May not different Degrees of Vibration of the above-mentioned Universal Medium occasion the Appearances of different Colours? I think the Electric Fluid is always the same; yet I find that weaker and stronger Sparks differ in apparent Colour; some white, blue, purple, red; the strongest, White; weak ones, red. Thus different Degrees of Vibration given to the Air produce the 7 different Sounds in Music, analogous to the 7 Colours, yet the Medium, Air, is the same.

This electrostatic friction machine is said to have belonged to Franklin.
(The British National Science Museum, London.)

Statuette of Franklin with an early electrostatic generator. *(Franklin Institute, Philadelphia.)*

EXPERIMENTS

AND

OBSERVATIONS

ON

ELECTRICITY,

MADE AT

Philadelphia in *America*,

BY

Mr. BENJAMIN FRANKLIN,

AND

Communicated in feveral Letters to Mr. P. COLLINSON, of *London*, F. R. S.

L O N D O N:
Printed and fold by E. CAVE, at *St. John's Gate.* 1751.
(Price 2 s. 6 d.)

Title page of Franklin's collected letters to Collinson on electricity. *(Yale University Library.)*

If the sun is not wasted by Expence of Light, I can easily conceive that he shall otherwise always retain the same Quality of Matter; tho' we should suppose him made of Sulphur constantly flaming. The Action of Fire only *separates* the Particles of Matter; it does not *annihilate* them: Water by Heat rais'd in Vapour, returns to the Earth in Rain. And if we could collect all the Particles of burning Matter that go off in Smoke, perhaps they might, with the Ashes, weigh as much as the Body before it was fired; and, if we could put them into the same Position with regard to each other, the Mass would be the same as before, and might be burnt over again. The Chemists have analys'd Sulphur, and find it compos'd, in certain Proportions, of Oil, Salt, and Earth; and, having by the Analysis discovered those Proportions, they can, of those Ingredients, make Sulphur. So we have only to suppose, that the Parts of the Sun's Sulphur, separated by Fire, rise into his Atmosphere, there, being freed from the immediate Action of the Fire, they collect into cloudy Masses, and growing by degrees too heavy to be longer supported, they descend to the Sun, and are burnt over again. Hence the Spots appearing on his Face, which are observ'd to diminish daily in Size, their consuming Edges being of particular Brightness.

From a letter to James Bowdoin
Queries and Conjectures relating to Magnetism and the Theory of the Earth

Philadelphia, May 31, 1788.

Let me add another Question or two, not relating indeed to Magnetism, but, however, to the Theory of the Earth.

Is not the finding of great Quantities of Shells and Bones of Animals (natural to hot Climates) in the cold ones of our

Considered an accurate likeness, this portrait of Franklin was painted by George D. Leslie after one by Mason Chamberlain. Franklin was 56 at this sitting. *(Yale University Art Gallery, gift of Avery Rockefeller.)*

present World, some proof that its Poles have been changed? Is not the Supposition, that the Poles have been changed, the easiest way of accounting for the Deluge, by getting rid of the old Difficulty how to dispose of its Waters after it was over? Since, if the Poles were again to be changed, and plac'd in the present Equator, the Sea would fall there about 15 Miles in height, and rise as much in the present polar Regions; and the Effect would be proportionable, if the new Poles were plac'd anywhere between the present and the Equator.

Does not the apparent Wrack of the Surface of this Globe thrown up into long Ridges of Mountains, with Strata in various Positions, make it probable, that its internal Mass is a Fluid; but a Fluid so dense as to float the heaviest of our Substances? Do we know the Limit of Condensation Air is capable of? Supposing it to grow denser *within* the Surface, in the same Proportion nearly as it does *without*, at what Depth may it be equal in Density with Gold?

Can we easily conceive how the Strata of the Earth could have been so derang'd, if it had not been a mere shell supported by a heavier Fluid? Would not such a suppos'd internal fluid Globe be immediately sensible of a Change in the Situation of the earth's Axis, alter its Form, and thereby burst the Shell, and throw up Parts of it above the rest? As if we would alter the Position of the Fluid contain'd in the Shell of an Egg, and place its longest Diameter where the shortest now is, the Shell must break; but would be much harder to break, if the whole internal Substance were as solid and hard as the Shell.

Might not a Wave, by any means rais'd in this supposed internal Ocean of extreamly dense Fluid, raise in some degree, as it passes the present Shell of incumbent Earth, and break it in some Places, as in Earthquakes? And may not the Progress of such Wave, and the Disorders it occasions among the Solids of the Shell, account for the rumbling Sound being first heard at a distance, augmenting as it approaches, and gradually dying away as it proceeds?

THE ART OF PROCURING PLEASANT DREAMS
Inscribed to Miss [Shipley], being written at her request

As a great part of our life is spent in sleep during which we have sometimes pleasant and sometimes painful dreams, it becomes of some consequence to obtain the one kind and avoid the other; for whether real or imaginary, pain is pain and pleasure is pleasure. If we can sleep without dreaming, it is well that painful dreams are avoided. If while we sleep we can have any pleasing dream, it is, as the French say, *autant de gagné*, so much added to the pleasure of life.

To this end it is, in the first place, necessary to be careful in preserving health, by due exercise and great temperance; for, in sickness, the imagination is disturbed, and disagreeable, sometimes terrible, ideas are apt to present themselves. Exercise should precede meals, not immediately follow them; the first promotes, the latter, unless moderate, obstructs digestion. If, after exercise, we feed sparingly, the digestion will be easy and good, the body lightsome, the temper cheerful, and all the animal functions performed agreeably. Sleep, when it follows, will be natural and undisturbed; while indolence, with full feeding, occasions nightmares and horrors inexpressible; we fall from precipices, are assaulted by wild beasts, murderers, and demons, and experience every variety of distress. Observe, however, that the

Franklin's pneumatic machine (air pump) is labeled: "These and all sorts of Mathematical Philosophical and Optical Instruments Accurately Made and Sold by George Adams. . . in Fleet Street, London." *(Independence National Historical Park.)*

quantities of food and exercise are relative things; those who move much may, and indeed ought to eat more; those who use little exercise should eat little. In general, mankind, since the improvement of cookery, eat about twice as much as nature requires. . . .

Another means of preserving health, to be attended to, is the having a constant supply of fresh air in your bedchamber. It has been a great mistake, the sleeping in rooms exactly closed, and in beds surrounded by curtains. No outward air that may come in to you is so unwholesome as the unchanged air, often breathed, of a close chamber. . . .

Confined air, when saturated with perspirable matter, will not receive more; and that matter must remain in our bodies, and occasion diseases; but it gives some previous notice of its being about to be hurtful, by producing certain uneasiness, slight indeed at first, which as with regard to the lungs is a trifling sensation, and to the pores of the skin a kind of restlessness, which is difficult to describe, and few that feel it know the cause of it. But we may recollect, that sometimes on waking in the night, we have, if warmly covered, found it difficult to get asleep again. We turn often without finding repose in any position. This fidgettiness (to use a vulgar expression for want of a better) is occasioned wholly by an uneasiness in the skin, owing to the retention of the perspirable matter — the bed-clothes having received their quantity, and being saturated, refusing to take any more. . . .

Here, then, is one great and general cause of unpleasing dreams. For when the body is uneasy, the mind will be disturbed by it, and disagreeable ideas of various kinds will in sleep be the natural consequences. The remedies, preventive and curative, follow:

1. By eating moderately (as before advised for health's sake) less perspirable matter is produced in a given time; hence the bed-clothes receive it longer before they are saturated, and we may therefore sleep longer before we are made uneasy by their refusing to receive any more.

2. By using thinner and more porous bed-clothes, which will suffer the perspirable matter more easily to pass through them, we are less incommoded, such being longer tolerable.

3. When you are awakened by this uneasiness, and find you cannot easily sleep again, get out of bed, beat up and turn your pillow, shake the bed-clothes well, with at least twenty shakes, then throw the bed open and leave it to cool; in the meanwhile, continuing undressed, walk about your chamber till your skin has had time to discharge its load, which it will do sooner as the air may be dried and colder. When you begin to feel the cold air unpleasant, then return to your bed, and you will soon fall asleep, and your sleep will be sweet and pleasant. . . .

One or two observations more will conclude this little piece. Care must be taken, when you lie down, to dispose your pillow so as to suit your manner of placing your head, and to be perfectly easy; then place your limbs so as not to bear inconveniently hard upon one another, as, for instance, the joints of your ankles; for, though a bad position may at first give but little pain and be hardly noticed, yet a continuance will render it less tolerable, and the uneasiness may come on while you are asleep, and disturb your imagination. These are the rules of the art. But, though they will generally prove effectual in producing the end intended, there is a case in which the most punctual observance of them will be totally fruitless. I need not mention the case to you, my dear friend, but my account of the art would be imperfect without it. The case is, when the person who desires to have pleasant dreams has not taken care to preserve, what is necessary above all things,

A Good Conscience.

From a letter to Mary (Polly) Stevenson

Craven Street, Aug. 10, 1761.

. . . It is certain that the Skin has *imbibing* as well as *discharging* Pores; witness the Effects of a Blister Plaister, &c. I have read, that a Man, hired by a Physician to stand by way of Experiment in the open Air naked during a moist Night, weighed near 3 Pounds heavier in the Morning. I have often observ'd myself, that, however thirsty I may have been before going into the Water to swim, I am never long so in the Water. These imbibing Pores, however, are very fine, perhaps fine enough in filtring to separate Salt from Water; for, tho' I have soak'd by Swimming, when a Boy, several Hours in the Day for several Days successively in Salt water, I never found my Blood and Juices salted by that means, so as to make me thirsty or feel a salt Taste in my Mouth; And it is remarkable that the Flesh of Sea Fish, tho' bred in Salt Water, is not Salt.

Hence I imagine, that, if People at Sea, distress'd by Thirst when their fresh Water is unfortunately spent, would make Bathing-Tubs of their empty Water-Casks, and, filling them with Sea Water, sit in them an hour or two each Day, they might be greatly reliev'd. Perhaps keeping their Clothes constantly wet might have an almost equal Effect; and this without Danger of catching Cold. Men do not

catch Cold by wet Clothes at Sea. Damp, but not wet Linen may possibly give Colds; but no one catches Cold by Bathing, and no Clothes can be wetter than Water itself. Why damp Clothes should then occasion Colds, is a curious Question, the Discussion of which I reserve for a future Letter, or some future Conversation.

Diir Pali, Ritsmṃnd, Dsulṃi 20.-68
Ɏii intended to hev sent iu ċhiz Pepers sunṃr, bṃt biiŋ bizi fargat it.
Mr Kolman hez mended deeli: bṃt iur gud Mṃċhṃr hez bin indispoz'd uiħ e slṃit Fivṃr, atended uiħ mṃts ħiibilnes and uirines. Si uiuld nat allau mi to send iu uṃrd av it at ċhi tṃim, and iz nau beter.
Ɏii uis iu to kansider ċhis Alfabet, and giv mi Instanses af sṃts Iŋlis Uṃrds and Saunds az iu mee ħink kannat perfektlṃi bi eksprest bṃi it. Ɏii am persueeded it mee bi kamplited bṃi iur help. Ði greeter difikṃlti uil bi to briŋ it into ius. Hauevṃr, if Amendments eer nevṃr atemted, and ħiŋs kantinu to gro uṃrs and uṃrs, ċhee mṃst kṃm to bi in a retsed Kandisṃn at last; sṃts indiid ṃi ħink aur Alfabet and Rṃitiŋ alredi in; bṃt if ui go an az ui hev dṃn e fiu Senturiz langer, aur uṃrds uil graduali siis to ekspres Saunds, ċhee uil onli stand far ħiŋs, az ċhi rittin uṃrds du in ċhi Tsuiniiz Languads, huits ṃi sṃspekt mṃit oridsinali hev bin e litiral Rṃitiŋ lṃik ċhat af Iurop, bṃt ħru ċhi Tseendsez in Pronṃsiesṃn braat an bṃi ċhi Kors af Eedses, and ħru ċhi abstinet Adhirens af ċhat Pipil to old Kṃstṃms and amṃŋ ṃċhṃrs to ċheer old manṃr ov Rṃitiŋ, ċhi oridsinal Saunds af Leters and Uṃrds eer last, and no langṃr kansidered. Ɏii am, mṃi diir Frend, Iurz afeksṃnetli,
B. FRANKLIN

Letter to Mary (Polly) Stevenson written in Franklin's phonetic alphabet and transcribed into modern type. (*Yale University Press and American Philosophical Society.*)

From a letter to Mary (Polly) Stevenson

Richmond, July 20, 1768

Dear Polly,

I intended to have sent you these Papers sooner, but being busy forgot it.

Mr. Coleman has mended daily; but your good Mother has been indispos'd with a slight Fever, attended with much feebleness and weariness. She would not allow me to send you word of it at the time and is now better.

I wish you to consider this Alphabet, and give me Instances of such English Words and Sounds as you may think can not perfectly be expressed by it. I am persuaded it may be completed by your help. The greater difficulty will be to bring it into use. However, if Amendments are never attempted and things continue to grow worse and worse they must come to be in a wretched Condition at last; such indeed I think our Alphabet and Writing already in; but if we go on as we have done a few Centuries longer, our words will gradually cease to express Sounds, they will only stand for things, as the written words do in the Chinese Language, which I suspect might originally have been a literal Writing like that of Europe, but through the Changes in Pronunciation brought on by the Course of Ages and through the obstinate Adherence of that People to old Customs, and among others to their old manner of Writing, the original Sounds of Letters and Words are lost, and no longer considered. I am, my dear Friend, Yours affectionately,

B. Franklin.

Characters.	Sounded as now in	Names of the Letters express'd in the reform'd Sounds and Characters	
o	old	o	the first Vowel naturally, and deepest sound; requires only to open the Mouth, and breathe thro' it.
a[a]¹	John, Folly	a	the next, requiring the Mouth open'd a little more or hollower.
a	man, can	a	the next, a little more.
e	mane, lane	e	the next, requires the Tongue to be a little more elevated ⎫ tho the Pipe alone will form
i	een, seen	i	the next, still a little more, ⎭ them, but not so easily.
u	tool, fool	u	the next, requires the Lips to be gather'd up, leaving a small Opening.
ɥ[ɥ; ꭹ]¹	um, un, as in umbrage, unto, &c.	ɥ	the next, a very short Vowel, the Sound of which we should express in our present Letters thus, *uh*, a short and not very strong Aspiration.
h	hunter, happy, high	huh	a stronger or more forcible Aspiration.
g	give, gather	gi	the first Consonant, being form'd by the Root of the Tongue, this is the present hard g.
k	keep, kick	ki	a kindred Sound, a little more acute, to be us'd instead of the hard c.
s[ʃ]¹	sh, ship, wish	ish	a new Letter, wanted in our Language, our sh, separately taken, not being proper Elements of the Sound.
ɡ[ɡ]¹	ng, ing, reaping, among	ing	a new Letter, wanted for the same Reason; these are form'd back in the Mouth.
n	end	en	form'd more forward in the Mouth, the Tip of the Tongue to the Roof of the Mouth.
r	art	ar	the same, the Tip of the Tongue a little loose or separate from the Roof of the Mouth.
t	teeth	ti	the Tip of the Tongue more forward, touching and then leaving the Roof.
d	deed	di	the same, touching a little fuller.
l	ell, tell	el	the same touching just about the Gums of the upper Teeth.
ħ[ħ]¹	th, think	eħ	the Tongue under and a little behind the upper Teeth, touching them nearly but so as to let the Breath pass between.
dh[ð; Ð]¹	dh, thy	edh	the same a little fuller.
s	essence	es	this Sound is form'd by the Breath passing between the moist End of the Tongue and the upper Teeth.
z	ez, wages	ez	the same a little denser and duller.
f	effect	ef	form'd by the lower Lip against the upper Teeth.
v	ever	ev	the same fuller and duller.
b	bees	bi	the lips put full together and open'd as the Air passes out.
p	peep	pi	the same but a thinner Sound.
m	ember	em	the closing of the Lips, while the e is sounding.

Franklin's phonetic alphabet. *(Yale University Press and American Philosophical Society.)*

From a letter to Giambatista Beccaria

London, July 13, 1762.

Reverend Sir,

Perhaps . . . it may be agreeable to you, as you live in a musical country, to have an account of the new instrument lately added here to the great number that charming science was before possessed of. . . .

You have doubtless heard the sweet tone that is drawn from a drinking-glass, by passing a wet finger round its brim. One Mr. *Puckeridge*, a gentleman from *Ireland*, was the first who thought of playing tunes, formed of these tones. He collected a number of glasses of different sizes, fixed them near each other on a table, and tuned them by putting into them water, more or less, as each note required. The tones were brought out by passing his fingers round their brims. . . . Being charmed by the sweetness of its tones, and the music he produced from it, I wished only to see the glasses disposed in a more convenient form, and brought together in a narrower compass, so as to admit of a greater number of tunes, and all within reach of hand to a person sitting before the instrument, which I accomplished, after various intermediate trials, and less commodious forms, both of glasses and construction, in the following manner.

The glasses are blown as near as possible in the form of hemisphere, having each an open neck or socket in the middle. [See Figure 1.] The thickness of the glass near the brim about a tenth of an inch, or hardly quite so much, but thicker as it comes nearer the neck. . . . The largest glass is nine inches diameter, and the smallest three inches. Between these there are twenty-three different sizes, differing from each other a quarter of an inch in diameter. To make a single instrument there should be at least six glasses blown of each size; and out of this number one may probably pick 37 glasses, (which are sufficient for three octaves with all the semitones) that will be each either the note one wants or a little sharper than that note, and all fitting so well into each other as to taper pretty regularly from the largest to the smallest. . . .

The glasses being chosen and every one marked with a diamond the note you intend it for, they are to be tuned by diminishing the thickness of those that are too sharp. This is done by grinding them round from the neck towards the brim, the breadth of one or two inches, as may be required. . . .

The glasses being thus tuned, you are to be provided with a case for them, and a spindle on which they are to be fixed. [See Figure 2.] My case is about three feet long, eleven inches every way wide within at the biggest end, and five inches at the smallest end; for it tapers all the way, to adapt it better to the conical figure of the set of glasses. This case opens in the middle of its height, and the upper part turns up by hinges fixed behind. The spindle which is of hard iron, lies horizontally from end to end of the box within, exactly in the middle, and is made to turn on brass gudgeons at each end. It is round, an inch diameter at the thickest end, and tapering to a quarter of an inch at the smallest. A square shank comes from its thickest end through the box, on which shank a wheel is fixed by a screw. This wheel serves as a fly to make the motion equable, when the spindle, with the glasses, is turned by the foot like a spinning-wheel. . . .

To fix the glasses on the spindle, a cork is first to be fitted in each neck pretty tight, and projecting a little without the neck, that the neck of one may not touch the inside of another when put together, for that would make a jarring. These corks are to be perforated with holes of different diameters, so as to suit that part of the spindle on which they are to be fixed. . . . The glasses thus are placed one in another, the largest on the biggest end of the spindle which is to the left hand; the neck of this glass is towards the wheel, and the next goes into it in the same position, only about an inch of its brim appearing beyond the brim of the first; thus proceeding. . . .

My largest glass is G, a little below the reach of a common voice, and my highest G, including three compleat octaves. . . .

This instrument is played upon, by sitting before the middle of the set of glasses as before the keys of a harpsichord, turning them with the foot, and wetting them now and then with a spunge and clean water. The fingers should be first a little soaked in water, and quite free from all greasiness; a little fine chalk upon them is sometimes useful, to make them catch the glass and bring out the tone more readily. Both hands are used, by which means different parts are played together. Observe, that the tones are best drawn out when the glasses turn *from* the ends of the fingers, not when they turn *to* them.

The advantages of this instrument are, that its tones are incomparably sweet beyond those of any other; that they may be swelled and softened at pleasure by stronger or weaker pressures of the finger, and continued to any length; and that the instrument, being once well tuned, never again wants tuning.

In honour of your musical language, I have borrowed from it the name of this instrument, calling it the Armonica.

ARMONICA.

Figure 1

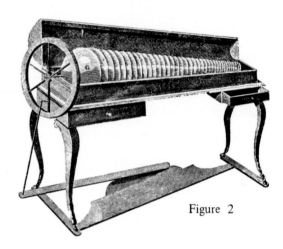

Figure 2

Franklin loved music and was quite accomplished at playing his invention, the (h)armonia, a musical instrument widely popular in Europe during his lifetime, though it later lost favor.
(Painting by A. Fostes; Bettmann Archive.)

From a letter to Jan Ingenhousz on the hot-air balloon
Passy, Jan. 16, 1784.

It appears, as you observe, to be a discovery of great Importance, and what may possibly give a new turn to human Affairs. Convincing Sovereigns of the Folly of wars may perhaps be one Effect of it; since it will be impracticable for the most potent of them to guard his Dominions. Five thousand Balloons, capable of raising two Men each, could not cost more than Five Ships of the Line; and where is the Prince who can afford so to cover his Country with Troops for its Defence, as that Ten Thousand Men descending from the Clouds might not in many places do an infinite deal of mischief, before a Force could be brought together to repel them? It is a pity that any national Jealousy should, as you imagine it may, have prevented the English from prosecuting the Experiment, since they are such ingenious Mechanicians, that in their hands it might have made a more rapid progress towards Perfection, and all the Utility it is capable of affording.

81

Backleaf: A highly imaginative painting, *Benjamin Franklin Drawing Electricity from the Sky*, ca. 1805, by Benjamin West, shows him an old sage seated on clouds, his electrical apparatus to the left and several cherubs to the right aiding him by flying the kite while he touches his knuckle to the electricized key. *(Philadelphia Museum of Art, Mr. and Mrs. Wharton Sinkler Collection.)*

A profile medallion of Franklin by James
Tassie, an artist employed in the English
Wedgwood works. *(Scottish
National Portrait Gallery.)*

Left: *Benjamin Franklin Before the Lords Council, 1774,*
by R. Whitechurch, captures the grave turning point in
Franklin's allegiance to Britian. After this denunciation, he
felt there was no hope for reconciliation between American
and English interests. *(Library of Congress.)*

Right: A chair from Franklin's elegant home on High Street (now Market Street) is displayed at the Franklin Institute in Philadelphia. The portrait of Franklin is by Thomas Sully. *(Franklin Institute, Philadelphia.)* Below: A library chair with steps to assist a reader to reach high shelves was one of Franklin's most useful devices. *(American Philosophical Society.)*

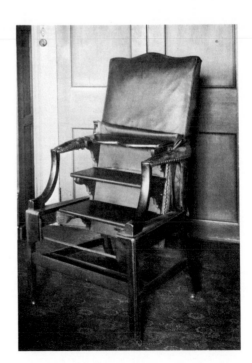

From a letter to George Whatley

Passy, May 23, 1785.

By Mr. Dollond's Saying, that my double Spectacles can only serve particular Eyes, I doubt he has not been rightly informed of their Construction. I imagine it will be found pretty generally true, that the same Convexity of Glass, through which a Man sees clearest and best at the Distance proper for Reading, is not the best for greater Distances. I therefore had formerly two Pair of Spectacles, which I shifted occasionally, as in travelling I sometimes read, and often wanted to regard the Prospects. Finding this Change troublesome, and not always sufficiently ready, I had the Glasses cut, and half of each kind associated in the same Circle. . . . By this means, as I wear my Spectacles constantly, I have only to move my Eyes up or down, as I want to see distinctly far or near, the proper Glasses being always ready. This I find more particularly convenient since my being in France, the Glasses that serve me best at Table to see what I eat, not being the best to see the Faces of those on the other Side of the Table who speak to me; and when one's Ears are not well accustomed to the Sounds of a Language, a Sight of the Movements in the Features of him that speaks helps to explain; so that I understand French better by the help of my Spectacles.

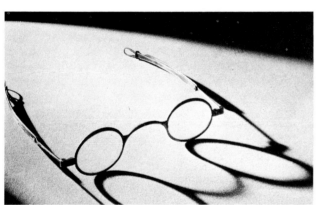

Franklin's regular glasses (not bifocals). To make bifocals, Franklin cut and joined the lower half from very convex reading glasses and the upper half from barely convex glasses for viewing distant objects. *(Franklin Institute, Philadelphia.)*

[Weary with sitting through the proceedings of the Pennsylvania Assembly, Franklin had, in his younger years, composed what he called "arithmetical curiosities," magic squares and a magic circle. In two letters to Peter Collinson, he described their properties. –Ed.]

From letters to Peter Collinson

The properties are,

1. That every straight row (horizontal or vertical) of 8 numbers added together, makes 260, and half each row half 260.

2. That [any] bent row of 8 numbers, ascending and descending diagonally, *viz.* from 16 ascending to 10, and from 23 descending to 17; and every one of its parallel bent rows of 8 numbers, make 260. . . . Also the parallel bent rows next to the above-mentioned, which are shortened to 3 numbers ascending, and 3 descending. . . . And, lastly, the 4 corner numbers, with the 4 middle numbers, make 260.

So this magical square seems perfect in its kind. . . .

Franklin watched with fascination many of the 1783 hot-air balloon ascensions in France, like this engraving of Peter de Rozier's and the Marquis d'Arlandes's ascent in the Garden of Versailles. When another balloonist, Montgolfier, began his ascensions, someone said, "What is the use of a balloon?" Franklin replied, "What is the use of a new-born baby." *(Bettmann Archive.)*

[In addition, Franklin composed a square of 16 (below) with the same properties of the square of 8, though the total would be 2,056 and "that a four square hole being cut in a piece of paper of such a size as to take in and show through it, just 16 of the little squares, when laid on the greater square, the sum of the 16 numbers so appearing through the hole, wherever it was placed on the the greater square, should likewise make 2056. . . . I make no questions but you will readily allow this square of 16 to be the most magically magical of any magic square ever made by any magician." –Ed.]

The magic square of 16 was an ingenious arithmetical exercise in arranging numbers so that specific rows of 16 (see text) add up to 2,056. *(Library of Congress.)*

In the quarter century before the American Revolution, there was no other leading American so familiar with American and English needs and desires, so fond of each country and so eager to keep a happy, just union between the two as Franklin. He held onto his imperialist dreams for England in North America nearly until the Revolution. He cheered every British gain gainst the Spanish and French in the New World, and for a time envisioned America as the next seat of English power. And yet, from his extensive travels as Postmaster General throughout the colonies, he had first-hand knowledge of the increasing injustices in commerce and government.

One of the earliest indications that Franklin was not satisfied with the relations between the colonies and the London government was his satire in *The Pennsylvania Gazette*, "Exporting of Felons to the Colonies," excerpted in this chapter. The same year, he wrote several protests against the government's commercial interference and restrictions.

Other intercolonial affairs soon involved him. With the onset of the French and Indian War (1754), he supported the need for a defensive colonial union: He wrote essays in his *Gazette*; campaigned for a milita in Assembly debates; published the cartoon "Join or Die" reproduced in this chapter (which later was widely used in the colonies); and drafted the Albany Plan of Union towards that end. His account of its mixed reception is included.

The year 1757 proved to be a dividing line in Franklin's activities: He sailed to London as representative to Parliament and King George III from the Pennsylvania Assembly. He did not return home permanently until 1785.

IV CITIZEN AND ADVOCATE

His presence in London was a result of longstanding problems. First was the antagonism between the largely Quaker Assembly of Pennsylvania and the Proprietary Party (descendants of William Penn and their appointed governors) over taxation. The Penns refused to pay on their large estates, and, of course, the other merchants and landowners found this unacceptable. Franklin was sent to petition for royal assistance.

The second reason for sending Franklin to London was to increase support among sympathetic legislators in Parliament for jeopardized American civil rights. There was no thought at this time about independence, but there was discontent with government encroachments on civil liberties.

During his first stay in Britain (1757-62), Franklin also had leisure for some experimentation and travel to Scotland (1759), Belgium and Holland (1761) where he was well-received in scientific circles. His lodging at #7 Craven Street, Strand (London), owned by Mrs. Margaret Stevenson, became a second home for him. His friendship with her and her daughter Mary (Polly) was lifelong.

His return to America (1762-64) for two years is related in his letter to Lord Kames, a Scottish judge and notorious hoaxer like Franklin. During this time the Pennsylvania frontier exploded with Pontiac's Rebellion against encroaching white settlements and the Paxton Boys' reprisal against unrelated Indians . The armed Paxton Boys marched to Philadelphia to confront the predominantly Quaker Assembly which they blamed for being too lenient with the Indians.   Franklin rode out to negotiate with the Paxton group. As he said, he was a very great man for about forty-eight hours when the Governor, John Penn, and the Assembly were frightened. After the fright passed, reprisals against Indians resumed, and John Penn proclaimed a bounty for Indian scalps. Franklin lost his Assembly seat in the election that followed. A majority of his supporters, however, remained in power, and he was elected to return to London to petition the King for a new colonial government.

In London, however, the Stamp Act took first priority. The government needed money to pay for its recently concluded French and Indian War and felt the colonies should pay their share for defense. Colonists were willing to pay, but felt that their own assemblies should raise the money. Parliament was less concerned, at this point, with the legality of their taxation than it was with getting the money. Before Franklin had time to lobby against it actively, the Stamp Act passed with little debate and received royal approval. Americans received the news with indignation and, in some places, violent opposition. American refusal to consume British goods

Congress Voting Independence, 1776,
by Edward Savage shows Franklin
an old man of 70, yet still in the thick
of politics, as he had been for 40 years.
(Historical Society of Pennsylvania.)

finally affected Parliament — but not before Franklin was summoned to testify before the House of Commons. His defense of the colonies was quick and learned; the bill was repealed eight days later.

For an interim of several months, Franklin traveled to Ireland and the Continent, where Irish patriots and French scientists (among others) received him with honor. He returned to London for ten more years of petitioning, acting officially as agent for four colonies — Massachusetts, Pennsylvania, New Jersey and Georgia — and unofficially for the others.

Franklin sensed the uneasy times to come, though he remained hopeful and conciliatory until what is called the "Scene in the Cockpit." In 1772, hoping to reconcile the Massachusetts populace with the King, he allowed private letters of the Massachusetts governor and lieutenant governor, Thomas Hutchinson and Andrew Oliver, to be circulated among friends in Boston. In these letters of 1768-69, Hutchinson and others, *Americans,* advocated military presence and suspension of English civil rights in the colonies as a means of keeping them in line. Franklin hoped that the colonists would see that their problems were not all with the English, but also with native Americans. Bostonians were outraged, and the Massachusetts House petitioned for Hutchinson's removal. Wild stories circulated on the means by which Franklin received the letters; two men dueled over it; Franklin refused to reveal his source, assuming all responsibility. London newspapers denounced him as an enemy to Britain's welfare, an incendiary. He was summoned by the Lords Council on Plantation Affairs to appear in the Cockpit (a Parliamentary chamber) while the Massachusetts petition was considered. What occurred there in January, 1774, was not a hearing but a one-sided diatribe by the Solicitor-General against Franklin personally, before many nobles and onlookers. Dr. Joseph Priestly recorded that "No person belonging to the Council behaved with decent gravity, except Lord North" while Franklin was ridiculed. Edmund Burke said the attack was "beyond all bounds of decency." Franklin remained silent the entire time.

Unofficial negotiations continued in private with meetings between sympathetic Englishmen and Franklin, but the American terms he insisted upon were too stiff. Early in 1775 news arrived that Deborah Franklin had died the preceding December. Franklin had given up hope now that he and the sympathetic English could prevail against the King, Lord North and the majority of Parliament that Americans were enemies of the Empire. He returned to America, arriving shortly before the Battle of Bunker Hill (June 1775). Instead of resting, he became engulfed in the activities of ten committees of the Continental Congress.

At the end of 1776, Congress elected Franklin, at age seventy, Arthur Lee and Silas Deane as commissioners to France, which appeared receptive to American interests. His last act before leaving America was to raise between three and four thousand pounds for a loan to Congress. A sad note to the end of this period in his life was William Franklin's decision to remain loyal to England. The split between father and son was never wholly reconciled, even after the war.

The St. James Park that Franklin referred to in his satire on felons and rattlesnakes looked exactly like the above in 1751. Engraving by H. Roberts. *(Historical Pictures Service, Chicago.)*

EXPORTING OF FELONS TO THE COLONIES
From *The Pennsylvania Gazette*, May 9, 1751
To The Printer of The Gazette

By a Passage in one of your late Papers, I understand that the Government at home will not suffer our mistaken Assemblies to make any Law for preventing or discouraging the Importation of Convicts from Great Britain, for this kind Reason, *'That such laws are against the Publick Utility, as they tend to prevent the* Improvement *and* Well Peopling *of the Colonies.'*

Such a tender *parental* Concern in our *Mother Country* for the *Welfare* of her *Children*, calls aloud for the highest *Returns* of Gratitude and Duty. This every one must be sensible of: But 'tis said, that in our present Circumstances it is absolutely impossible for us to make *such* as are adequate to the Favour. I own it; but nevertheless let us do our Endeavour. 'Tis something to show a grateful Disposition.

In some of the uninhabited Parts of these Provinces, there are Numbers of these venomous Reptiles we call Rattlesnakes; Felons-convict from the Beginning of the World: These, whenever we meet with them, we put to Death, by Virtue of an old Law, *Thou shalt bruise his Head.* But as this is a sanguinary Law, and may seem too cruel; and as however mischievous those Creatures are with us, they may possibly change their Natures, if they were to change the Climate; I would humbly propose, that this general Sentence of *Death* be changed for *Transportation.*

In the Spring of the Year, when they first creep out of their Holes, they are feeble, heavy, slow, and easily taken; and if a small Bounty were allow'd *per* Head, some Thousands might be collected annually, and *transported* to *Britain.* There I would propose to have them carefully distributed in *St. James's Park*, in the *Spring-Gardens* and other Places of Pleasure about *London*; in the Gardens of all the Nobility and Gentry throughout the Nation; but particularly in the Gardens of the *Prime Ministers*, the *Lords of Trade* and *Members of Parliament*; for to them we are *most particularly* obliged.

There is no human Scheme so perfect, but some Inconveniencies may be objected to it: Yet when the Conveniencies far exceed, the Scheme is judg'd rational, and fit to be executed. Thus Inconveniencies have been objected to that *good* and *wise* Act of Parliament, by virtue of which all the *Newgates* and *Dungeons* in *Britain* are emptied into the Colonies. It has been said, that these Thieves and Villains introduc'd among us, spoil the Morals of Youth in the Neighbourhoods that entertain them, and perpetrate many horrid Crimes: But let not *private Interests* obstruct *publick* Utility. Our *Mother* knows what is best for us. What is a little *Housebreaking, Shoplifting*, or *Highway Robbing*; what is a *Son* now and then *corrupted* and *hang'd*, a Daughter *debauch'd* and *pox'd*, a Wife *stabb'd*, a Husband's *Throat cut*, or a Child's *Brains beat out* with an Axe, compar'd with this 'Improvement and Well Peopling of the Colonies!'

Thus it may perhaps be objected to my Scheme, that the *Rattle-Snake* is a mischievous Creature, and that his changing his Nature with the Clime is a mere Supposition, not yet confirm'd by sufficient Facts. What then? Is not Example more prevalent than Precept? And may not the honest rough British Gentry, by a Familiarity with these Reptiles, learn to *creep*, and to *insinuate*, and to *slaver*, and to *wriggle* into Place (and perhaps to *poison* such as stand

88

in their Way) Qualities of no small Advantage to Courtiers! In comparison of which 'Improvement and Publick Utility,' what is a *Child* now and then kill'd by their venomous Bite, ... or even a favourite *Lap Dog*?

I would only add, that this exporting of Felons to the Colonies, may be consider'd as a *Trade*, as well as in the Light of a *Favour*, Now all Commerce implies Returns: Justice requires them: There can be no Trade without them. And *Rattle-Snakes* seem the most *suitable Returns* for the *Human Serpents* sent us by our *Mother* Country. In this, however, as in every other Branch of Trade, she will have the Advantage of us. She will reap *equal* Benefits without equal Risque of the Inconveniencies and Dangers. For the *Rattle-Snake* gives Warning before he attempts his Mischief; which the Convict does not. I am

> Yours, &c.
> Americanus.

Autobiography

Philadelphia, August, 1788.

In 1754, war with France being again apprehended, a congress of commissioners from the different colonies was, by order of the Lords of Trade, to be assembled at Albany, there to confer with the chiefs of the Six Nations concerning the means of defending both their country and ours....

A cartoon, "Join or Die" was Franklin's device for urging colonial union — with English support — against the French and Indians. It appeared May 9, 1754, in his *Pennsylvania Gazette,* just before he presented his Albany Plan of Union. *(Franklin Institute, Philadelphia.)*

Franklin had an ivory miniature painted by C. Dixon in 1757 for his sister, Jane Mecom, to wear as a pendant. *(Museum of Fine Arts, Boston, gift of Franklin Greene Balch.)*

In our way thither, I projected and drew a plan for the union of all the colonies under one government, so far as might be necessary for defense, and other important general purposes.... It then appeared that several of the commissioners had form'd plans of the same kind. A previous question was first taken, whether a union should be established, which pass'd in the affirmative unanimously. A committee was then appointed, one member from each colony, to consider the several plans and report. Mine happen'd to be preferr'd, and, with a few amendments, was accordingly reported.

By this plan the general government was to be administered by a president-general, appointed and supported by the crown, and a grand council was to be chosen by the representatives of the people of the several colonies, met in their respective assemblies. The debates upon it in congress went on daily, hand in hand with the Indian business. Many objections and difficulties were started, but at length they were all overcome, and the plan was unanimously agreed to, and copies ordered to be transmitted to the Board of Trade and to the assemblies of the several provinces. Its fate was singular: the assemblies did not adopt it, as they all thought there was too much *prerogative* in it, and in England it was judg'd to have too much of the *democratic.*...

... The different and contrary reasons of dislike to my plan makes me suspect that it was really the true medium; and I am still of opinion it would have been happy for both sides of the water if it had been adopted. The colonies, so united, would have been sufficiently strong to have defended themselves; there would then have been no need of troops from England; of course, the subsequent pretence for taxing America, and the bloody contest it occasioned, would have been avoided. But such mistakes are not new; history is full of the errors of states and princes.

> *"Look round the habitable world, how few*
> *Know their own good, or, knowing it, pursue!"*

Those who govern, having much business on their hands, do not generally like to take the trouble of considering and carrying into execution new projects. The best public measures are therefore seldom *adopted from previous wisdom, but forc'd by the occasion.*

TOWN MEETING.

*In Rivers and bad Governments,
the lightest Things swim at top.
— Poor Richard's Almanack.*

From a letter to Governor Shirley
On the Imposition of Direct Taxes Upon the Colonies Without Their Consent.

Wednesday Morning [December 18, 1754.]

Sir,

I mentioned it yesterday to your Excellency as my opinion, that excluding the *people* of the colonies from all share in the choice of the grand council, would probably give extreme dissatisfaction, as well as the taxing them by act of Parliament, where they have no representative . In matters of general concern to the people, and especially where burthens are to be laid upon them, it is of use to consider, as well what they will be apt to think and say, as what they ought to think; I shall therefore, as your Excellency requires it of me, briefly mention what of either kind occurs to me on this occasion.

First they will say, and perhaps with justice, that the body of the people in the colonies are as loyal, and as firmly attached to the present constitution, and reigning family, as any subjects in the king's dominions.

That there is no reason to doubt the readiness and willingness of the representatives they may choose, to grant from time to time such supplies for the defence of the country, as shall be judged necessary, so far as their abilities will allow.

That the people in the colonies, who are to feel the immediate mischiefs of invasion and conquest by an enemy in the loss of their estates, lives and liberties, are likely to be better judges of the quantity of forces necessary to be raised and maintained, forts to be built and supported, and of their own abilities to bear the expence, than the parliament of England at so great a distance.

That governors often come to the colonies merely to make fortunes, with which they intend to return to Britain; are not always men of the best abilities or integrity; have many of them no estates here, nor any natural connexions with us, that should make them heartily concerned for our welfare; and might possibly be fond of raising and keeping up more forces than necessary, from the profits accruing to themselves, and to make provision for their friends and dependants. . . .

That the parliament of England is at a great distance, subject to be misinformed and misled by such Governors and Councils, whose united interests might probably secure them against the effect of any complaint from hence.

That it is supposed an undoubted right of Englishmen, not to be taxed but by their own consent given through their representatives.

That the colonies have no representatives in parliament.

That to propose taxing them by parliament, and refuse them the liberty of choosing a representative council . . . shews suspicion of their loyalty to the crown, or of their regard for their country, or of their common sense and understanding, which they have not deserved. . . .

A late 18th century engraving shows the kind of turmoil that sometimes occurred in colonial assemblies. *(Library of Congress.)*

That it would be treating them as a conquered people, and not as true British subjects. . . .

In short, as we are not suffered to regulate our trade, and restrain the importation and consumption of British superfluities (as Britain can the consumption of foreign superfluities) our whole wealth centers finally amongst the merchants and inhabitants of Britain, and if we make them richer, and enable them better to pay their taxes, it is nearly the same as being taxed ourselves, and equally beneficial to the crown. . . .

These, and such kind of things as these, I apprehend, will be thought and said by the people. . . . Dangerous animosities and feuds will arise between the governors and governed; and every thing go into confusion.

From a letter to Peter Collinson

Philadelphia, June 26, 1755

. . . I am heartily sick of our present Situation; I like neither the Governor's Conduct, nor the Assembly's; and having some Share in the Confidence of both, I have endeavour'd to reconcile 'em but in vain, and between 'em they make me very uneasy. I was chosen last Year in my Absence and was not at the Winter Sitting when the House sent home that Address to the King, which I am afraid was both ill-judg'd and ill-tim'd. If my being able now and then to influence a good Measure did not keep up my Spirits I should be ready to swear never to serve again as an Assembly Man, since both Sides expect more from me than they ought, and blame me sometimes for not doing what I am not able to do, as well as for not preventing what was not in my Power to prevent. The Assembly ride restive; and the Governor tho' he spurs with both heels, at the same time reins-in with both hands, so that the Publick Business can never move forward, and he remains like St. George on the Sign, Always a Horseback and never going on. Did you never hear this old Catch?

> *Their was a mad Man – He had a mad Wife,*
> *And three mad Sons beside;*
> *And they all got upon a mad Horse*
> *And madly they did ride.*

'Tis a Compendium of our Proceedings and may save you the Trouble of reading them.

From a letter to Reverend George Whitefield

New York, July 2, 1756

You mention your frequent wish that you were a Chaplain to an American Army. I sometimes wish that you and I were jointly employ'd by the Crown, to settle a Colony on the Ohio. I imagine we could do it effectually, and without putting the Nation to much expence. But I fear we shall never be called upon for such a Service. What a glorious Thing it would be, to settle in that fine Country a large strong Body of Religious and Industrious People! What a Security to the other Colonies; and Advantage to Britain, by Increasing her People, Territory, Strength, and Commerce. Might it not greatly facilitate the Introduction of pure Religion among the Heathen, if we could, by such a Colony, show them a better Sample of Christians than they commonly see in our Indian Traders, the most vicious and abandoned Wretches of our Nation? . . . Life, like a dramatic Piece, should not only be conducted with Regularity, but methinks it should finish handsomely. Being now in the

last Act, I begin to cast about for something fit to end with. Or if mine be more properly compar'd to an Epigram, as some of its few Lines are but barely tolerable, I am very desirous of concluding with a bright Point. In such an Enterprise I could spend the Remainder of Life with Pleasure; and I firmly believe God would bless us with Success, if we undertook it with a sincere Regard to his Honour, the Service of our gracious King, and (which is the same thing) the Public Good.

From PLAN FOR SETTLING TWO WESTERN COLONIES IN NORTH AMERICA, WITH REASONS FOR THE PLAN

The great country back of the Appalachian Mountains, on both sides of the Ohio, and between that river and the Lakes is now well known, both to the English and French, to be one of the finest in North America, for the extreme richness and fertility of the land; the healthy temperature of the air, and mildness of the climate; the plenty of hunting, fishing, and fowling; the facility of trade with the Indians; and the vast convenience of inland navigation or water-carriage by the Lakes and great rivers, many hundreds of leagues around.

From these natural advantages it must undoubtedly (perhaps in less than another century) become a populous and powerful dominion; and a great accession of power either to England or France. . . .

A single old colony does not seem strong enough to extend itself otherwise than inch by inch. It cannot venture a settlement far distant from the main body, being unable to support it; but if the colonies were united under one governor-general and grand council, agreeably to the Albany plan, they might easily, by their joint force, establish one or more new colonies, whenever they should judge it necessary or advantageous to the interest of the whole.

But if such union should not take place, it is proposed that two charters be granted, each for some considerable part of the lands west of Pennsylvania and the Virginian mountains, to a number of the nobility and gentry of Britain; with such Americans as shall join them in contributing to the settlement of those lands, either by paying a proportion of the expense of making such settlements, or by actually going thither in person, and settling themselves and families.

That as many and as great privileges and powers of government be granted to the contributors and settlers, as his Majesty in his wisdom shall think most fit for their benefit and encouragement, consistent with the general good of the British empire. . . .

Such settlements may better be made now, than fifty years hence; because it is easier to settle ourselves, and thereby prevent the French settling there, as they seem now to intend, than to remove them when strongly settled.

If these settlements are postponed, then more forts and stronger, and more numerous and expensive garrisons must be established, to secure the country, prevent their settling, and secure our present frontiers; the charge of which may probably exceed the charge of the proposed settlements, and the advantage nothing near so great.

From a letter to Mrs. Deborah Franklin

London, Jan. 21, 1758

... I begin to think I shall hardly be able to return before this time twelve months. I am for doing effectually what I came about; and I find it requires both time and patience. You may think, perhaps, that I can find many amusements here to pass the time agreeable. 'Tis true, the regard and friendship I meet with from persons of worth, and the conversation of ingenious men, give me no small pleasure; but at this time of life, domestic comforts afford the most solid satisfaction, and my uneasiness at being absent from my family, and longing desire to be with them, make me often sigh in the midst of cheerful company.

[*Henry Home, Lord Kames, was a noted jurist, author and practical joker who had been Franklin's host at his estate in Berwick, Scotland. The "reduction of Canada" was the British seizure of Quebec in September of 1759, the beginning of the end of French domination of Canada and the closing of the Seven Years' War. Franklin was worried that, in closing peace terms with France, Britain would prefer to keep the rich sugar island of Guadeloupe, return Canada to France and endanger frontier colonial safety. —Ed.*]

From a letter to Lord Kames

London, January 3, 1760.

No one can more sincerely rejoice than I do, on the reduction of Canada; and this is not merely as I am a colonist, but as I am a Briton. I have long been of opinion, that the *foundations of the future grandeur and stability of the British empire lie in America*; and though, like other foundations, they are low and little seen, they are, nevertheless, broad and strong enough to support the greatest political structure human wisdom ever yet erected. I am therefore by no means for restoring Canada. If we keep it, all the country from the St. Lawrence to the Mississippi will in another century be filled with British people. Britain itself will become vastly more populous, by the immense increase of its commerce; the Atlantic sea will be covered with your trading ships; and your naval power, thence continually increasing, will extend your influence round the whole globe, and awe the world! If the French remain in Canada, they will continually harass our colonies by the Indians, and impede if not prevent their growth; your progress to greatness will at best be slow, and give room for many accidents that may for ever prevent it. But I refrain, for I see you begin to think my notions extravagant, and look upon them as the ravings of a mad prophet.

The year 1760 saw the demise of French power in North America with the British victory at Quebec. This English cartoonist affirms Britain as the only rightful owner of northern North America, a view with which Franklin agreed. *(Library of Congress.)*

Craven Street, London, June 2, 1765.

You require my history from the time I set sail for America [1762]. . . .

On the 1st of November, I arrived safe and well at my own home, after an absence of near six years, found my wife and daughter well; the latter grown quite a woman, with many amiable accomplishments acquired in my absence; and my friends as hearty and affectionate as ever, with whom my house was filled for many days, to congratulate me on my return. I had been chosen yearly during my absence to represent the city of Philadelphia in our

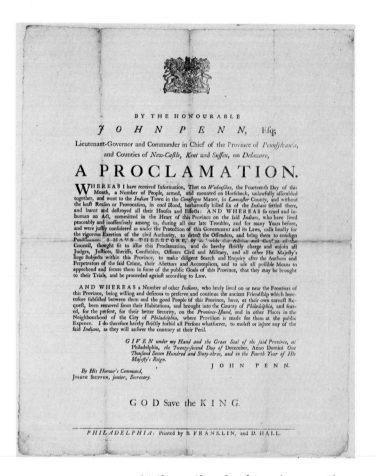

At the outbreak of two insurrections by Pennsylvania settlers, led by a group called the Paxton Boys, against neighboring Indians in 1763, Governor John Penn issued this proclamation offering protection to the surviving Indians. Franklin became deeply involved in settling the dispute. *(Library of Congress.)*

provincial Assembly; and, on my appearance in the House, they voted me £3000 Sterling for my services in England, and their thanks delivered by the Speaker. In February following my son arrived with my new daughter; for, with my consent and approbation, he married soon after I left England a very agreeable West India lady, with whom he is very happy. I accompanied him into his government [New Jersey], where he met with the kindest reception from people of all ranks, and has lived with them ever since in

the greatest harmony. A river only parts that province and ours, and his residence is within seventeen miles of me, so that we frequently see each other.

In the spring of 1763, I set out on a tour through all the northern Colonies to inspect and regulate the Postoffices in the several provinces. In this journey I spent the summer, travelled about 1600 miles, and did not get home till the beginning of November. The Assembly sitting through the following winter, and warm disputes arising between them and the Governor, I became wholly engaged in public affairs; for, besides my duty as an Assemblyman, I had another trust to execute, that of being one of the Commissioners appointed by law to dispose of the public money appropriated to the raising and paying an army to act against the Indians, and defend the frontiers. And then in December, we had two insurrections of the back inhabitants of our province, by whom twenty poor Indians were murdered, that had, from the first settlement of the province, lived among us, under the protection of our government. This gave me a good deal of employment; for, as the rioters threatened farther mischief, and their actions seemed to be approved by an increasing party, I wrote a pamphlet entitled *A Narrative [of the Late Massacres in Lancaster County, 1764]*, (which I think I sent you) to strengthen the hands of our weak Government, by rendering the proceedings of the rioters unpopular and odious.

"The Counter Medly," 1764, deals with the political campaign of that year, when Franklin lost his Assembly seat. *(Historical Society of Pennsylvania.)*

This had a good effect; and afterwards, when a great body of them with arms marched towards the capital, in defiance of the Government, with an avowed resolution to put to death 140 Indian converts then under its protection, I formed an Association at the Governor's request, for his and their defence, we having no militia. Near 1000 of the citizens accordingly took arms; Governor Penn made my house for some time his headquarters, and did every thing by my advice; so that, for about forty-eight hours, I was a very great man; as I had been once some years before, in a time of public danger; But the fighting face we put on, and

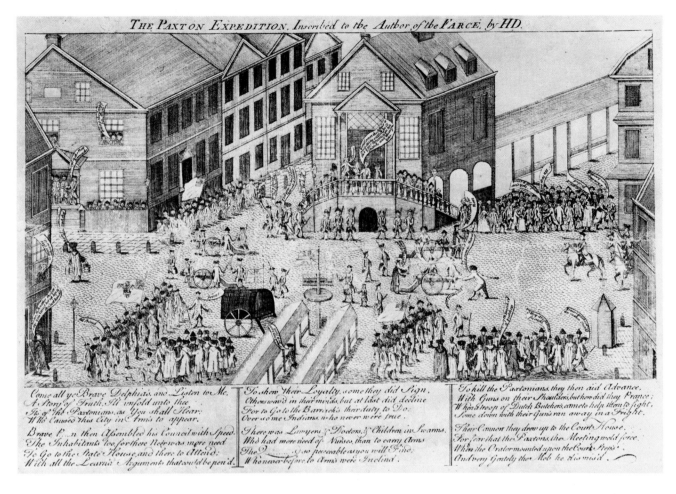

A cartoon, "Franklin and the Quakers,"
attacks them for their "friendly association with the Indians. A group of Quakers
sits at center discussing the Paxton's
march to Philadelphia to confront the
Quaker-dominated Assembly.
Franklin, who had antagonized Dutch, Irish,
Scots and Germans with his satirical
pamphlets, *Cool Thoughts* and *A
Narrative of the Late Massacres*, is charac-
terized with a bag of money, a scientific
letter and words to imply he enjoys dis-
cord. *(Historical Society of Pennsylvania.)*

the reasonings we used with the insurgents, (for I went at
the request of the Governor and Council, with three others,
to meet and discourse them,) having turned them back and
restored quiet to the city, I became a less man than ever;
for I had, by these transactions, made myself many enemies
among the populace; and the Governor, (with whose family
our public disputes had long placed me in an unfriendly
light, and the services I had lately rendered him not being
of the kind that make a man acceptable,) thinking it a
favourable opportunity, joined the whole weight of the proprietary interest to get me out of the Assembly; which was
accordingly effected at the last election, by a majority of
about 25 in 4000 voters. The House, however, when they
met in October, approved of the resolutions taken while I
was Speaker, of petitioning the crown for a change of
Government, and requested me to return to England, to
prosecute that petition; which service I accordingly undertook, and embarked at the beginning of November last,
being accompanied to the ship, sixteen miles, by a caval-
cade of three hundred of my friends, who filled our sails
with their good wishes, and I arrived in thirty days at
London.

Here I have been ever since, engaged in that and other
public affairs relating to America, which are like to continue some time longer upon my hands.

95

[In England, Franklin was at first unaware of the degree of opposition to the Stamp Act in America. He felt patience and moderation were necessary to obtain the larger goal of removing the arbitrary colonial governments. Thus the "outrages by those misguided people" — the vocal opposition by Patrick Henry of Virginia and others in Pennsylvania and Massachusetts — appeared unwise. Charles Thomson was to become secretary of the Continental Congress, 1774-89. —Ed.]

From a letter to Charles Thomson,

London, July 11, 1765.

Dear Friend,

I am extremely obliged by your kind Letters of April 12th and 14th, and thank you for the intelligence they contain. The Outrages continually committed by those misguided people, will doubtless tend to convince all the considerate on your side of the water, of the weakness of our present Government, and the necessity of a Change. I am sure it will contribute toward hastening that Change here so that upon the whole, Good will be brought out of Evil; but yet I grieve to hear of such horrid disorders. The Letters and accounts boasted of from the Proprietor, of his being sure of retaining the Government, as well as those of the sums offered for it, which the people will be obliged to pay, &c., are all idle Tales, fit only for knaves to propagate, and Fools to believe. A little Time will *dissipate all the smoke* they can raise to conceal the real state of things. . . .

Depend upon it, my good neighbour, I took every step in my power to prevent the passing of the Stamp Act. Nobody could be more concerned in interest than myself to oppose it sincerely and heartily. But the Tide was too strong against us. The nation was provoked by American Claims of Independence, and all Parties joined in resolving by this act to settle the point. We might as well have hindered the sun's setting. That we could not do. But since 'tis down, my Friend, and it may be long before it rises again, let us make as good a night of it as we can. We may still light candles. Frugality and Industry will go a great way toward indemnifying us. Idleness and Pride tax with a heavier hand than Kings and Parliaments; if we can get rid of the former, we may easily bear the latter.

[This section of a satire on British treatment of the colonies' resistance to the Stamp Act has been attributed to Franklin. He spent much of his time in the ten years from 1765-1775 defending America by means of such articles in London newspapers. Grenville was the minister under whom the Stamp Act came into being. —Ed.]

To the Printer of the Public Advertiser

January 23, 1766

Now in order to bring these People to a proper Temper, I have a Plan to propose, which I think cannot fail, and which will be entirely consistent with the Oeconomy at present so much in Vogue. It is so cheap a Way of going to work, that even Mr. G— G—, [George Grenville] that great Oeconomost, could have no reasonable Objection to it.

Let Directions be given, that Two Thousand Highlanders be immediately raised, under proper Officers of their own. It ought to be no Ojection, that they were in the Rebellion in Forty-five: If Roman Catholics, the better. The C—l at present in the P—ze [Portuguese] Service may be at their Head. Transport them early in the Spring to Quebec: They with the Canadians, natural Enemies to our Colonists, who would voluntarily engage, might make a Body of Five or Six Thousand Men; and I doubt not, by artful Management, and the Value of two or three Thousand Pounds in Presents, with the Hopes of Plunder, as likewise a Gratuity for every Scalp, the Savages on the Frontiers might be engaged to join, at least they would make a Diversion, which could not fail of being useful. I could point out a very proper General to command the Expedition; he is of a very sanguine Disposition, and has an inordinate Thirst for Fame, and besides has the Hearts of the Canadians. He might march from Canada, cross the Lakes, and fall upon these People without their expecting or being prepared for him, and with very little Difficulty over-run the whole Country.

The Business might be done without employing any of the Regular Troops quartered in the Country, and I think it would be best they should remain neuter, as it is to be feared they would be rather backward in embruing their Hands in the Blood of their Brethren and Fellow Subjects.

I would propose, that all the Capitals of the several Provinces should be burnt to the Ground, and that they cut the Throats of all the Inhabitants, Men, Women, and Children, and scalp them, to serve as an Example; that all the Shipping should be destroyed, which will effectually prevent Smuggling, and save the Expence of Guarda Costas.

No Man in his Wits, after such terrible Military Execution, will refuse to purchase stamp'd Paper. If any one should hesitate, five or six Hundred Lashes in a cold frosty Morning would soon bring him to Reason.

If the Massacre should be objected to, as it would too much depopulate the Country, it may be replied, that the Interruption this Method would occasion to Commerce, would cause so many Bankruptcies, such Numbers of Manufacturers and Labourers would be unemployed, that, together with the Felons from our Gaols, we should soon be enabled to transport such Numbers to repeople the Colonies, as to make up for any Deficiency which Example made it Necessary to sacrifice for the Public Good. Great Britain might then reign over a loyal and submissive People, and be morally certain, that no Act of Parliament would ever after be disputed. Your's,

Pacificus.

A Letter Concerning the Stamp Act

To the printer of the *Gazetteer*, January 15, 1766.

Give me leave, Master John Bull, to remind you, that you are related to all mankind; and therefore it less becomes you than anybody, to affront and abuse other nations. But you have mixed with your many virtues a pride, a haughtiness, and an insolent contempt for all but yourself, that, I am afraid, will, if not abated, procure you one day or other a handsome drubbing. Besides your rudeness to foreigners, you are far from being civil even to your own family. The Welch you have always despised for submitting to your government; but why despise your own English, who conquered and settled Ireland for you; who conquered and settled America for you? Yet these you now think you may treat as you please, because forsooth, they are a *conquered* people. Why despise the Scotch, who fight and die for you all over the world? Remember you courted Scot-

land for one hundred years, and would fain have had your wicked will of her. She virtuously resisted all your importunities; but at length kindly consented to become your lawful wife. You then solemnly promised to love, cherish, and honour her, as long as you both should live; and yet you have ever since treated her with the utmost contumely, which you now begin to extend to your common children.

The only known original of Franklin's Stamp Act cartoon shows Britannia dismembered, deserted, with her ships lying idle in the background, implying the disastrous effects on the empire from unfairly taxing the colonies. *(Library Company of Philadelphia.)*

But, pray, when your enemies are uniting in a Family Compact against you, can it be discreet in you to kick up in your own house a Family Quarrel? And at the very time you are inviting foreigners to settle on your lands, and when you have more to settle than ever you had before, is it prudent to suffer your lawyer, Vindex, to abuse those who have settled there already, because they cannot yet speak "plain English?" — It is my opinion Master Bull, that the Scotch and Irish, as well as the Colonists are capable of speaking much plainer English that they ever yet spoke, but which I hope they will never be provoked to speak.

Homespun.

Odometer used by Franklin as Postmaster General and given to him by Thomas Jefferson. *(Franklin Institute, Philadelphia.)*

[*The excerpts below from the record of Franklin's examination before the House of Commons are partial indication of his great range of knowledge and the quick and capable defense he provided as America's advocate. Questions were posed by many different members, some antagonists, some friends who posed their questions to Franklin's and America's advantage. Eight days after the Examination, a Repealing Bill passed both Houses and received the king's assent within a few weeks. —Ed.*]

THE REPEAL. — or the Funeral Procession, of MISS AMERIC-STAMP.

"The Repeal, or the Funeral Procession of Miss Americ-Stamp" depicts English politicians, with George Grenville holding a symbolic casket, and churchmen who supported the Stamp Act. In the background, ships and cargo are ready to sail to the colonies again. The Repeal was greeted with extravagant joy in Pennsylvania, where the governor, mayor and leading men drank a toast to "our worthy and faithful agent, Dr. Franklin." *(Library of Congress.)*

THE EXAMINATION OF DOCTOR BENJAMIN FRANKLIN, IN THE BRITISH HOUSE OF COMMONS, RELATIVE TO THE REPEAL OF THE AMERICAN STAMP ACT, IN 1766.

Q. From the thinness of the back settlements, would not the stamp act be extremely inconvenient to the inhabitants, if executed?

A. To be sure it would; as many of the inhabitants could not get stamps when they had occasion for them without taking long journeys, and spending perhaps Three or Four Pounds, that the Crown might get Six pence.

Q. Are not the Colonies, from their circumstances, very able to pay the stamp duty?

A. In my opinion there is not gold and silver enough in the Colonies to pay the stamp duty for one year.

Q. Don't you know that the money arising from the stamps was all to be laid out in America?

A. I know it is appropriated by the act to the American service; but it will be spent in the conquered Colonies, where the soldiers are, not in the Colonies that pay it.

Q. Is there not a balance of trade due from the Colonies where the troops are posted, that will bring back the money to the old colonies?

A. I think not. I believe very little would come back. I know of no trade likely to bring it back. I think it would come from the Colonies where it was spent directly to England; for I have always observed, that in every Colony the more plenty the means of remittance to England, the more goods are sent for, and the more trade with England carried on.

Q. What was the temper of America toward Great Britain, before the year 1763?

A. The best in the world. They submitted willingly to the government of the Crown, and paid, in all their courts, obedience to acts of parliament. Numerous as the people are in the several provinces, they cost you nothing in forts, citadels, garrisons, or armies, to keep them in subjection. They were governed by this country at the expence only of a little pen, ink and paper. They were led by a thread. They had not only a respect, but an affection for Great-Britain; for its Laws, its customs and manners, and even a fondness for its fashions, that greatly increased the commerce. Natives of Britain were always treated with particular regard; to be an Old England man was, of itself, a character of some respect, and gave a kind of rank among us.

. . . . . .

98

William Pitt, Earl of Chatham (1708-78), led a ministry briefly in 1766-67 and habitually spoke out against government policy towards the colonies. He was not able to unite a party against the King's administration and never advocated American independence, yet he was popular in the colonies for his strong stand against George III. *(National Portrait Gallery, London.)*

Jonathan Shipley was a staunch supporter of American liberties and a life-long friend to Franklin. *(Courtesy, Yale University Library.)*

William Strahan (1715-1785), the King's Printer, was Franklin's most intimate friend in England. Their long personal and business relations were always smooth, and Strahan almost convinced Franklin to settle in England, if only Deborah Franklin had been willing. *(National Portrait Gallery, London.)*

Q. In what light did the people of America use to consider the parliament of Great Britain?

A. They considered the parliament as the great bulwark and security of their liberties and privileges, and always spoke of it with the utmost respect and veneration. Arbitrary ministers, they thought, might possibly, at times attempt to oppress them; but they relied on it, that the parliament, on application, would always give redress. They remembered, with gratitude, a strong instance of this, when a bill was brought into parliament, with a clause, to make royal instructions laws in the colonies, which the House of Commons would not pass, and it was thrown out.

Q. And have they not still the same respect for parliament?

A. No, it is greatly lessened.

Q. To what causes is that owing?

A. To a concurrence of causes; the restrains lately laid on their trade, by which the bringing of foreign gold and silver into the Colonies was prevented; and prohibition of making paper money among themselves; and then demanding a new and heavy tax by stamps; taking away, at the same time, trials by juries, and refusing to receive and hear their humble petitions.

Q. Don't you think they would submit to the stamp-act, if it was modified, the obnoxious parts taken out, and the duty reduced to some particulars, of small moment?

A. No; they will never submit to it.

. . . . . .

In America from 1775-76, Franklin worked on 10 committees of the second Continental Congress, and here he speaks before one. He was involved in defense preparations to pay for and supply a Pennsylvania militia and in plans for fortifications and armed boats. He helped plan a post office and served as its first Postmaster General. Other committee work included Indian affairs, engraving and printing continental money, considering Lord North's conciliatory offer, employing packetships, drawing up plans for foreign treaties and for protecting commerce, and secretly corresponding with "friends in Great Britain, Ireland, and other parts of the world." Though usually appearing the calm elder statesman, during these years Franklin zealously campaigned to raise a spirit of independence among Americans.
(Franklin Institute, Philadelphia.)

Q. Can any thing less than a military force carry the stamp act into execution?

A. I do not see how a military force can be applied to that purpose.

Q. Why may it not?

A Suppose a military force sent into America, they will find nobody in arms; what are they then to do? They cannot force a man to take stamps who chooses to do without them. They will not find a rebellion; they may indeed make one.

Q. If the act is not repealed, what do you think will be the consequences?

A. A total loss of the respect and affection the people of America bear to this country, and of all the commerce that depends on that respect and affection.

Q. Is the American stamp act an equal tax on the country?

A. I think not.

Q. Why so?

A. The greatest part of the money must arise from lawsuits for the recovery of debts, and be paid by the lower sort of people, who were too poor easily to pay their debts. It is, therefore, a heavy tax on the poor, and a tax upon them for being poor.

. . . . . .

Q. What used to be the pride of the Americans?

A. To indulge in the fashions and manufactures of Great Britain.

Q. What is now their pride?

A. To wear their old clothes over again, till they can make new ones.

Some Americans were preparing for independence when Franklin returned home after 11 years (1764-75) of representing colonial interests in London. Within a year, in 1776, independence was declared. An idealized *Raising of the Liberty Pole*, by John McRae pictures the event. *(Kennedy Galleries, New York.)*

Overleaf: Franklin returned to America about a month before the first major battle of the Revolution, the Battle of Bunker's Hill, June 17, 1775. An anonymous painter captured the action in this panorama, *Attack on Bunker's Hill, with the Burning of Charles Town. (National Gallery of Art, gift of Edgar William and Bernice Chrysler Garbisch.)*

The State House, Philadelphia, where the
Declaration of Independence was adopted and
the Constitution was drafted. From a
drawing by Charles Willson Peale.
(Historical Society of Pennsylvania.)

The Liberty Bell was used on many
occasions prior to and after its ringing
at the public reading of the Declaration
of Independence, July 8, 1776. It rang
in 1757 when the Pennsylvania Assembly
sent Franklin to England to seek redress of grievances and in 1765, 1768 and 1770
to protest taxation and other impositions
by Parliament.It rang in 1783 to proclaim
peace and in 1799 to toll Washington's
death. It cracked and was repaired several
times. Presently it is irreparable and
hangs in the Pennsylvania State House
called Independence Hall.

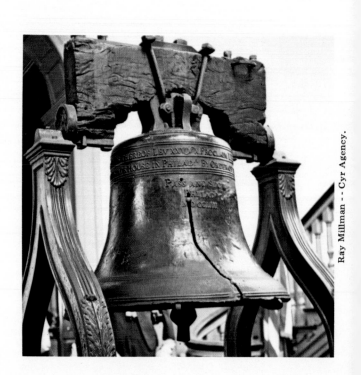

Ray Millman -- Cyr Agency.

Franklin was one of Pennsylvania's 25 delegates to the conference of the Committee of Safety in June 1776 that foreswore allegiance to the English king and which voted to form a constitution. The five who drew up the Declaration of Independence stand together in the center of this painting by an unknown artist: Adams, Sherman, Livingston, Jefferson and Franklin. Washington is seated on the right. On July 8, Franklin was elected president of the Constitutional Convention. *(Insurance Company of North America.)*

[*Franklin spent the years after the repeal of the Stamp Act until the eve of the American Revolution in London, with visits to other parts of the British Isles and to the Continent. His time was greatly taken up in trying to smooth over the growing hostility between the American and British interests, until 1775, when he and colonial leaders decided reconciliation on former terms of colony and mother country was impossible. He returned to America then, in time to become involved in the revolutionary preparations by the Continental Congress.—Ed.*]

[*Thomas Jefferson's account of Franklin's response to the changes imposed on the draft of the Declaration of Independence by the Continental Congress:*]

"I have made it a rule, whenever in my power, to avoid becoming the draughtsman of papers to be reviewed by a public body. I took my lesson from an incident which I will relate to you. When I was a journeyman printer, one of my companions, an apprentice hatter, having served out his time, was about to open shop for himself. His first concern was to have a handsome signboard, with a proper inscription. He composed it in these words, 'John Thompson, *Hatter, makes* and *sells hats* for ready money,' with the figure of a hat subjoined; but he thought he would submit it to his friends for their amendments. The first he showed it to thought the word '*Hatter*' tautologous, because followed by the words 'makes hats,' which showed he was a hatter. It was struck out. The next observed that the word '*makes*' might as well be omitted, because his customers would not care who made the hats. If good and to their mind, they would buy, by whomsoever made. He struck it out. A third said he thought the words '*for ready money*' were useless, as it was not the custom of the place to sell on credit; every one who purchased expected to pay. They were parted with, and the inscription now stood, 'John Thompson sells hats.' '*Sells hats?*' says his next friend. 'Why, nobody will expect you to give them away; what then is the use of that word?' It was stricken out, and '*hats*' followed it, the rather as there was one painted on the board. So the inscription was reduced ultimately to 'John Thompson,' with the figure of a hat subjoined."

As the Congressional delegates were about to sign the Declaration of Independence, the popular story goes, John Hancock said, "We must be unanimous; there must be no pulling different ways, we must all hang together," to which Franklin replied, "We must indeed hang together, or, most assuredly, we shall all hang separately."

105

Franklin arrived in France after a raw November voyage, so weak he could hardly stand and not yet expected by friends or the government. The British ambassador in France was certain he came to gain French aid, though other Britons hoped he was running away from a lost cause. It soon was apparent he came for and was gaining French support.

Arriving in 1777, in ordinary dress and fur cap to keep his head warm (most men in upper levels of French society wore powdered wigs), Franklin appeared to the French as the home-spun Quaker philosopher they had expected. "Poor Richard," as he was pictured by the middle and lower classes, was already familiar, for his *Way to Wealth* from the *Almanack* had been widely published in France. Soon, as one of Franklin's editors says, "The enthusiasm for *le grand Franklin* became a passion . . . idolatry." As a symbol of democracy, Franklin was deified in an almost unparalleled way.

Franklin made the best of this favor, for certainly the American cause needed all possible support. He kept the fur cap, unfashionable spectacles and thoroughly enjoyed being the primitive sage. His private letters show he was amused with seeing his image reproduced on plaques, snuffboxes, mugs, miniature paintings and the like. There is a story that King Louis XVI, tired of hearing a noblewoman's continual praise of Franklin, presented her with a chamberpot with his picture on the bottom. Despite all the adulation, however gratifying, Franklin remained aware of the quick changes of fortune he had endured as a public figure.

V AMBASSADOR IN PARIS

The political scene Franklin entered was complex. His official home, the Hôtel de Valentinois in Passy, a suburb of Paris, was enmeshed by a network of British spies. He knew this, as did the French, and the Paris police were told to guard against "sinister-looking persons seen lurking around" his home. A British double agent, Edward Bancroft, was already a confidant of Silas Deane (another U.S. commissioner) and, soon after, Franklin, who had met Bancroft in London in the Royal Society. Neither Franklin or Deane suspected Bancroft, but the third commissioner, Arthur Lee, was suspicious of him and nearly everyone in the embassy. (Bancroft's role was not proven until a century after his death.) Franklin, feeling it was impossible to discover every spy, decided to act quite openly, perhaps thinking this would confuse the English. Franklin has been criticized for ignoring usual precautions by some historians, yet others interpret his actions as shrewd: He played the French and British animosities against each other. While the French hesitated to ally with America, Franklin let it be known that he still met with the English to reconcile differences. On the other hand, the English spies kept their government informed of every gain he and the other commissioners made in getting "secret" French aid.

All this while, Congress depended on Franklin for French loans and good will. In addition to the official duties of commissioner, Franklin found himself undertaking other responsibilities. He never received the secretary Congress promised, so he and his grandson kept the huge correspondence files. Franklin served as a judge of admiralty who commissioned privateers to harass and embarrass British merchants, judged the legality of captures, and ordered the prizes to be sold and distributed. Though he later despised privateering, these actions gave him some leverage in exchanging prisoners and gaining supplies.

Other endeavors were the improvement of prisoner-of-war condtions and purchase of military supplies. The most fatiguing work, he said, was accounting for all the bills of exchange Congress drew on its French bank account, for which Franklin alone secured eighteen million livres (over $3,600,000) by 1782. Without French aid (totaling over $8,000,000 by 1783), and thus without Franklin's work in France, the Revolutionary War would not have succeeded.

In his final public service in France, Franklin worked with John Jay, John Adams, Henry Laurens and Thomas Jefferson in successfully concluding peace negotiations with England in September of 1783, about one year after the British surrender at Yorktown. Franklin had been continually in touch with Englishmen who also hoped to end the war, but declined all their

AND ELDER STATESMAN AT HOME

An allegorical engraving, ca. 1778, by Etienne Palliere, of Franklin's arrival in
France shows him as he was popularily recognized, in fur cap and glasses. Louis XVI
is the figure to his right in armor. Various pagan gods prepare armaments, others make
thunder, and another saves a distressed woman (presumably American) from the
British lion. *(Yale University Art Gallery,William Smith Mason Collection.)*

early offers for a separate peace, excluding France. It was essential that
America have equal commerical and political rights with all Europeans.

Returning to America in 1785, Franklin expected he could at last find
repose. Though physically he needed rest, Franklin was by no means ready
to retire. He sincerely felt a duty to perform public offices, but it must have
flattered him to be chosen President of Pennsylvania and elected a
Counsellor for Philadelphia. In the summer of 1787 he attended the
Constitutional Convention, where his usefulness proved to be, as in the past,
in reconciling opposing factions. A friend commented, "Dr. Franklin
exhibits daily a spectacle of transcendent benevolence." His chief contribution to the document was supporting the Connecticut Compromise, whereby
two kinds of elected representation, House and Senate, satisfied both large
and small states. The next year he served as President of the Pennsylvania
Society for Promoting the Abolition of Slavery, for which he wrote the
satire, *Speech of Allah Bismillah,* against slavery.

His last two years were spent in retirement and waning health with his
daughter and among friends. Alert to the end, he wrote the satire mentioned
above only a few weeks before he died. His interest in science continued, as
did interest in the affairs of his new nation and the upheavals in France. The
effects of pleurisy when he was young finally took effect on his weakened
body; an absess in his lungs broke, he nearly suffocated, then fell into a
coma. He died April 17, 1790, at eighty-four years.

BENJAMIN FRANKLIN.

Né à Boston, dans la nouvelle Angleterre le 17 Janvier 1706.

Dessiné par C. N. Cochin Chevalier de l'Ordre du Roi, en 1777 et Gravé par Aug. de S.ᵗ Aubin Graveur de la Bibliothèque du Roi.

Se vend à Paris chés C. N. Cochin aux Galleries du Louvre, et chés Aug. de S.ᵗ Aubin, rue des Mathurins.

From a letter to Mrs. Thompson [at Lille]
Paris, February 8, 1777.

. . . I know you wish you could see me; but, as you can't, I will describe myself to you. Figure me in your mind as jolly as formerly, and as strong and hearty, only a few years older; very plainly dress'd, wearing my thin gray strait hair, that peeps out under my only *Coiffure*, a fine Fur Cap, which comes down my Forehead almost to my Spectacles. Think how this must appear among the Powder'd Heads of Paris! I wish every gentleman and Lady in France would only be so obliging as to follow my Fashion, comb their own Heads as I do mine, dismiss their *Friseurs*, and pay me half the Money they paid to them. You see, the gentry might well afford this, and I could then enlist those *Friseurs*, who are at least 100,000, and with the Money I would maintain them, make a Visit with them to England, and dress the Heads of your Ministers and Privy Counsellors; which I conceive to be at present *un peu dérangées* ["a little disturbed"]. Adieu, Madcap; and believe me ever, your affectionate Friend and humble Servant,

B. Franklin

From a letter to Mrs. Elizabeth Partridge
Passy, Oct. 11, 1779.

You mention the Kindness of the French Ladies to me. I must explain that matter. This is the civilest nation upon Earth. Your first Acquaintances endeavour to find out what you like, and they tell others. If 'tis understood that you like Mutton, dine where you will you find Mutton. Somebody, it seems, gave it out that I lov'd Ladies; and then every body presented me their Ladies (or the Ladies presented themselves) to be *embrac'd*, that is to have their Necks kiss'd. For as to kissing of Lips or Cheeks it is not the Mode here, the first, is reckon'd rude, & the other may rub off the Paint. The French Ladies have however 1000 other ways of rendering themselves agreeable; by their various Attentions and Civilities, & their sensible Conversation. 'Tis a delightful People to live with.

[The Sale of the Hessians *is attributed to Franklin and was written to shame the British for employing German mercenaries to fight the colonists. Nearly 30,000 Germans were dispatched by petty German princes who received head money for each man sent and for each man killed.* —Ed.]

THE SALE OF THE HESSIANS

From the Count De Schaumbergh to the Baron Hohendorf, Commanding the Hessian Troops in America.
Rome, February 18, 1777.

Monsieur Le Baron: — On my return from Naples, I received at Rome your letter of the 27th December of last year. I have learned with unspeakable pleasure the courage our troops exhibited at Trenton, and you cannot imagine my joy on being told that of the 1,950 Hessians engaged in the fight, but 345 escaped. There were just 1,605 men

killed, and I cannot sufficiently commend your prudence in sending an exact list of the dead to my minister in London. This precaution was the more necessary, as the report sent to the English ministry does not give but 1,455 dead. This would make 483,450 florins instead of 643,500 which I am entitled to demand under our convention. You will comprehend the prejudice which such an error would work in my finances, and I do not doubt you will take the necessary pains to prove that Lord North's list is false and yours correct.

The court of London objects that there were a hundred wounded who ought not to be included in the list, nor paid for as dead; but I trust you will not overlook my instructions to you on quitting Cassel, and that you will not have tried by human succor to recall the life of the unfortunates whose days could not be lengthened but by the loss of a leg or an arm. That would be making them a pernicious present, and I am sure they would rather die than live in a condition no longer fit for my service. I do not mean by this that you should assassinate them; we should be humane, my dear Baron, but you may insinuate to the surgeons with entire propriety that a crippled man is a reproach to their profession, and that there is no wiser course than to let every one of them die when he ceases to be fit to fight.

I am about to send to you some new recruits. Don't economize them. Remember glory before all things. Glory is true wealth. There is nothing degrades the soldier like the love of money. He must care only for honour and reputation, but this reputation must be acquired in the midst of dangers. A battle gained without costing the conqueror any blood is an inglorious success, while the conquered cover themselves with glory by perishing with their arms in their hands. Do you remember that of the 300 Lacedaemonians who defended the defile of Thermopylae, not one returned? How happy should I be could I say the same of my brave Hessians!

It is true that their king, Leonidas, perished with them: but things have changed, and it is no longer the custom for princes of the empire to go and fight in America for a cause with which they have no concern. And besides, to whom should they pay the thirty guineas per man if I did not stay in Europe to receive them? Then, it is necessary also that I be ready to send recruits to replace the men you lose. For this purpose I must return to Hesse. It is true, grown men are becoming scarce there, but I will send you boys. Besides, the scarcer the commodity the higher the price. I am assured that the women and little girls have begun to till our lands, and they get on not badly. You did right to send back to Europe that Dr. Crumerus who was so successful in curing dysentery. Don't bother with a man who is subject to looseness of the bowels. That disease makes bad soldiers. One coward will do more mischief in an engagement than ten brave men will do good. Better that they burst in their barracks than fly in a battle, and tarnish the glory of our arms. Besides, you know that they pay me as killed for all who die from disease, and I don't get a farthing for runaways. My trip to Italy, which has cost me enormously, makes it desirable that there should be a great mortality among them. You will therefore promise promotion to all who expose themselves; you will exhort them to seek glory in the midst of dangers; you will say to Major Maundorff that I am not at all content with his saving the 345 men

Left: Franklin's fur cap and glasses were considered sensational when he appeared thus dressed as New World ambassador. This 1777 engraving was reworked on countless items like watches, prints and medallions. Etched by A. de Saint Aubin after a drawing by C.N. Cochin. *(The Philadelphia Museum of Art.)*

who escaped the massacre of Trenton. Through the whole campaign he has not had ten men killed in consequence of his orders. Finally, let it be your principal object to prolong the war and avoid a decisive engagement on either side, for I have made arrangements for a grand Italian opera, and I do not wish to be obliged to give it up. Meantime I pray God, my dear Baron de Hohendorf, to have you in his holy and gracious keeping.

[*Dr. Samuel Cooper, of Boston, was an old friend of Franklin who shared political and scientific interests. —Ed.*]

From a letter to Samuel Cooper

Paris, May 1, 1777.

I rejoice with you in the happy Change of Affairs in America last Winter. I hope the same Train of Success will continue thro' the Summer. Our Enemies are disappointed in the Number of additional Troops they purposed to send over. What they have been able to muster will not probably recruit their Army to the State it was in the beginning of last Campaign; and ours I hope will be equally numerous, better arm'd, and better clothed, than they have been heretofore.

All Europe is on our Side of the Question, as far as Applause and good Wishes can carry them. Those who live under arbitrary Power do nevertheless approve of Liberty, and wish for it; they almost despair of recovering it in Europe; they read the Translations of our separate Colony Constitutions with Rapture; and there are such Numbers everywhere, who talk of Removing to America, with their Families and Fortunes, as soon as Peace and our Independence shall be established, that 'tis generally believed we shall have a prodigious Addition of Strength, Wealth, and Arts, from the Emigrations of Europe; and 'tis thought, that, to lessen or prevent such Emigrations, the Tyrannies established there must relax, and allow more Liberty to their People. Hence 'tis a Common Observation here, that our Cause is *the Cause of all Mankind*, and that we are fighting for their Liberty in defending our own. 'Tis a glorious task assigned'd us by Providence; which has, I trust, given us Spirit and Virtue equal to it, and will at last crown it with Success. I am ever, my dear Friend, yours most affectionately,

B. F[ranklin].

From the COMPARISON OF GREAT BRITAIN AND THE UNITED STATES IN REGARD TO THE BASIS OF CREDIT IN THE TWO COUNTRIES

[1777]

With regard to Frugality in Expences; the Manner of Living in America is in general more simple and less Expensive than in England. Plain Tables, plain Clothing, plain Furniture in Houses, few Carriages of Pleasure. In America an expensive Appearance hurts Credit, and is therefore avoided; in England it is often put on with a View of gaining Credit, and continued to Ruin. In *publick* Affairs, the Difference is still greater. In England Salaries of Officers and Emoluments of office are Enormous. The King has a Million Sterling per Annum, and yet cannot maintain his Family free of Debt; Secretaries of State, Lords of the Treasury, Admiralty, &c., have vast Appointments. . . . This

*While you, great George, for knowledge hunt
And sharp conductors change for blunt
The Empire's out of joint.
Franklin another course pursues
And all your thunder heedless views
By keeping to the point.*
— Anonymous popular lines.

* At the outbreak of the American Revolution, King George III insisted all lightning rods have blunt ends, for he refused to use the rebel Franklin's design for pointed rods.

Lord Frederick North (1732-92) was Prime Minister throughout the American Revolution and executor of George III's policies. *(National Portrait Gallery, London.)*

is all paid by the People, who are oppress'd by the Taxes so occasioned, and thereby rendered less able to contribute to the Payment of necessary national Debts. In America, Salaries, where indispensable, are extreamly low; but much of publick Business is done gratis. The Honour of serving the Publick ably and faithfully is deemed sufficient. *Public Spirit* really exists there, and has great Effects. In England it is universally deemed a NonEntity, and whoever pretends to it is laugh'd at as a fool, or suspected as a Knave. The Committees of Congress . . . all attend the Business of their respective Functions without any Salary or Emolument whatever, tho' they spend in it much more of their Time, than any Lord of Treasury or Admiralty in England can afford from his Amusements. . . .

George III of England (1738-1820) by Allan Ramsay. King George fully supported English measures oppressive to the colonies which lead to the American Revolution. *(Colonial Williamsburg.)*

The industrious country that Franklin wanted America to be was epitomized in its leading city, Philadelphia. Pictured is the New Market at the corner of Shippen and Second streets. *(Courtesy, The New-York Historical Society.)*

With regard to Prudence in General Affairs, and the Advantages they expect from the Loan desired. The Americans are Cultivators of Land; those engag'd in Fishery and Commerce are a small Number, compar'd with the Body of the People. They have ever conducted their several Governments with Wisdom, avoiding Wars and vain, expensive Projects, delighting only in their peaceable Occupations, which must, considering the Extent of their yet uncultivated Territory, find them Employment still for Ages. Whereas England, ever unquiet, ambitious, avaricious, imprudent, and quarrelsome, is half her Time engag'd in some War, or other, always at an expence infinitely greater than the advantages proposed if it could be obtained. . . . Indeed, there is scarce a Nation in Europe, against which she has not made War on some frivolous Pretext or other, and by this means has imprudently accumulated a Debt, that has brought her on the Verge of bankruptcy. But the most indiscrete of all her Wars is the present against America, with whom she might for ages have preserv'd her profitable connection by only a just and equitable Conduct. She is now acting like a mad Shop-keeper, who should attempt, by beating those that pass his Door, to make them come in and be his Customers. . . . America, on the other Hand, aims only at establishing her Liberty, and that Freedom of Commerce which will be advantageous to all Europe; while the Abolishing of the Monopoly which she has hitherto labour'd under, will be an Advantage sufficiently ample to repay the Debt, she may contract to accomplish it.

[*David Hartley, Franklin's close friend, was attached to Lord Rockingham, and both sympathized with the colonies. Thus he was later elected to act as British plenipotentiary in Paris, where he helped draw the peace treaty between America and England. —Ed.*]

From a letter to David Hartley

Passy, Oct. 14, 1777.

Happy should I have been, if the honest warnings I gave, of the fatal separation of interests, as well as of affections, that must attend the measures commenced while I was in England, had been attended to, and the horrid mischief of this abominable war been thereby prevented. I should still be happy in any successful endeavours for restoring peace, consistent with the liberties, the safety, and honour of America. As to our submitting to the government of Great Britain, it is vain to think of it. . . . It is now impossible to persuade our people, as I long endeavoured, that the war was merely ministerial, and that the nation bore still a good will to us. The infinite number of addresses printed in your gazettes, all approving this conduct of your government towards us, and encouraging our destruction by every possible means, the great majority in Parliament constantly manifesting the same sentiments, and the popular public rejoicings on occasion of any news of the slaughter of an innocent and virtuous people, fighting only in defence of their just rights; these, together with the recommendations of the same measures by even your celebrated moralists and divines, in their writings and sermons, that are cited approved and applauded in your great national assemblies; all join in convincing us, that you are no longer the magnan-

(continued on p. 118)

David Martin's "Thumb Portrait" of Franklin was painted in London in 1766. The portrait hung in the chamber of the Pennsylvania Executive Council, then later in Charles Willson Peale's Philadelphia Museum, and finally was given to the White House collection. *(The White House, gift of Mr. and Mrs. Walter H. Annenberg.)*

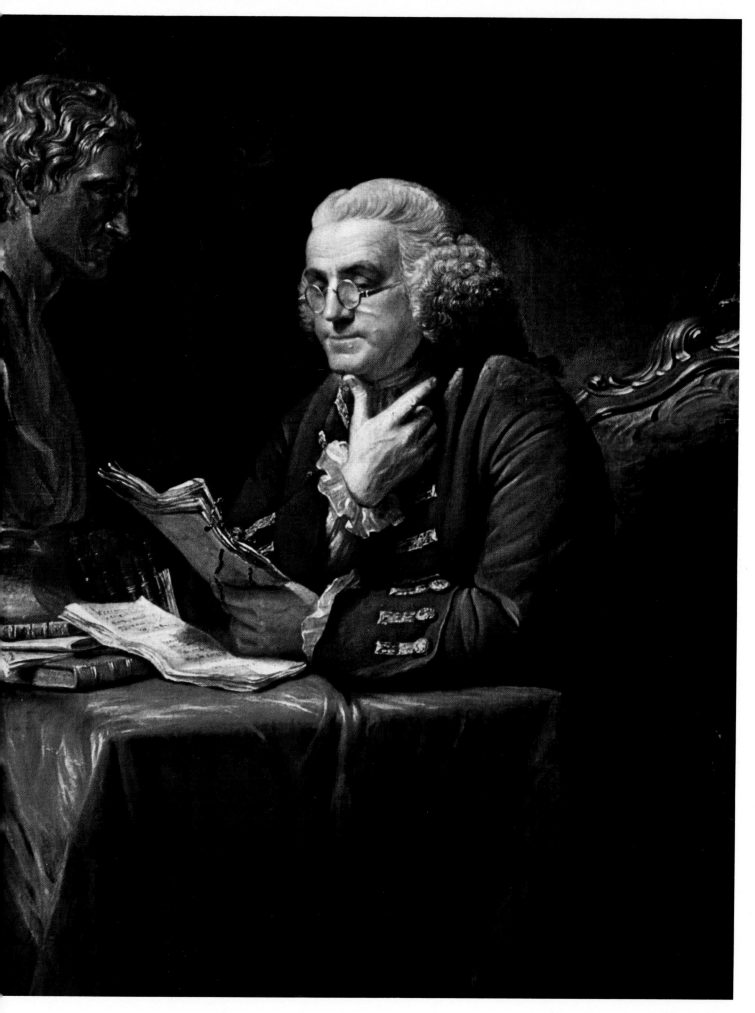

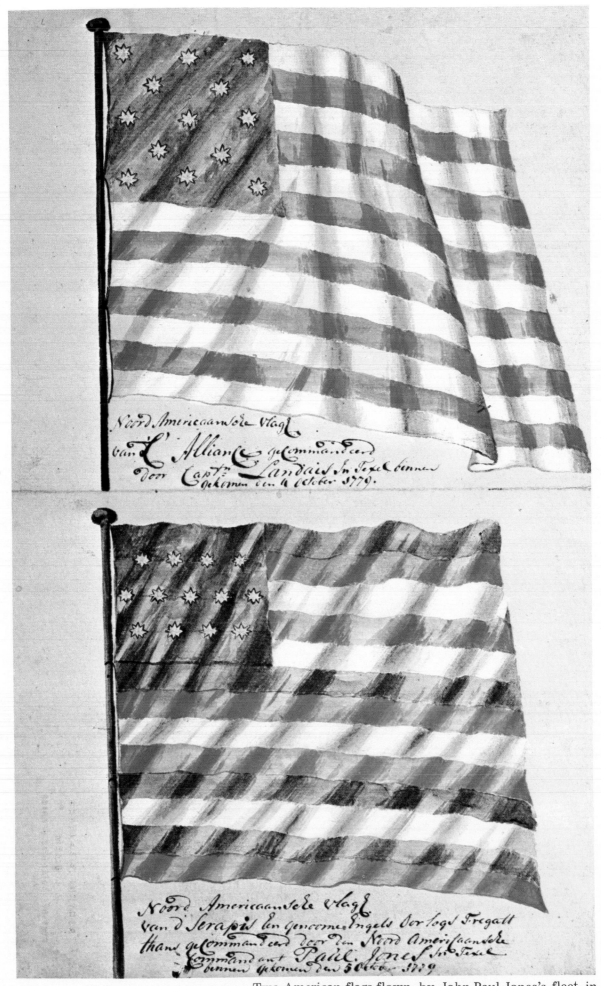

Two American flags flown by John Paul Jones's fleet in 1779 during his famous battle on the *Bonhomme Richard*. The Dutch made these watercolor sketches to refute the British claim that Jones was a pirate sailing under no recognized nation's flag. The top flag was the *Alliance's* and the lower was flown on the *Serapis* after Jones captured it. *(Courtesy, Chicago Historical Society.)*

114

There never was a good war nor a bad peace. — Letter to Josiah Quincy.

Above: *Moment in the afternoon, II August 1778*, a sea battle between British and French fleets. *(Library of Congress.)*

The famous sea battle between Commodore John Paul Jones's *Bonhomme Richard* and the English *Serapis* in 1779 was painted by Richard Elliot. In the fight, Jones lost his ship, although he defeated the *Serapis*, and a quarrel started between Jones and American Captain Peter Landais, commander of the accompanying ship *Alliance*, over conduct in the battle. Franklin was called on to try mediation and inquiry into the battle and he soon was expected to act as consul for many other naval affairs. *(U.S. Naval Academy Museum, Annapolis.)*

Prinz Carl Regiment.
Chef und Gen: Lieut Se: Hochfürstl: Durcht: Prinz Carl
Commandeur Gen: May: v. Borck.

Dritter Regiment

Above: The English hired mercenary soldiers from petty princes in Germany who were eager to have an income for themselves and their troops when they were unoccupied in continental quarrels. *(Anne S.K. Brown Military Collection, Providence, R.I.)*

The German soldier on the left, a grenadier in Landgraves's Third Guard Regiment, and the Hessians above in the Prinz Carl Regiment look like the pawns they came to be in the American Revolution. Franklin's 1777 satire, *The Sale of the Hessians*, spotlighted their condition. *(Anne S.K. Brown Military Collection, Providence, R.I.)*

L'AMÉRIQUE INDÉPENDANTE

Dédiée au Congrès des Etats unis de l'Amérique

Borel invenit et delineavit 1778.   *J.C. le Vaßeur Sculptor Regis et Majestm Imperm et Regm Sculp*

A Paris chez l'Auteur rue Boucherat au coin de la rue Xaintonge   *Par leur très humble et très obeissant Serviteur Borel.*

L'*Amerique Independante,* 1778, engraving by
J.C. Le Vasseur after Antoine Borel. A romanized
Franklin protects an Indian maiden, America, who
embraces the pedestal of a statue of Liberty. Minerva
guards from above with sword and shield; Prudence
stands at Franklin's shoulder and Courage threatens
both Britain and Neptune, who have fallen into the water.
Agriculture and Commerce, to the left, look on
with pleasure. *(The Philadelphia Museum of Art.)*

117

Silas Deane (1737-89) was Congress's first foreign agent. In France with Lee and Franklin, he obtained supplies for the American army, but also speculated privately in stocks. *(Emmet Collection, New York Public Library.)*

which your drafts on me here shall be punctually honour'd. You could then be able to speak with some certainty to the point in Parliament, and this might be attended with good effect.

To Mrs. Sarah Franklin Bache

Passy, June 3, 1779.

Dear Sally,

I have before me your letters of October 22d and January 17th. They are the only ones I received from you in the course of eighteen months. If you knew how happy your letters make me, and considered how many miscarry, I think you would write oftener. . . .

The clay medallion of me you say you gave to Mr. Hopkinson was the first of the kind made in France. A variety of others have been made since of different sizes; some to be set in the lids of snuffboxes, and some so small as to be worn in rings; and the numbers sold are incredible. These, with the pictures, busts, and prints, (of which copies upon copies are spread everywhere,) have made your father's face as well known as that of the moon, so that he durst not do any thing that would oblige him to run away, as his phiz would discover him wherever he should venture to show it. It is said by learned etymologists, that the name *doll*, for the images children play with, is derived from the word Idol. From the number of *dolls* now made of him, he may be truly said, *in that sense*, to be *i-doll-ized* in this country. . . .

I was charmed with the account you gave me of your industry, the tablecloths of your own spinning, &c.; but the latter part of the paragraph, that you had sent for linen

(continued from p.112)

imous and enlightened nation, we once esteemed you, and that you are unfit and unworthy to govern us, as not being able to govern your own passions.

But, as I have said, I should be nevertheless happy in seeing peace restored. For tho', if my friends and the friends of liberty and virtue, who still remain in England, could be drawn out of it, a continuance of this war to the ruin of the rest would give me less concern, I cannot, as that removal is impossible, but wish for peace for their sakes, as well as for the sake of humanity, and preventing further carnage.

This wish of mine, ineffective as it may be, induces me to mention to you, that, between nations long exasperated against each other in war, some act of generosity and kindness towards prisoners on one side has softened resentment, and abated animosity on the other, so as to bring on an accommodation. You in England, if you wish for peace, have at present the opportunity of trying this means, with regard to the prisoners now in your goals. They complain of very severe treatment. . . .

. . . Some considerable act of kindness towards our people would take off the reproach of inhumanity in that respect from the nation, and leave it where it ought with more certainty to lay, on the conductors of your war in America. This I hint to you, out of some remaining good will to a nation I once sincerely loved. . . .

If you could have leisure to visit the gaols in which they are confined, and should be desirous of knowing the truth relative to the treatment they receive, I wish you would take the trouble of distributing among the most necessitous according to their wants, two or three hundred pounds, for

Arthur Lee (1740-92), co-agent to France, assisted in negotiating a treaty with and aid from Louis XVI. Lee later served in the Continental Congress but opposed adoption of the Constitution. *(Emmet Collection, New York Public Library.)*

Sarah Franklin Bache (1758-1810),
Franklin's daughter, kept ties with both her
father and brother William, who remained
loyal to the English when his father supported revolution. *(The Metropolitan
Museum of Art, Wolfe Fund.)*

mend the holes, they will come in time to be lace; and
feathers, my dear girl, may be had in America from every
cock's tail. . . .

Present my affectionate regards to all friends that inquire after me . . . and write oftener, my dear child, to your
loving father,

B. Franklin.

William Franklin (1731?-1813), a son, was a
general, Governor of New Jersey and Loyal-
ist during the Revolution, to his father's
great despair. Portrait attributed to
Mather Brown. *(Frick Art Reference
Library, Mrs. J. M. Castle, Jr. Collection.)*

from France, because weaving and flax were grown dear,
alas, that dissolved the charm; and your sending for long
black pins, and lace, and feathers! disgusted me as much as
if you had put salt into my strawberries. The spinning, I
see, is laid aside, and you are to be dressed for the ball! You
seem not to know, my dear daughter, that, of all the dear
things in this world, idleness is the dearest, except mischief. . . .

When I began to read your account of the high prices of
goods, "a pair of gloves, $7; a yard of common gauze, $24,
and that it now required a fortune to maintain a family in a
very plain way, " I expected you would conclude with
telling me, that everybody as well as yourself was grown
frugal and industrious; and I could scarce believe my eyes in
reading forward, that "there never was so much pleasure
and dressing going on;" and that you yourself wanted black
pins and feathers from France to appear, I suppose, in the
mode! . . . The War indeed may in some degree raise the
prices of goods, and the high taxes which are necessary to
support the war may make our frugality necessary; and, as I
am always preaching that doctrine, I cannot in conscience
or in decency encourage the contrary, by my example, in
furnishing my children with foolish modes and luxuries. I
therefore send all the articles you desire, that are useful and
necessary, and omit the rest; for, as you say you should
"have great pride in wearing any thing I send, and showing
it as your father's taste," I must avoid giving you an opportunity of doing that with either lace or feathers. If you
wear your cambric ruffles as I do, and take care not to

William Temple Franklin (1756-1843),
a grandson, served as Franklin's secretary
in Paris and later started to collect his
voluminous writings. Painting by John
Trumbull. *(Yale University Art Gallery.)*

119

[Franklin wrote this in response to what is now the famous battle between John Paul Jones's Bonhomme Richard *and the English* Serapis *and* Countess of Scarborough, *in which the* Bonhomme Richard *was so badly battered that it sank after several days. —Ed.]*

From a letter to John Paul Jones

Passy, Oct. 15, 1779.

Dear Sir,

I received the Account of your Cruise and Engagement with the *Serapis*, which you did me the honour to send me from the Texel. I have since received your Favor of the 8th, from Amsterdam. For some Days after the Arrival of your Express, scarce any thing was talked of at Paris and Versailles, but your cool Conduct and persevering Bravery during that terrible Conflict. You may believe, that the Impression on my Mind was not less strong than on that of others; but I do not choose to say in a letter to yourself all I think on such an Occasion.

From a letter to the Commissioners of the Navy for the Eastern Department, Boston

Passy, October 17, 1779.

The Cruise of our little American Squadron, under Commodore Jones, intended partly to intercept the Baltic Trade, has had some Success, tho' not all that was hoped for. The Coasts of Britain and Ireland have been greatly alarmed, apprehending Descents, it being supposed that he had land forces with him. This has put the Enemy to much Expence in marching Troops from place to place. Several valuable Prizes have been made of Merchant-Ships. . . . These two are safely arrived at Bergen, in Norway; two smaller Prizes are arrived in France, and a Number of Colliers have been burnt or ransomed. The Baltic fleet was met with, and the two Men-of War who convoyed them, viz., the *Serapis*, a new ship of 44 Guns, and the *Countess of Scarborough*, of 20 Guns are taken after a long and bloody engagement, and are brought into the Texel. But the merchant-Ships escaped during the conflict, for which the *Alliance* and one of the other Ships are blamed, whether justly or not may be enquired into. Our Commodore's ship was so shatter'd that she could not be kept afloat, and the People being all taken out of her, she sank the Second Day after the Engagement. The rest of the Squadron are refitting in the Texel, from which neutral Place they will be obliged soon to depart with their prizes and Prisoners, near 400. I wish they may arrive safe in France, for I suppose thy English will endeavour to intercept them. Jones' Bravery and Conduct in the Action has gain'd him great honour.

From a letter to George Washington

Passy, March 5, 1780.

Should peace arrive after another Campaign or two, and afford us a little Leisure, I should be happy to see your Excellency in Europe, and to accompany you, if my Age and Strength would permit, in visiting some of its ancient and most famous Kingdoms. You would, on this side of the Sea, enjoy the great Reputation you have acquir'd, pure and free from those little Shades that the Jealousy and

Envy of a Man's Countrymen and Cotemporaries are ever endeavouring to cast over living Merit. Here you would know, and enjoy, what Posterity will say of Washington. For 1000 Leagues have nearly the same Effect with 1000 Years. The feeble Voice of those grovelling Passions cannot extend so far either in Time or Distance. At present I enjoy that Pleasure for you, as I frequently hear the old Generals of this martial Country, (who study the Maps of America, and mark upon them all your Operations,) speak with sincere Approbation and great Applause of your conduct; and join in giving you the Character of one of the greatest Captains of the Age.

I must soon quite the Scene, but you may live to see our Country flourish, as it will amazingly and rapidly after the War is over. Like a Field of young Indian Corn, which long Fair weather and Sunshine had enfeebled and discolored, and which in that weak State, by a Thunder Gust, of violent Wind, Hail, and Rain, seem'd to be threaten'd with absolute Destruction; yet the Storm being past, it recovers fresh Verdure, shoots up with double Vigour, and delights the Eye, not of its Owner only, but of every observing Traveller.

[Washington never took up Franklin's offer to visit Europe. —Ed.]

JOHN PAUL JONES.

Tels hommes rarement se peuvent presenter,
Et quand le ciel les donne, il faut en profiter.

A portrait of John Paul Jones (1747-92), by J. M. Moreau the Younger, was made soon after his brilliant naval victory against the English in 1779. Louis XVI made Jones a chevalier and sent a golden sword. *(Louisiana State Museum, New Orleans.)*

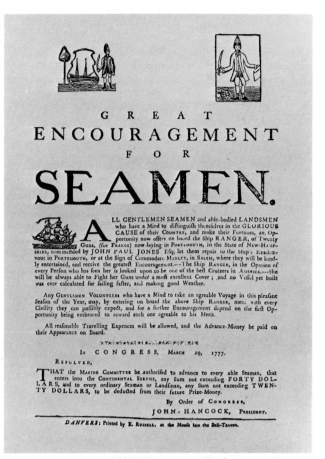

A 1777 poster calls for gentlemen volunteers to join John Paul Jones's *Ranger*. The greatest inducement was prize money from captured ships. *(Courtesy, Essex Institute, Salem, Massachusetts.)*

[Charles Gravier, Comte de Vergennes, was the French Minister of Foreign Affairs who sympathized with the policy of making grants to America. —Ed.]

To Comte de Vergennes

Passy, Sept. 20, 1780.

Sir,

Since I had the Honour of speaking to your Excellency on the Subject of a farther Loan of Money to the United States, our Banker Mr. Grand has given me a State of the Funds necessary to be provided, which I beg Leave to lay before you.

I have frequently written to Congress to draw no farther upon me, but to make me Remittances; for that the inevitable Expences of France in this War were immense; and that I could not presume to make repeated Applications for more Money with any Prospect of Success. Your Excellency will see this acknowledg'd in their late Letters to me; of which I inclose Copies; and that they would have avoided drawing on me any more, if the present Conjuncture in which they were oblig'd to make vast Preparations to act effectually with your Troops, had not laid them under the absolute Necessity.

The present State of their Currency rendering it insufficient for the Maintaining of their Troops, they provide for a great Part of the Expence by furnishing Provisions in kind; but some more hard Money than came in by Taxes, was wanted, and could only be obtain'd by these fresh Drafts.

From a letter to Samuel Huntington, President of Congress

Passy, May 31, 1780.

. . . The Congress have drawn on me very considerably . . . which has sometimes greatly embarrass'd me, but I have duly accepted and found means to pay their Drafts; so that their Credit in Europe has hitherto been well supported. But, if every Agent of Congress in different Parts of the World is permitted to run in Debt, and draw upon me at pleasure to support his Credit, under the Idea of its being necessary to do so for the Honour of Congress, the Difficulty upon me will be too great, and I may in fine be obliged to protest the Interest Bills. I therefore beg that a Stop may be put to such irregular Proceedings. . . .

. . . In the Newspapers that I send, the Congress will see authentic Pieces expressing the Sense of the European Powers on the Subject of Neutral Navigation. I hope to receive the Sense of Congress for my future Government, and for the Satisfaction of the Neutral Nations now entering into the Confederacy, which is considered here as a great Stroke against England.

In Truth, that Country appears to have no Friends on this Side the Water; no other Nation wishes it Success in its present War, but rather desires to see it effectually humbled; no one, not even their old Friends the Dutch, will afford them any assistance. Such is the mischievous Effect of Pride, Insolence, and Injustice on the Affairs of Nations, as well as on those of private Persons!

George Washington (1732-99), by Gilbert Stuart. Franklin compared Washington to Joshua of old, who commanded sun and moon to stand still, and they obeyed him. *(Courtesy, Museum of Fine Arts, Boston.)*

Their former unexpected Drafts had already absorb'd much of the Money put into my hands, and I am now put into a Situation that distresses me exceedingly. I dread the Consequences of protesting their Bills. The Credit of the Congress being thereby destroy'd at home, the People will be unable to act or exert their Force. The Enemy will find them in a State similar to that of being bound hand and foot.

We have had Hopes of some Aid from Spain; but they are vanished.

The Expectation of a Loan in Holland, has also failed.

I submit these important Circumstances to your Excellency's wise Consideration. The States will be well able in a few Years of Peace, to repay all that shall be advanc'd to them in this time of Difficulty: and they will repay it with Gratitude. The Good Work of establishing a free Government *for them*, and a free Commerce with them *for France*, is nearly compleated. It is pity it should now miscarry for want of 4 or 5 millions of Livres, to be furnished, not immediately but in the Course of the ensuing Year.

With the greatest & most sincere Respect, I have the honour to be,

[B. Franklin]

To John Adams

Passy, Oct. 2, 1780.

Sir,

By all our late Advices from America, the Hopes you express that our Countrymen, instead of amusing themselves any longer with delusive Dreams of Peace, would bend the whole Force of their Minds to find out their own Strength and Resources, and to depend upon themselves, are actually accomplished. All the Accounts I have seen agree that the Spirit of our People was never higher than at present, nor their Exertions more vigorous.

. . . Our Credit and Weight in Europe depend more on what we do than on what we say; And I have long been humiliated with the Idea of our running about from Court to Court begging for Money and Friendship, which are the more withheld, the more eagerly they are solicited, and would perhaps have been offer'd if they had not been ask'd. The suppos'd Necessity is our only Excuse. The Proverb says, *God helps them that help themselves*. And the World too in this Sense is very godly.

From a letter to Joseph Priestley

Passy near Paris, June 7, 1782.

I should rejoice much, if I could once more recover the Leisure to search with you into the Works of Nature; I mean the *inanimate*, not the *animate* or moral part of them, the more I discover'd of the former, the more I admir'd them; the more I know of the latter, the more I am disgusted with them. Men I find to be a Sort of Beings very badly constructed, as they are generally more easily provok'd than reconcil'd, more disposed to do Mischief to each other than to make Reparation, much more easily deceiv'd than undeceiv'd, and having more Pride and even Pleasure in killing than in begetting one another. . . .

. . . In what Light we are viewed by superior Beings, may be gathered from a Piece of late West India News, which

Charles Gravier, Count de Vergennes (1717-87), French Foreign Minister, supported Franklin's request for aid to Americans principally out of dislike for the English. *(Emmet Collection, New York Public Library.)*

possibly has not yet reached you. A young Angel of Distinction being sent down to this world on some Business, for the first time, had an old courier-spirit assigned him as a Guide. They arriv'd over the Seas of Martinico, in the middle of the long Day of obstinate Fight between the Fleets of Rodney and De Grasse. When, thro' the Clouds of smoke, he saw the Fire of the Guns, the Decks covered with mangled Limbs, and Bodies dead or dying; the ships sinking, burning, or blown into the Air; and the Quantity of Pain, Misery, and Destruction, the Crews yet alive were thus with so much Eagerness dealing round to one another; he turn'd angrily to his Guide, and said, "You blundering Blockhead, you are ignorant of your Business; you undertook to conduct me to the Earth, and you have brought me into Hell!" "No, sir," says the Guide, "I have made no mistake; this is really the Earth, and these are men. Devils never treat one another in this cruel manner; they have more Sense, and more of what Men (vainly) call *Humanity*."

But to be serious, my dear old Friend, I love you as much as ever, and I love all the honest Souls that meet at the London Coffee-House. I only wonder how it happen'd, that they and my other Friends in England came to be such good Creatures in the midst of so perverse a Generation. I long to see them and you once more, and I labour for Peace with more Earnestness, that I may again be happy in your sweet society.

To Samuel Cooper

Passy, Dec. 26, 1782.

Dear Sir,

We have taken some good steps here towards a peace. Our independence is acknowledged; our boundaries as good and extensive as we demanded; and our fishery more so than the Congress expected. I hope the whole preliminaries will be approved, and with the definitive treaty, when made, give entire satisfaction to our country. But there are so many interests to be considered between five nations, and so many claims to adjust, that I can hardly flatter myself to see the peace soon concluded, though I wish and pray for it, and use my best endeavours to promote it.

I am extremely sorry to hear language from Americans on this side the water, and to hear of such language from your side, as tends to hurt the good understanding that has hitherto so happily subsisted between this court and ours. There seems to be a party with you that wish to destroy it. If they could succeed, they would do us irreparable injury. It is our firm connection with France, that gives us weight with England, and respect throughout Europe. If we were to break our faith with this nation, *on whatever pretence*, England would again trample on us, and every other nation despise us. We cannot, therefore, be too much on our guard, how we permit the *private resentments* of particular persons to enter into our public counsels. . . . .

In my opinion, the true political interest of America consists in observing and fulfilling, with the greatest exactitude, the engagements of our alliance with France, and behaving at the same time towards England, so as not entirely to extinguish her hopes of a reconciliation.

[*Jonathan Shipley, Bishop of Asaph, was an old friend of Franklin and it was at Shipley's country estate that Franklin had spent some of his happiest times in England and where he wrote part of his* Autobiography. –Ed.]

From a letter to Jonathan Shipley

Passy, March 17, 1783.

Let us now forgive and forget. Let each Country seek its Advancement in its own internal Advantages of Arts and Agriculture, not in retarding or preventing the Prosperity of the other. America will, with God's blessing, become a great and happy Country; and England, if she has at length gained Wisdom, will have gained something more valuable, and more essential to her Prosperity, than all she has lost; and will still be a great and respectable Nation.

[*Robert R. Livingston was a delegate to the Continental Congress, one of the Committee of five to draft the Declaration of Independence, first Chancellor of New York and administered the oath of office to George Washington at his inauguration as President of the United States. –Ed.*]

From a letter to Robert R. Livingston

Passy, July 22, 1783.

I ought not, however, to conceal from you, that one of my Colleagues [John Adams] is of a very different Opinion from me in these Matters. He thinks the French Minister one of the greatest Enemies of our Country, that he would have straightened our Boundaries, to prevent the Growth of

LOUIS SEIZE,
Roi de France et de Navarre;

Né à Versailles le 25 Août 1754, et mort à Paris le 21 Janvier 1793.

Louis XVI (1754-93), was France's absolute monarch who supported the American Revolution. *(Emmet Collection, New York Public Library.)*

our People; contracted our Fishery, to obstruct the Increase of our Seamen; and retained the Royalists among us, to keep us divided; that he privately opposes all our negociations with foreign Courts, and afforded us, during the War, the Assistance we receiv'd, only to keep it alive, that we might be so much the more weaken'd by it; that to think of Gratitude to France is the greatest of Follies, and that to be influenc'd by it would ruin us. . . .

If I were not convinc'd of the real Inability of this Court to furnish the further Supplys we ask'd, I should suspect these Discourses of a Person in his Station might have influenced the Refusal; but I think they have gone no farther than to occasion a Suspicion, that we have a considerable Party of Antigallicans in America, who are not Tories, and consequently to produce some doubts of the Continuance of our Friendship. As such Doubts may herafter have a bad Effect, I think we cannot take too much care to remove them; and it is, therefore, I write this, to put you on your guard, (believing it my duty, tho' I know that I hazard by it a mortal Enmity), and to caution you respecting the Insinuations of this Gentleman against this Court, and the Instances he supposes of their ill will to us, which I take to be as imaginary as I know his Fancies to be, that Count de V. and myself are continually plotting against him, and employing the News-Writers of Europe to depreciate his Character, &c. But as Shakespeare says, "Trifles light as Air," &c. I am persuaded, however, that he means well for his Country, is always an honest Man, often a wise one, but sometimes, and in some things, absolutely out of his senses.

From a letter to Elias Boudinot, President of Congress
Passy, September 10, 1783.

Sir:--

On the 3d instant [September 3] definitive treaties of peace were concluded between all the late belligerent powers, except the Dutch, who, the day before, settled and signed preliminary articles of peace with Britain.

We most sincerely and cordially congratulate Congress and our country in general on this happy event, and we hope that the same kind Providence which has led us through a rigorous war to an honourable peace will enable us to make a wise and moderate use of that inestimable blessing. . . .

. . . Much, we think, will depend on the success of our negotiations with England. If she could be prevailed upon to agree to a liberal system of commerce, France, and perhaps some other nations, will follow her example; but if she should prefer an extensive monopolizing plan, it is probable that her neighbours will continue to adhere to their favourite restrictions.

Were it certain that the United States could be brought to act as a nation, and would jointly and fairly conduct their commerce on principles of exact reciprocity with all nations, we think it probable that Britain would make extensive concessions. But, on the contrary, while the prospect of disunion in our council, or want of power and energy in our executive department exists, they will not be apprehensive of retaliation, and consequently lose their principal motive to liberality. Unless, with respect to all foreign nations and transactions, we uniformly act as an entire united nation, faithfully executing and obeying the constitutional acts of Congress on those subjects, we shall soon find ourselves in the situation in which all Europe wishes to see us, viz., as unimportant consumers of her manufactures and productions, and as useful labourers to furnish her with raw materials.

(continued on p. 129)

"The Reconciliation between Britania [sic] and her Daughter America," published 1782. *(The Metropolitan Museum of Art, gift of William D. Huntington.)*

FRANKLIN'S RECEPTION AT THE COURT OF FRANCE, 1778.

RESPECTFULLY DEDICATED TO THE PEOPLE OF THE UNITED STATES

Franklin's Reception in the Court of France, 1778, by J. Smith. Louis XVI and Marie Antoinette are the seated figures. *(Library of Congress.)*

Left: A Limoge china tea set given to Franklin in France and used by him in Philadelphia. *(Franklin Institute, Philadelphia.)*

125

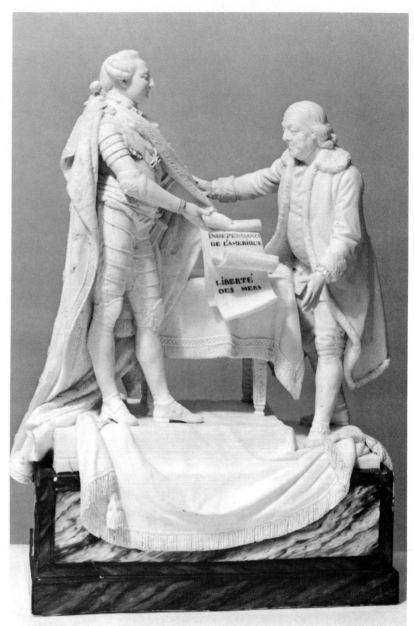

Porcelain statuette of Louis XVI and Franklin,
ca. 1785, by Lemire (Charles Sauvage). The
French king extends a document inscribed
"American independence" and "freedom of
the seas," the two points essential in the
French-American alliance of 1778. *(Courtesy,
Henry Francis du Pont Winterthur Museum.)*

The American peace commissioners at the preliminary
negotiations and final Treaty of Paris were (l. to r.):
John Jay, John Adams, Franklin, Henry Laurens, and
Franklin's grandson and secretary, William Temple
Franklin. Unfinished painting by Benjamin West.
(Courtesy, Henry Francis du Pont Winterthur Museum.)

Ben Franklin's Belles, by Norman Rockwell.
Among the talented women of France who became
Franklin's social companions were duchesses, countesses
and ladies whose fame rested in ability as writers, wits,
mistresses and musicians and in what the French call the
joi de vivre, "joy of living." *(Collection of Mr. Joseph Hennage.)*

We beg leave to assure Congress that we shall apply our best endeavours to execute the new commission to their satisfaction, and punctually obey such instructions as they may be pleased to give us relative to it. . . .

. . . With great respect we have the honour to be, sir, your Excellency's most obedient and most humble servants,

John Adams
[Signed]   B. Franklin
John Jay

From a letter to William Franklin

Passy, Aug. 16, 1784.

Dear Son,

I received your Letter of the 22d past, and am glad to find that you desire to revive the affectionate Intercourse, that formerly existed between us. It will be very agreable to me; indeed nothing has ever hurt me so much and affected me with such keen Sensations, as to find myself deserted in my old Age by my only Son; and not only deserted, but to find him taking up Arms against me, in a Cause, wherein my good Fame, Fortune and Life were all at Stake. You conceived, you say, that your Duty to your King and Regard for your Country requir'd this. I ought not to blame you for differing in Sentiment with me in Public Affairs. We are Men, all subject to Errors. Our Opinions are not in our own Power; they are form'd and govern'd much by Circumstances, that are often as inexplicable as they are irresistible. Your Situation was such that few would have censured your remaining Neuter, *tho' there are Natural Duties which precede poltical ones, and cannot be extinguish'd by them.*

John Adams (1735-1826), by C. W. Peale. Adams served with Franklin as commissioner to France, as peace negotiator and later became second U. S. President. *(Independence National Historical Park.)*

John Jay (1745-1829), like Adams, was anti-French, but served in Paris during peace negotiations with England. Later he became first U. S. Chief Justice. *(Culver Pictures.)*

Speech in the Constitutional Convention; on the Subject of Salaries

[June 2, 1787]

Sir, there are two Passions which have a powerful Influence in the Affairs of Men. These are *Ambition* and *Avarice*; the Love of Power and the Love of Money. Separately, each of these has great Force in prompting Men to Action; but when united in View of the same Object, they have in many Minds the most violent Effects. Place before the Eyes of such Men a Post of *Honour*, that shall at the same time be a Place of *Profit*, and they will move Heaven and Earth to obtain it. . . .

Besides these Evils, Sir, tho' we may set out in the Beginning with moderate Salaries, we shall find, that such will not be of long Continuance. Reasons will never be wanting for propos'd Augmentations; and there will always be a Party for giving more to the Rulers, that the Rulers may be able in Return to give more to them. Hence, as all History informs us, there has been in every State and Kingdom a constant kind of Warfare between the Governing and the Governed; the one striving to obtain more for its Support, and the other to pay less. . . . The more the People are discontented with the Oppression of Taxes, the greater Need the Prince has of Money to distribute among his Partisans, and pay the Troops that are to suppress all Resistance, and enable him to plunder at Pleasure. . . . It will be said, that we do not propose to establish Kings. I know it. But there is a natural Inclination in Mankind to kingly Government. It sometimes relieves them from Aristocratic Domination. They had rather have one Tyrant than 500. It gives more of the Appearance of Equality among Citizens; and that they like. I am apprehensive, therefore, – perhaps too apprehensive, – that the Government of these States may

Franklin returned from Europe in 1785, two years after the peace treaty, during which time he worked on commercial agreements. *(Bettmann Archives.)*

in future times end in a Monarchy. But this Catastrophe, I think, may be long delay'd, if in our propos'd System we do not sow the Seeds of Contention, Faction, and Tumult, by making our Posts of Honour Places of Profit. . . .

Motion for Prayers in the Constitutional Convention
Mr. President,

The small Progress we have made, after 4 or 5 Weeks' close Attendance and continual Reasonings with each other, our different Sentiments on almost every Question, several of the last producing as many *Noes* as *Ayes*, is, methinks, a melancholy Proof of the Imperfection of the Human Understanding. We indeed seem to feel our own want of political Wisdom, since we have been running all about in Search of it. We have gone back to ancient History for Models of Government . . . and we have view'd modern States all round Europe, but find none of their Constitutions suitable to our Circumstances.

In this Situation of this Assembly, groping, as it were, in the dark to find Political Truth, and scarce able to distinguish it when presented to us, how has it happened, Sir, that we have not hitherto once thought of humbly applying to the Father of Lights to illuminate our Understandings? . . . I have lived, Sir, a long time; and the longer I live, the more convincing proofs I see of this Truth, *that* God *governs in the Affairs of Men.* And if a Sparrow cannot fall to the Ground without his Notice, is it probable that an Empire can rise without his Aid? We have been assured, Sir, in the Sacred Writing, that "except the Lord build the House, they labour in vain that build it." I firmly believe this; and I also believe, that, without his concurring Aid, we shall succeed in this political Building no better than the Builders of Babel. . . .

I therefore beg leave to move,

That henceforth Prayers, imploring the Assistance of Heaven and its Blessing on our Deliberation, be held in this Assembly every morning before we proceed to Business;

and that one or more of the Clergy of this city be requested to officiate in that Service.

Speech in the Convention
at the Conclusion of its Deliberations
Mr. President,

I confess, that I do not entirely approve of this Constitution at present; but, Sir, I am not sure I shall never approve it; for, having lived long, I have experienced many instances of being obliged, by better information or fuller consideration, to change my opinions even on important subjects, which I once thought right, but found to be otherwise. It is therefore that, the older I grow, the more apt I am to doubt my own judgment of others. Most men, indeed, as well as most sects in religion, think themselves in possession of all truth, and that wherever others differ from them, it is so far error. . . . But, though, many private Persons think almost as highly of their own infallibility as of that of their Sect, few express it so naturally as a certain French Lady, who, in a little dispute with her sister, said, "But I meet with nobody but myself that is *always* in the right . . . ."

In these sentiments, Sir, I agree to this Constitution, with all its faults, – if they are such; because I think a general Government necessary for us, and there is no *form* of government but what may be a blessing to the people, if well administered; and I believe, farther, that this is likely to be well administered for a course of years, and can only end in despotism, as other forms have done before it, when the people shall become so corrupted as to need despotic government, being incapable of any other. I doubt, too, whether any other Convention we can obtain, may be able to make a better constitution; for, when you assemble a number of men, to have the advantage of their joint wisdom, you inevitably assemble with those men all their prejudices, their passions, their errors of opinion, their local interests, and their selfish views. From such an assembly can a *perfect* production be expected? It therefore astonishes me, Sir, to find this system approaching so near to perfection as it does; and I think it will astonish our enemies, who are waiting with confidence to hear, that our councils are confounded like those of the builders of Babel, and that our States are on the point of separation, only to meet hereafter for the purpose of cutting one another's throats. Thus I consent, Sir, to this Constitution, because I expect no better, and because I am not sure that it is not the best. . . .

From a letter to David Hartley
Philadelphia, Dec. 4, 1789.

The Convulsions in France are attended with some disagreeable Circumstances; but if by the Struggle she obtains and secures for the Nation its future Liberty, and a good Constitution, a few Years' Enjoyment of those Blessings will amply repair all the Damages their Acquisition may have occasioned. God grant, that not only the Love of Liberty, but a thorough Knowledge of the Rights of Man, may pervade all the Nations of the Earth, so that a Philosopher may set his Foot anywhere on its Surface, and say, "This is my Country."

Our Constitution is in actual operation; everything appears to promise that it will last; but in this world nothing is certain but death and taxes.
— Letter to Jean Baptiste Le Roy.

The first map of the United States, 1783, engraved by Abel Buel. *(I. N. Phelps Stokes Collection, Prints Division, New York Public Library, Astor, Lenox and Tilden Foundations.)*

To the editor of the *Federal Gazette*

March 23d, 1790.

Sir,

Reading last night in your excellent Paper the speech of Mr. Jackson in Congress against their meddling with the Affair of Slavery, or attempting to mend the Condition of the Slaves, it put me in mind of a similar One made about 100 Years since by Sidi Mehemet Ibrahim, a member of the Divan of Algiers, which may be seen in Martin's Account of his Consulship, anno 1687. It was against granting the Petition of the Sect called *Erika,* or Purists, who pray'd for the Abolition of Piracy and Slavery as being unjust. Mr. Jackson does not quote it; perhaps he has not seen it. If, therefore, some of its Reasonings are to be found in his eloquent Speech, it may only show that men's Interests and Intellects operate and are operated on with surprising similarity in all Countries and Climates, when under similar Circumstances. The African's Speech, as translated, is as follows.

"Allah Bismillah, &c. God is great, and Mahomet is his Prophet.

"Have these *Erika* considered the Consequences of granting their Petition? If we cease our Cruises against the Christians, how shall we be furnished with the Commodities their Countries produce, and which are so necessary for us? If we forbear to make Slaves of their People, who in this hot Climate are to cultivate our Lands? Who are to perform the common Labours of our City, and in our Families? Must we not then be our own Slaves? . . . If we then cease taking and plundering the Infidel Ships, and making Slaves of the Seamen and Passengers, our Lands will become of no Value for want of Cultivation; the Rents of Houses in the City will sink one half; and the Revenues of Government arising from its Share of Prizes be totally destroy'd! And for what? To gratify the whims of a whimsical Sect, who would have us, not only forbear making more Slaves, but even to manumit those we have.

"But who is to indemnify their Masters for the Loss? Will the State do it? Is our Treasury sufficient? Will the *Erika* do it? Can they do it? Or would they, to do what they think Justice to the Slaves, do a greater Injustice to the Owners? And if we set our Slaves free, what is to be done with them? Few of them will return to their Countries; they know too well the greater Hardships they must there be subject to; they will not embrace our holy Religion; they will not adopt our Manners; our People will not pollute themselves by intermarrying with them. Must we maintain them as Beggars in our Streets, or suffer our Properties to be the Prey of their Pillage? For Men long accustom'd to Slavery will not work for a Livelihood when not compell'd. And what is there so pitiable in their present Condition? Were they not Slaves in their own Countries?

"Are not Spain, Portugal, France, and the Italian states govern'd by Despots, who hold all their Subjects in Slavery, without Exception? Even England treats its Sailors as Slaves. . . . Is their Condition then made worse by their falling into our Hands? No; they have only exchanged one Slavery for another, and I may say a better; for here they are brought into a Land where the Sun of Islamism gives forth its Light, and shines in full Splendor, and they have an Opportunity of making themselves acquainted with the true Doctrine, and thereby saving their immortal Souls. . . .

. . . Here their Lives are in Safety. They are not liable to be impress'd for Soldiers, and forc'd to cut one another's Christian Throats, as in the Wars of their own Countries.

"How grossly are they mistaken in imagining Slavery to be disallow'd by the Alcoran [Koran]! Are not the two Precepts, to quote no more, *'Masters, treat your Slaves with kindness; Slaves, serve your Masters with Cheerfulness and Fidelity,'* clear proofs to the contrary? Nor can the Plundering of Infidels be in that sacred Book forbidden, since it is well known from it, that God has given the World, and all that it contains, to his faithful Mussulmen, who are to enjoy it of Right as fast as they conquer it. Let us then hear no more of this detestable Proposition, the Manumission of Christian Slaves. . . . I have therefore no doubt, but this wise Council will prefer the Comfort and Happiness of a whole Nation of true Believers to the Whim of a few *Erika,* and dismiss their Petition."

The result was, as Martin tells us, that the Divan came to this Resolution; "The Doctrine, that Plundering and Enslaving the Christians is unjust, is at best problematical; but that it is the Interest of this State to continue the Practice, is clear, therefore let the Petition be rejected."

And it was rejected accordingly.

And since like Motives are apt to produce in the Minds of Men like Opinions and Resolutions, may we not, Mr. Brown, venture to predict, from this Account, that the Petitions to the Parliament of England for abolishing the Slave-Trade, to say nothing of other Legislatures, and the Debates upon them, will have a similar Conclusion? I am, Sir, your constant Reader and humble servant,

Historicus.

Unfailing wit was part of Franklin's success as a writer. His *Gazette* and *Poor Richard's Almanack* were filled with facetious predictions, tales and editorial comments that gained him immediate popularity. This chapter includes samples of his droll humor: a few lines from "Alice Addertongue," one of Franklin's pen names in the *Gazette*; the *Speech of Polly Baker*; his hoax, "A Parable Against Persecution, Genesis LI;" the bagatelles, or humorous allegories, "The Whistle," "The Ephemera" and "Dialogue Between Franklin and the Gout;" and his "Morals of Chess." Other political satires have been placed earlier in this book with the events of their time.

Franklin's spontaneous humor and the joys he found in friends and family and his playful intrigues with women deserve special attention. There has been much speculation about Franklin's feelings towards his wife, Deborah. Franklin's marriage, though it lacks all the romance that makes good stories, was a long and contented one, as he describes in his letters to Catherine Ray in this chapter. Excluding the year preceding Deborah's death (she was ill and lonely while Franklin negotiated in London), their affection never failed.

VI PHILOSOPHER, FRIEND AND HUMORIST

Much more has been made of Franklin's relationships with other women: the early intrigues he so regretted; his feelings for Catherine Ray, a coy, young relation; his affection for Polly Stevenson, the daughter of his English landlady, and her girlfriends; for the daughters of his friends, such as Georgina Shipley; and of course, to his fondness for many women friends in France, especially Mesdames Brillon and Helvétius. Warmth and intimacy are the tone of all Franklin's private letters, to men or women, boys or girls; his paternalistic style has been amusingly interpreted at times, and literal-minded biographers have counted some of his young friends, whom he would call "my daughter," as his offspring. This is not to deny his early affairs (mentioned in the *Autobiography*), his delight in women's company, or relish for playing the witty love games of words and suggestions so enjoyed in cultured eighteenth-century France and England. Yet Franklin, by the time he was twenty-four, had come to respect marriage as the happiest state because it was the healthiest. He encouraged his young friends, such as Polly Stevenson and Catherine Ray, to find good mates for themselves, though he teased Catherine and cheerfully pleaded that she unfairly refused his offer to teach her "multiplication and addition," according to the rules of their word game.

In France, his two most intimate friends were Anne-Louise Brillon and Anne-Catherine Helvétius. Franklin was a widower whose family lived across an ocean. Madame Helvétius was widowed, thirteen years younger than Franklin, independent and bohemian. Madame Brillon was a recognized musician, an intellect and many years younger than her prosaic, philandering husband. The comforts of Madame Brillon's home — young children to remind him of his own grandchildren, good music, dinners, chess and agreeable conversation — were a restorative to Franklin. She revered and loved him as she had her late father, and he was elated to have a "daughter" so accomplished. Yet, in their letters and in his bagatelle, "The Ephemera," included in this chapter, it appears that Franklin's gallantry had a serious import, though Madame Brillon insisted that their pleasures together would have to be reserved for paradise. He implored Christian charity, and she referred him to philosophy: ". . . the gentleman, great philosopher that he is, goes by the doctrines of Anacreon (writer of love poems) and Epicure (devotee of sensual pleasure), but the lady is a Platonist."

At Madame Helvétius' country estate, he found a more madcap existence, stimulating and intellectual, though Madame was more an exuberant individualist than an intellect. Abigail Adams was not so favorably impressed with Madame Helvétius when they met, but her description of the French lady is amusing:

She entered the room with a careless, jaunty air; upon seeing the ladies who were strangers to her, she bawled out, "Ah! mon Dieu,

A whimsical-looking Franklin is
preserved in the 1790 aquatint by Pierre
Michel Alix after a painting by L. M. Vanloo.
(The Philadelphia Museum of Art.)

where is Franklin? Why did you not tell me
there were ladies here? . . . How I look!''

. . . Her hair was frizzled; over it she
had a small straw hat, with a dirty gauze
half-handkerchief behind. She had a black
gauze scarf thrown over her shoulders.

. . . When we went into the room to
dine, she was placed between the Doctor
and Mr. Adams. She carried on the chief
of the conversation at dinner, frequently
locking her hand into the Doctor's, and
sometimes spreading her arms upon the
backs of both the gentlemen's chairs, then
throwing her arm carelessly upon the
Doctor's neck.

I should have been greatly astonished at
this conduct, if the good Doctor had told
me that in this lady I should see a genuine
Frenchwoman . . . one of the best women
in the world . . . .

Around her disordered home at Auteuil, Madame
Helvétius drew the philosophers, scientists, poets,
theologians and historians of the age "as straws
about a fine piece of amber," according to
Franklin. The "Academie d'Auteuil," as it was
facetiously called, included, besides Franklin, the
learned Abbés de la Roche and Morellet and the
brilliant young medical theorist P.G. Cabanis, three
who lived on Madame's estate (an arrangement

which met the disapproval of John and Abigail
Adams), and Baron Turgot and Denis Diderot, the
encyclopedist, and others. Madame Helvétius —
"Notre Dame d'Auteuil," Franklin named her —
was once beautiful and still retained regal bearing
when Franklin met her. He was openly devoted to
her and proposed marriage. She refused, in defer-
ence to the memory of her late husband, she said.

Franklin never got the marriage he hoped for,
though he continued to write her even after he left
France. His last letter to Madame Helvétius from
Philadelphia in 1788 reads (translation):

I cannot let this chance go by, my dear
friend, without telling you that I love you
always, and that I am feeling well. I think
endlessly of the pleasures I enjoyed in the
sweet society of Auteuil. And often, in my
dreams, I dine with you, I sit beside you on
one of your thousand sofas, or I walk with
you in your beautiful garden.

A final and significant aspect of Franklin's private life is his feeling and writing on religion. This
chapter includes a section from *Articles of Belief
and Acts of Religion* and his version of *The Lord's
Prayer*. These speak for what he valued most in
the conduct of life. A letter to a Philadelphia
friend restates his constant belief: "If men rest in
Hearing and Praying, as all too many do, it is as
if a Tree should Value itself on being watered and
putting forth Leaves, tho' it never produced any
Fruit."

133

> *It seems . . . that happiness in this life rather depends on internals than externals; and that, besides the natural effects of wisdom and virtue, vice and folly, there is such a thing as a happy or an unhappy constitution.*
> — Letter to Hugh Roberts.

Franklin was 72 when his portrait by J. F. de L'Hospital was made of him in France at the beginning of his years as ambassador and revolutionary idol. He radiates the same good humor that earned him an early reputation in America for his writing. *(University of Pennsylvania Collection.)*

[*Franklin composed many facetious letters from "readers" like Alice Addertongue, Celia Single and Anthony Afterwit to entertain and gain subscribers to his* Gazette. *Addertongue made a strong defense of scandal as* censure *done for the good of her country-folk. —Ed.*]

From a letter from Alice Addertongue

Printed in *The Pennsylvania Gazette*, September 12, 1732

. . . 'Tis a Principle with me, that none ought to have a greater Share of Reputation, than they really deserve; if they have, 'tis an Imposition upon the Publick. I know it is every one's Interest, and therefore believe they endeavour to conceal all their Vices and Follies; and I hold that those People are *extraordinary* foolish or careless, who suffer a Fourth of their Failings to come to publick Knowledge. Taking then the common Prudence and Imprudence of Mankind in a Lump, I suppose none suffer above *one Fifth* to be discovered: Therefore, when I hear of any person's Misdoing, I think I keep within Bounds if in relating it I only make it *three times* worse than it is; and I reserve to myself the Privilege of charging them with one Fault in four, which for aught I know, they may be entirely innocent of. You see there are but few so careful of doing Justice as myself. What Reason then have Mankind to complain of *Scandal*? In a general way the worst that is said of us is only half what *might* be said, if all our Faults were seen.

THE SPEECH OF POLLY BAKER, attributed to Franklin.
[Before 1747]

Thomas Jefferson tells an interesting story concerning it: "The Doctor and Silas Deane were in conversation one day at Passy on the numerous errors in the Abbé's [Raynal] *Histoire des deux Indes* when he happened to step in. After the usual salutations, Silas Deane said to him 'the Doctor and myself, Abbé, were just speaking of the errors of fact into which you have been led in your history.' 'Oh no, Sir,' said the Abbé, 'that is impossible. I took the greatest care not to insert a single fact for which I had not the most unquestionable authority.' 'Why,' says Deane, 'there is the story of Polly Baker, and the eloquent apology you have put into her mouth when brought before a court of Massachusetts to suffer punishment under a law, which you cite, for having had a bastard. I know there never was such a law in Massachusetts.' 'Be assured,' said the Abbé, 'you are mistaken, and that that is a true story. I do not immediately recollect indeed the particular information on which I quote it, but I am certain that I had for it unquestionable authority.' Doctor Franklin who had been for some time shaking with restrained laughter at the Abbé's confidence in his authority for the tale, said, 'I will tell you, Abbé, the origin of that story. When I was a printer and editor of a newspaper, we were sometimes slack of news and to amuse our customers, I used to fill up our vacant columns with anecdotes, and fables, and fancies of my own, and this of Polly Baker is a story of my own making, on one of those occasions.' The Abbé without the least disconcert, exclaimed with a laugh, 'Oh, very well, Doctor, I had rather relate your stories than other men's truths.' " (*The Writings of Thomas Jefferson*, Vol X.)

The Speech of Miss Polly Baker before a Court of Judicature, at Connecticut near Boston in New England; where she was prosecuted the fifth time, for having a Bastard Child: Which influenced the Court to dispense with her Punishment, and which induced one of her Judges to marry her the next Day — by whom she had fifteen Children.

"May it please the honourable bench to indulge me in a few words: I am a poor, unhappy woman, who have no money to fee lawyers to plead for me, being hard put to it to get a living. . . . This is the fifth time, gentlemen, that I have been dragg'd before your court on the same account; twice I have paid heavy fines, and twice have been brought to publick punishment, for want of money to pay those fines. This may have been agreeable to the laws, and I don't dispute it; but since laws are sometimes unreasonable in themselves, and therefore repealed; and others bear too hard on the subject in particular circumstances, and therefore there is left a power somewhere to dispense with the execution of them; I take the Liberty to say, that I think this law, by which I am punished, both unreasonable in itself, and particularly severe with regard to me, who have always lived an inoffensive life in the neighbourhood where I was born, and defy my enemies (if I have any) to say I ever wrong'd any man, woman, or child. Abstracted from the law, I cannot conceive (may it please your honours) what the nature of my offense is. I have brought five fine children into the world, at the risque of my life; I have maintain'd them well by my own industry, without burdening the township, and would have done it better, if it had not been for the heavy charges and fines I have paid. Can it be a crime (in the nature of things, I mean) to add to the king's subjects, in a new country, that really wants people? I own it, I should think it rather a praiseworthy than a punishable action. I have debauched no other woman's husband, nor enticed any other youth; these things I never was charg'd with; nor has any one the least cause of complaint against me, unless, perhaps, the ministers of justice, because I have had children without being married, by which they have missed a wedding fee. But can this be a fault of mine? I appeal to your honours. You are pleased to allow I don't want sense; but I must be stupefied to the last degree, not to prefer the honourable state of wedlock to the condition I have lived in. I always was, and still am willing to enter into it; and doubt not my behaving well in it, having all the industry, frugality, fertility, and skill in economy appertaining to a good wife's character. I defy any one to say I ever refused an offer of that sort: on the contrary, I readily consented to the only proposal of marriage that ever was made me, which was when I was a virgin, but too easily confiding in the person's sincerity that made it, I unhappily lost my honour by trusting to his; for he got me with child, and then forsook me.

"That very person, you all know, he is now become a magistrate of this country; and I had hopes he would have appeared this day on the bench, and have endeavoured to moderate the Court in my favour; then I should have scorn'd to have mentioned it; but I must now complain of

Franklin's image, which artists portrayed with as many faces as the moon, looks surprisingly unheroic in this French 1783 pencil sketch. *(Walters Art Gallery.)*

it, as unjust and unequal, that my betrayer and undoer, the first cause of all my faults and miscarriages (if they must be deemed such), should be advanced to honour and power in this government that punishes my misfortunes with stripes and infamy. I should be told, 'tis like, that were there no act of Assembly in the case, the precepts of religion are violated by my transgressions. If mine is a religious offense, leave it to religious punishments. You have already excluded me from the comforts of your church communion. Is not that sufficient? You believe I have offended heaven, and must suffer eternal fire: Will not that be sufficient? What need is there then of your additional fines and whipping? I own I do not think as you do, for, if I thought what you call a sin was really such, I could not presumptuously commit it. But, how can it be believed that heaven is angry at my having children, when to the little done by me towards it, God has been pleased to add his divine skill and admirable workmanship in the formation of their bodies, and crowned the whole by furnishing them with rational and immortal souls?

"Forgive me, gentlemen, if I talk a little extravagantly on these matters; I am no divine, but if you, gentlemen, must be making laws, do not turn natural and useful actions into crimes by your prohibitions. But take into your wise consideration the great and growing number of batchelors in the country, many of whom, from the mean fear of the expences of a family, have never sincerely and honourably courted a woman in their lives; and by their manner of living leave unproduced (which is little better than murder) hundreds of their posterity to the thousandth generation. Is not this a greater offense against the publick good than mine? Compel them, then, by law, either to marriage, or to pay double the fine of fornication every year. What must poor young women do, whom customs and nature forbid to solicit the men, and who cannot force themselves upon husbands, when the laws take no care to provide them any, and yet severely punish them if they do their duty without them; the duty of the first and great command of nature and nature's God, *increase and multiply*; a duty, from the steady performance of which nothing has been able to deter me, but for its sake I have hazarded the loss of the publick esteem, and have frequently endured publick disgrace and punishment; and therefore ought, in my humble opinion, instead of a whipping, to have a statue erected to my memory."

[Following is one account of Franklin telling his version of "A Parable Against Persecution." This comes from the papers of William Parsons, surveyor-general of Pennsylvania, though there are other versions longer than this. —Ed.]

A PARABLE AGAINST PERSECUTION, GENESIS LI

Dr. Franklin in England about 1755 Supporting Dr. Locke's Treatise book on Toleration was much difficulted in Argument with Lady Jane, a maiden Sister to the Earl of Thanet who opposed the doctrine. After several fruitless Attempts the Doctor told Lady Jane that if she would consult her Bible she would find Locke's Doctrine fully supported [,] upon which Lady Jane with an air of triumph Arrose from the chair [,] took from beneath the cushion a large Bible & The Doctor received it at her hand Saying [,] you will find it in the 51st chapter of Genesis [:] And

Abraham was standing at the Door of his Tent looking by the way of the Wilderness and behold a Man came leaning on his Staff, and Abr. said unto the Man [,] Stranger turn in, and tarry with me this Night, and the Man answered and said unto Abr. Nay! but I will tarry under this Oak. And Abr. press'd him and he turned in. And Abr. sat Meat before him, but the man called not on the Lord to Bless it; wherefore Abraham was wroth; & turned him out by the Way whence he came, Now at Midnight the Lord called unto Abr. & Abraham said here am I Lord—and the Lord said unto him [,] where is the Stranger? Abr. answered and said unto the Lord: he would not call on thy Name to bless his Meat; wherefore I turned him out with blows. And the Lord said unto Abr. Have I not born with him this 100 and 60 and 8 years, and couldest not thou, who are thyself a Sinner bear with him one Night.

[*Genesis LI does not exist as part of the Bible, but Franklin's friend, Benjamin Vaughan, wrote that Franklin knew it from memory and had it bound up as a leaf of his Bible, by which he was better able to fool his listeners and even scholars. —Ed.*]

[*Franklin and young Catherine Ray met at a mutual friend's home in 1755 and became good friends; their correspondence lasted the rest of Franklin's life. His letters to her and several other women friends were his indulgence in lighthearted humor. —Ed.*]

From a letter to Miss Catherine Ray [at Block Island]

Philadelphia, Sept. 11, 1755.

Begone, business, for an hour, at least, and let me chat a little with my Katy . . . .

You ask in your last, how I do, and what I am doing, and whether everybody loves me yet, and why I make them do so.

In regard to the first, I can say, thanks to God, that I do not remember I was ever better. I still relish all the pleasures of life, that a temperate man can in reason desire, and through favour I have them all in my power . . . . As to the second question, I must confess (but don't you be jealous), that many more people love me now, than ever did before; for since I saw you I have been enabled to do some general services to the country, and to the army, for which both have thanked and praised me, and say they love me. They say so, as you used to do; and if I were to ask any favours of them, they would, perhaps, as readily refuse me; so that I find little real advantage in being beloved, but it pleases my humour.

Now it is near four months since I have been favoured with a single line from you; but I will not be angry with you, because it is my fault. I ran in debt to you three or four letters . . . . But believe me, I am honest; and, tho' I should never make equal returns, you shall see I will keep fair accounts . . . . The small news, the domestic occurrences among our friends, the natural pictures you draw of persons, the sensible observations and reflections you make, and the easy, chatty manner in which you express every thing, all contribute to heighten the pleasure; and the more as they remind me of those hours and miles, that we talked away so agreeably, even in a winter journey, a wrong road, and a soaking shower. . . .

I commend your prudent resolutions, in the article of granting favours to lovers. But if I were courting you, I could not hardly approve such conduct. I should even be malicious enough to say you were too knowing, and tell you the old story of the Girl and the Miller. I enclose you the songs you write for, and with them your Spanish letter with a translation. I honour that honest Spaniard for loving you. It showed the goodness of his taste and judgement. But you must forget him, and bless some worthy young Englishman.

You have spun a long thread, five thousand and twenty-two yards. It will reach almost from Rhode Island hither. I wish I had hold of one end of it, to pull you to me. But you would break it rather than come. The cords of love and friendship are longer and stronger, and in times past have drawn me farther; even back from England to Philadelphia. I guess that some of the same kind will one day draw you out of that Island.

I was extremely pleased with the turf you sent me. The Irish people, who have seen it, say it is the right sort; but I cannot learn that we have any thing like it here. The

Jasperware medallions like the above, modeled after a 1777 design by J. B. Nini, were widespread in France, being sold and shipped by the case. These "fur cap" medallions were amazingly successful in popularizing Franklin's mission to France. (*Courtesy, The Henry Francis du Pont Winterthur Museum.*)

cheeses, particularly one of them, were excellent. All our friends have tasted it, and all agree that it exceeds any English cheese they ever tasted. Mrs. Franklin was very proud, that a young lady should have so much regard for her old husband, as to send him such a present. We talk of you every time it comes to table. She is sure you are a sensible girl, and a notable housewife, and talks of bequeathing me to you as a legacy; but I ought to wish you a better, and hope she will live these hundred years; for we are grown old together, and if she has any faults, I am so used to 'em that I don't perceive 'em; as the song says,

A silver tankard with the Franklin coat of arms, owned and probably used by Franklin. *(Franklin Institute, Philadelphia.)*

"Some faults we have all, and so has my Joan.
But then they're exceedingly small;
And, now I am used, they are like my own,
I scarcely can see 'em at all.
My dear friends,
I scarcely can see 'em at all."

Indeed, I begin to think she has none, as I think of you. And since she is willing I should love you, as much as you are willing to be loved by me, let us join in wishing the old lady a long life and a happy.

Autobiography

Passy, near Paris, 1784.

I had been religiously educated as a Presbyterian; and tho' some of the dogmas of that persuasion, such as *the eternal decrees of God, election, reprobation, etc.*, appeared to me unintelligible, others doubtful, and I early absented myself from the public assemblies of the sect, Sunday being my studying day, I never was without some religious principles. I never doubted, for instance, the existence of the Deity; that he made the world, and govern'd it by his Providence; that the most acceptable service of God was the doing good to man; that our souls are immortal; and that all crime will be punished, and virtue rewarded, either here or hereafter. These I esteem'd the essentials of every religion; and, being to be found in all the religions we had in our country, I respected them all, tho' with different degrees of respect, as I found them more or less mix'd with other articles, which, without any tendency to inspire, promote, or confirm morality, serv'd principally to divide us, and make us unfriendly to one another. This respect to all, with an opinion that the worst had some good effects, induc'd

me to avoid all discourse that might tend to lessen the good opinion another might have of his own religion; and as our province increas'd in people, and new places of worship were continually wanted, and generally erected by voluntary contribution, my mite for such purpose, whatever might be the sect, was never refused.

. . . I had some years before compos'd a little Liturgy, or form of prayer, for my own private use (viz., in 1728), entitled, *Articles of Belief and Acts of Religion*. I return'd to the use of this, and went no more to the public assemblies. My conduct might be blameable, but I leave it, without attempting further to excuse it; my present purpose being to relate facts, and not to make apologies for them.

[ARTICLES OF BELIEF AND ACTS OF RELIGION *was composed of Franklin's statement of First Principles, as related in the* Autobiography, *followed by a litany of Adoration, a reading from a devotional piece, several minutes of silence, singing of Milton's "Hymn to the Creator," then his Petition. –Ed.*]

Petition

Inasmuch as by Reason of our Ignorance We cannot be certain that many Things, which we often hear mentioned in the Petitions of Men to the Deity, would prove real Goods, if they were in our Possession, and as I have reason to hope and believe that the Goodness of my Heavenly Father will not withold from me a suitable share of Temporal Blessings, if by a Virtuous and holy Life I conciliate his Favour and Kindness, Therefore I presume not to ask such things, but rather humbly and with a Sincere Heart, express my earnest desires that he would graciously assist my Continual Endeavours and Resolutions of eschewing Vice and embracing Virtue; which Kind of Supplications will *at least be thus far beneficial, as they remind me* in a solemn manner of my Extensive duty.

. . . That I may be preserved from Atheism & Infidelity, Impiety, and Profaneness, and, in my Addresses to Thee, carefully avoid Irreverence and ostentation, Formality and odious Hypocrisy, – Help me, O Father! . . .

That I may be sincere in Friendship, faithful in trust, and Impartial in Judgment, watchful against Pride, and against Anger (that momentary Madness), – Help me, O Father!

That I may be just in all my Dealings, temperate in my Pleasures, full of Candour and Ingenuity, Humanity and Benevolence, – Help me, O Father! . . .

That I may possess Integrity and Evenness of Mind, Resolution in Difficulties, and Fortitude under Affliction; that I may be punctual in performing my promises, Peaceable and prudent in my Behaviour, – Help me, O Father!

That I may have Tenderness for the Weak, and reverent Respect for the Ancient; that I may be Kind to my Neighbours, good natured to my Companions, and hospitable to Strangers, – Help me, O Father! . . .

That I may be honest and open-hearted, gentle, merciful, and good, cheerful in spirit, rejoicing in the Good of others, – Help me, O Father! . . .

And forasmuch as ingratitude is one of the most odious of vices, let me not be unmindful gratefully to acknowledge the favours I receive from Heaven.

Thanks

For peace and liberty, for food and raiment, for corn, and wine, and milk, and every kind of healthful nourishment, – Good God, I thank thee!

For the common benefits of air and light; for useful fire and delicious water, – Good God, I thank thee!

For knowledge, and literature, and every useful art, for my friends and their prosperity, and for the fewness of my enemies, – Good God, I thank thee!

For all thy innumerable benefits; for life, and reason, and the use of speech; for health, and joy, and every pleasant hour, – My good God, I thank thee!

A NEW VERSION OF THE LORD'S PRAYER

[1768?]

Old Version	New Version, by BF.
1. Our Father which are in Heaven.	1. Heavenly Father,
2. Hallowed be thy Name.	2. May all revere thee.
3. Thy Kingdom come.	3. And become thy dutiful Children and faithful Subjects.
4. Thy Will be done on Earth as it is in Heaven.	4. May thy Laws be obeyed on Earth as perfectly as they are in Heaven.
5. Give us this Day our daily Bread.	5. Provide for us this Day as thou has hitherto daily done.
6. Forgive us our Debts as we forgive our Debtors.	6. Forgive us our Trespasses, and enable us likewise to forgive those that offend us.
[7.] And lead us not into Temptation, but deliver us from Evil.	7. Keep us out of Temptation, and deliver us from Evil.

Reasons for the Change of Expression

Old Version. *Our Father which are in Heaven*

New V. *Heavenly Father*, is more concise, equally expressive, and better modern English.

Old. *Hallowed be thy Name*. This seems to relate to an Observance among the Jews not to pronounce the proper or peculiar Name of God, they deeming it a Profanation so to do. We have in our Language no proper Name for God; the Word God being a common or general Name, expressing all chief Objects of Worship, true or false. The Word hallowed is almost obsolete; People now have but an imperfect Conception of the Meaning of the Petition. It is therefore proposed to change the Expression into

New. *May all revere thee.*

Old V. *Thy Kingdom come.* This Petition seems suited to the then Condition of the Jewish Nation. Originally their State was a Theocracy: God was their King. Dissatisfied with that kind of Government, they desired a visible earthly King in the manner of the Nations round them. They had such King's accordingly; but their Happiness was not increas'd by the Change, and they had reason to wish and pray for a Return of the Theocracy, or Government of God. Christians in these Times have other Ideas when they speak of the Kingdom of God, such as are perhaps more adequately express'd by

New V. *And become thy dutiful Children and faithful Subjects.*

Old V. *Thy Will be done on Earth as it is in Heaven.* More explicitly,

New V. *May thy Laws be obeyed on Earth as perfectly as they are in Heaven.*

Old V. *Give us this Day our daily Bread.* Give us what is *ours*, seems to put in a Claim of Right, and to contain

too little of the grateful Acknowledgement and Sense of Dependance that becomes Creatures who live on the daily Bounty of their Creator. Therefore it is changed to

New V. *Provide for us this Day, as thou hast hitherto daily done.*

Old V. *Forgive us our Debts as we forgive our Debtors.* Matthew. *Forgive us our Sins, for we also forgive every one that is indebted to us.* Luke. Offerings were *due* to God on many Occasions by the Jewish Law, which when People could not pay, or had forgotten as Debtors are apt to do, it was proper to pray that those Debts might be forgiven. Our Liturgy uses neither the *Debtors* of Matthew, nor the *indebted* of Luke, but instead of them speaks of *those that trespass against us.* Perhaps the Considering it as a Christian Duty to forgive Debtors, was by the Compilers thought an inconvenient Idea in a trading Nation. There seems however something presumptious in this Mode of Expression, which has the Air of proposing ourselves as an Example of Goodness fit for God to imitate. *We hope you will at least be as good as we are;* you see we forgive one another, and therefore we pray that you would forgive us. Some have considered it in another Sense, *Forgive us as we forgive others*; i.e. If we do not forgive others we pray that thou wouldst not forgive us. But this being a kind of conditional *Imprecation* against ourselves, seems improper in such a Prayer; and therefore it may be better to say humbly and modestly

New V. *Forgive us our Trespasses, and enable us likewise to forgive those that offend us.* This instead of assuring that we have already in and of ourselves the Grace of Forgiveness, acknowledges our Dependance on God, the Fountain of Mercy, for any Share we may have of it, praying that he would communicate of it to us.

Old V. *And lead us not into Temptation.* The Jews had a Notion, that God sometimes tempted, or directed or permitted the Tempting of People. Thus it was said he tempted Pharaoh; directed Satan to tempt Job; and a false Prophet to tempt Ahab, &c. Under this Persuasion it was natural for them to pray that he would not put them to such severe Trials. We now suppose that Temptation, so far as it is supernatural, comes from the Devil only; and this Petition continued, conveys a Suspicion which in our present Conceptions seems unworthy of God, therefore might be altered to

New V. *Keep us out of Temptation.*

[*Franklin addressed this "bagatelle" to Madame Brillon, whom he described as "a lady of most respectable character and pleasing conversation; mistress of an amiable family in this neighborhood, with which I spend an evening twice in every week. She has, among other elegant accomplishments, that of an excellent musician; and . . . she kindly entertains me and my grandson with little concerts, a cup of tea, and a game of chess." –Ed.*]

THE EPHEMERA
An Emblem of Human Life

1778

You may remember, my dear friend, that when we lately spent that happy day in the delightful garden and sweet society of the Moulin Joly [a friend's country home], I stopt a little in one of our walks, and stayed some time behind the company. We had been shown numberless skeletons of a kind of little fly, called an ephemera, whose successive generations, we were told, were bred and expired within the day. I happened to see a living company of them on a leaf, who appeared to be engaged in conversation. You know I understand all the inferior animal tongues: my too great application to the study of them is the best excuse I can give for the little progress I have made in your charming language. I listened through curiosity to the discourse of these little creatures; but as they, in their national vivacity, spoke three or four together, I could make but little of their conversation. I found, however, by some broken expressions that I heard now and then, they were disputing warmly on the merit of two foreign musicians, one a *cousin*, the other a *moscheto*; in which dispute they spent their time, seemingly as regardless of the shortness of life as if they had been sure of living a month. Happy people! thought I, you live certainly under a wise, just, and mild government, since you have no public grievances to complain of, nor any subject of contention but the perfections and imperfections of foreign music. I turned my head from them to an old grey-headed one, who was single on another leaf, and talking to himself. Being amused with his soliloquy, I put it down in writing, in hopes it will likewise amuse her to whom I am so much indebted for the most pleasing of all amusements, her delicious company and heavenly harmony.

"It was," said he, "the opinion of learned philosophers of our race, who lived and flourished long before my time, that this vast world, the Moulin Joly, could not itself subsist more than eighteen hours; and I think there was some foundation for that opinion, since, by the apparent motion of the great luminary that gives life to all nature, and which

Franklin looks like a stern moralist in this painting by Joseph Wright, though in fact he was apt to forgive readily his own and others' faults. *(The Pennsylvania Academy of the Fine Arts, Joseph and Sarah Harrison Collection.)*

in my time has evidently declined considerably towards the ocean at the end of our earth, it must then finish its course, be extinguished in the waters that surround us, and leave the world in cold and darkness, necessarily producing universal death and destruction. I have lived seven of those hours, a great age, being no less than four hundred and twenty minutes of time. How very few of us continue so long! I have seen generations born, flourish, and expire. My present friends are the children and grandchildren of the friends of my youth, who are now, alas, no more! And I must soon follow them; for, by the course of nature, though still in health, I cannot expect to live above seven or eight minutes longer. What now avails all my toil and labor, in amassing honey-dew on this leaf, which I cannot live to enjoy! What the political struggles I have been engaged in, for the good of my compatriot inhabitants of this bush, or my philosophical studies for the benefit of our race in general! for, in politics, what can laws do without morals? Our present race of ephemerae will in a course of minutes become corrupt, like those of other and older bushes, and consequently as wretched. And in philosophy how small our progress! Alas! art is long, and life is short! My friends would comfort me with the idea of a name, they say, I shall leave behind me; and they tell me I have lived long enough to nature and to glory. But what will fame be to an ephemera who no longer exists? And what will become of all history in the eighteenth hour, when the world itself, even the whole Moulin Joly, shall come to its end, and be buried in universal ruin?"

To me, after all my eager pursuits, no solid pleasures now remain, but the reflection of a long life spent in meaning well, the sensible conversation of a few good lady ephemerae, and now and then a kind smile and a tune from the ever amiable *Brillante*.

B. Franklin

Christ Church, Philadelphia, in 1778. *(Library of Congress.)*

The Cascades at the Palace of Versailles were part of the formal gardens. Franklin was received in the palace by Louis XVI and conducted peace negotiations here. *(Historical Pictures Service, Chicago.)*

From Mme. Brillon to Dr. Franklin

11th May, 1779.

You are quite right, my good Papa, true happiness should consist for us only in peace of mind; it is not in our power to change the nature of those with whom we live, nor to prevent the contrarieties that surround us. It is a wise man who speaks, and who tries to advise his too sensitive daughter by teaching her the truth. Oh, my Papa, I beg for your friendship, your healthy philosophy; my heart listens and submits to you. Give me the strength that it may take the place of an indifference your child can never feel. But admit, my friend, that for one who knows how to love, ingratitude is a frightful ill; that it is hard for a woman who would give her life without hesitation to insure her husband's happiness to see the result of her care and her desires taken away by intrigue, and falseness. Time will make all right: my Papa has said so, and I believe it. But my Papa has also said that time is the stuff of which life is made. My life, my friend, is made of fine and thin stuff, that grief tears cruelly; if I had anything to reproach myself with, I should long have ceased to exist. My soul is pure, simple, frank. I dare to tell my Papa so; I dare to tell him that it is worthy of him; I dare still assure him that my conduct, which he has considered wise, will not belie itself, that I will await justice in patience, that I will follow the advice of my honourable friend with firmness and confidence.

Adieu, you whom I love so much, — my kind Papa. Never call me anything but "my daughter." Yesterday you called me "Madame," and my heart shrank, I examined myself, to see whether I had done you any wrong, or if I had some failings that you would not tell me of. Pardon, my friend; I am not reproaching you, I am accusing myself of a weakness. I was born much too sensitive for my happiness and for that of my friends; cure me, or pity me, if you can do one and the other.

Tomorrow, Wednesday, you will come to tea, will you not? Believe, my Papa, that the pleasure I take in receiving you is shared by my husband, my children, and my friends; I cannot doubt it, and I assure you of it.

THE WHISTLE
From a letter to Madame Brillon

Passy, November 10, 1779.

I am charmed with your description of Paradise, and with your plan of living there; and I approve much of your conclusion, that, in the mean time, we should draw all the good we can from this world. In my opinion, we might all draw more good from it than we do, and suffer less evil, if we would take care not to give too much for *whistles.* For to me it seems, that most of the unhappy people we meet with, are become so by neglect of that caution.

You ask what I mean? You love stories, and will excuse my telling one of myself.

When I was a child of seven years old, my friends, on a holiday, filled my pocket with coppers. I went directly to a shop where they sold toys for children; and, being charmed with the sound of a *whistle,* that I met by the way in the hands of another boy, I voluntarily offered and gave all my money for one. I then came home, and went whistling all over the house, much pleased with my *whistle,* but disturbing all the family. My brothers, and sisters, and cousins, understanding the bargain I had made, told me I had given four times as much for it as it was worth; put me in mind what good things I might have bought with the rest of the money; and laughed at me so much for my folly, that I cried with vexation; and the reflection gave me more chagrin than the *whistle* gave me pleasure.

140

This however was afterwards of use to me, the impression continuing on my mind; so that often, when I was tempted to buy some unnecessary thing, I said to myself, *Don't give too much for the whistle*; and I saved my money.

As I grew up, came into the world, and observed the actions of men, I thought I met with many, very many, who *gave too much for the whistle*.

When I saw one too ambitious of court favour, sacrificing his time in attendance on levees, his repose, his liberty, his virtue, and perhaps his friends, to attain it, I have said to myself, *This man gives too much for his whistle*.

When I saw another fond of popularity, constantly employing himself in political bustles, neglecting his own affairs, and ruining them by that neglect, *He pays, indeed*, said I, *too much for his whistle*.

If I knew a miser, who gave up every kind of comfortable living, all the pleasure of doing good to others, all the esteem of his fellow-citizens, and the joys of benevolent friendship, for the sake of accumulating wealth, *Poor man*, said I, *you pay too much for your whistle*.

When I met with a man of pleasure, sacrificing every laudable improvement of the mind, or of his fortune, to mere corporeal sensations, and ruining his health in their pursuit, *Mistaken man*, said I, *you are providing pain for yourself, instead of pleasure; you give too much for your whistle*.

If I see one fond of appearance, or fine clothes, fine houses, fine furniture, fine equipages, all above his fortune, for which he contracts debts, and ends his career in a prison, *Alas!* say I, *he has paid dear, very dear, for his whistle*.

Presumed sketch of Franklin and a friend, by Charles Willson Peale. *(American Philosophical Society.)*

Fair Venus calls; her voice obey,
In beauty's arms spend night and day.
The joys of love all joys excell,
And loving's certainly doing well.
(Chorus) Oh! No! / Not so!
For honest souls know,
Friends and a bottle still bear the bell.
— Poem for L'Abbé de la Rouche.

When I see a beautiful, sweet-tempered girl married to an ill-natured brute of a husband, *What a pity*, say I, *that she should pay so much for a whistle!*

In short, I conceive that great part of the miseries of mankind are brought upon them by the false estimates they have made of the value of things, and by their *giving too much for their whistles*.

To Madame Brillon

Passy March 10.

I am charm'd with the goodness of my spiritual guide, and resign myself implicitly to her Conduct, as she promises to lead me to heaven in so delicious a Road when I could be content to travel thither even in the roughest of all ways with the pleasure of her Company.

How kindly partial to her Penitent in finding him, on examining his conscience, guilty of only one capital sin and to call that by the gentle name of Foible!

I lay fast hold of your promise to absolve me of all Sins past, present, & future, on the easy & pleasing Condition of loving God, America and my guide above all things. I am in Rapture when I think of being absolv'd of the future.

People commonly speak of Ten Commandments. — I have been taught that there are twelve. The first was in-

Of his house at Passy, Franklin said, "It is a fine House, situated in a neat Village, on high Ground, half a Mile from Paris, with a large Garden to walk in." Sketch by Victor Hugo. *(New York Public Library, Astor, Lenox and Tilden Foundations.)*

crease & multiply & replenish the earth. The twelfth is, A new Commandment I give unto you, *that you love one another*. It seems to me that they are a little misplaced, And that the last should have been the first. However I never made any difficulty about that, but was always willing to obey them both whenever I had an opportunity. Pray tell me my dear Casuist, whether my keeping religiously these two commandments tho' not in the Decalogue, may not be accepted in Compensation for my breaking so often one of the ten I mean that which forbids Coveting my neighbour's wife, and which I confess I break constantly God forgive me, as often as I see or think of my lovely Confessor, and I am afraid I should never be able to repent of the Sin even if I had the full Possession of her.

And now I am Consulting you upon a Case of Conscience I will mention the Opinion of a certain Father of the church which I find myself willing to adopt though I am not sure it is orthodox. It is this, that the most effectual way to get rid of a certain Temptation is, as often as it returns, to comply with and satisfy it.

Pray instruct me how far I may venture to practice upon this Principle?

But why should I be so scrupulous when you have promised to absolve me of the future?

Adieu my charming Conductress and believe me ever with the sincerest Esteem & affection.

Your most obed't hum. Serv.
[B. F.]

From MORALS OF CHESS

[1779]

The Game of Chess is not merely an idle Amusement. Several very valuable qualities of the Mind, useful in the course of human Life, are to be acquir'd or strengthened by it, so as to become habits, ready on all occasions. For Life is a kind of Chess, in which we often have Points to gain, & Competitors or Adversaries to contend with; and in which there is a vast variety of good and ill Events, that are in some degree the Effects of Prudence of the want of it. By playing at Chess, then, we may learn,

I. *Foresight*, which looks a little into futurity, and considers the Consequences that may attend an action; for it is continually occurring to the Player, "If I move this piece, what will be the advantages or disadvantages of my new situation? What Use can my Adversary make of it to annoy me? What other moves can I make to support it, and to defend myself from his attacks?"

II. *Circumspection*, which surveys the whole Chessboard, or scene of action; the relations of the several pieces and situations, the Dangers they are respectively exposed to, the several possibilities of their aiding each other, the probabilities that the Adversary may make this or that move, and attack this or the other Piece, and what different Means can be used to avoid his stroke, or turn its consequences against him.

III. *Caution*, not to make our moves too hastily. This habit is best acquired by observing the laws of the Game;

A relaxed portrait of Franklin was
engraved in 1781 by François Denis Nee, after
a drawing by L. C. Carmontelle.
At home in Passy, Franklin found that,
"I have an abundance of Acquaintance, dine
abroad Six Days in seven. Sundays I reserve to dine at home, with such Americans
as pass this Way; and I then have my Grandson
Ben, with some other American Children from
his school." *(Philadelphia Museum of Art.)*

A garden scene at Versailles is the epitome of the lavish estates to which Franklin was invited by his French friends of nobility. *(Historical Pictures Service, Chicago.)*

such as, *If you touch a Piece, you must move it somewhere; if you set it down, you must let it stand*. And it is therefore best that these rules should be observed, as the Game becomes thereby more the image of human Life, and particularly of War. . . .

And *lastly*, we learn by Chess the habit of not being discouraged by present appearances in the state of our affairs, the habit of hoping for a favorable Change, and that of persevering in the search of resources. The Game is so full of Events, there is such a variety of turns in it, the Fortune of it is so subject to sudden Vicissitudes, and so frequently, after long contemplation, discovers the means of extricating one's self from a supposed insurmountable Difficulty, that one is encouraged to continue the Contest to the last, in hopes of Victory from our own skill, or at least of getting a stalemate, from the Negligence of our Adversary. . . .

That we may therefore be induced more frequently to choose this beneficial amusement, in preference to others which are not attended with the same advantages, every Circumstance that may increase the pleasure of it should be regarded. . . .

Therefore, first, if it is agreed to play according to the strict rules, then those rules are to be exactly observed by both parties, and should not be insisted on for one side, while deviated from by the other — for this is not equitable.

Secondly, if it is agreed not to observe the rules exactly, but one party demands indulgencies, he should then be as willing to allow them to the other.

Thirdly, no false move should ever be made to extricate yourself out of difficulty, or to gain an advantage. There can be no pleasure in playing with a person once detected in such unfair practice.

Fourthly, if your adversary is long in playing, you ought not to hurry him, or express any uneasiness at his delay. You should not sing, nor whistle, nor look at your watch, nor take up a book to read, nor make a tapping with your feet on the floor, or with your fingers on the table, nor do any thing that may disturb his attention. For all these things displease; and they do not show your skill in playing, but your craftiness or your rudeness.

Fifthly, you ought not to endeavour to amuse and deceive your adversary, by pretending to have made bad moves, and saying that you have now lost the game, in order to make him secure and careless, and inattentive to your schemes: for this is fraud and deceit, not skill in the game. . . .

Lastly, if the game is not to be played rigorously, according to the rules above mentioned, then moderate your desire of victory over your adversary, and be pleased with one over yourself. Snatch not eagerly at every advantage offered by his unskilfulness or inattention; but point out to him kindly, that by such a move he places or leaves a piece in danger and unsupported; that by another he will put his king in a perilous situation, &c. By this generous civility (so opposite to the unfairness above forbidden) you may, indeed, happen to lose the game to your opponent; but you will win what is better, his esteem, his respect, and his affection, together with the silent approbation and goodwill of impartial spectators.

Right: A marble bust of Franklin, done with very delicate craftsmanship by J. A. Houdon, 1780. *(William Rockhill Nelson Gallery of Art, Atkins Museum of Fine Arts.)*

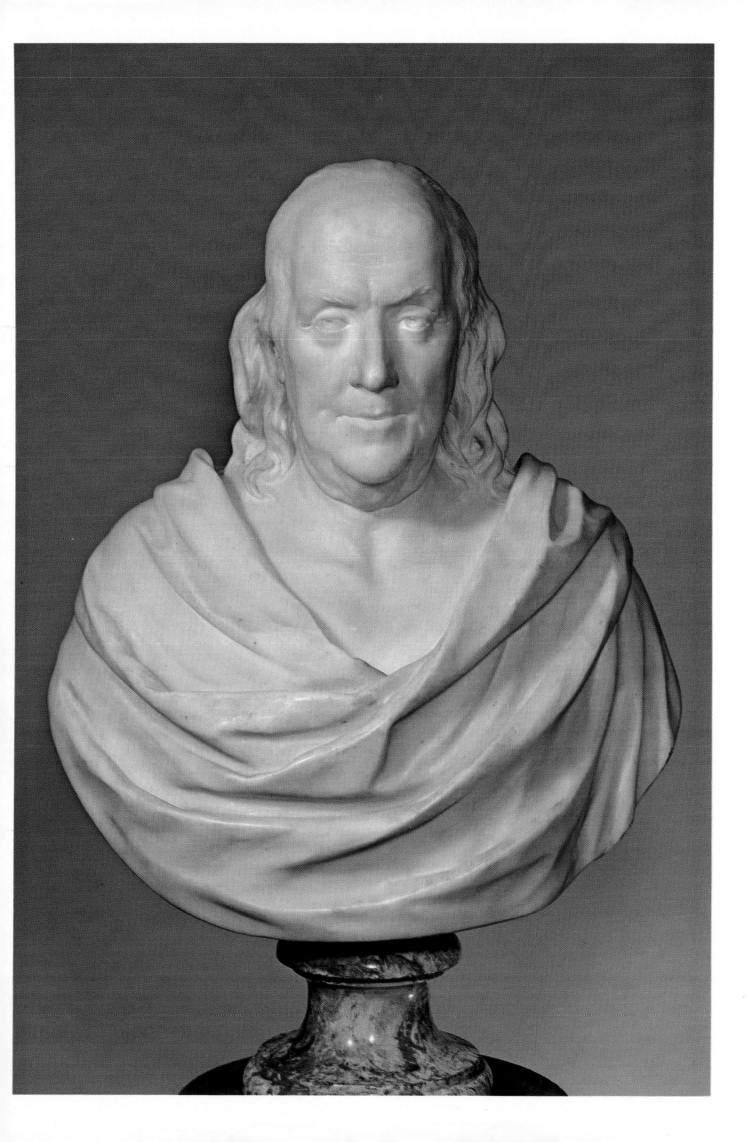

The "rising sun" chair was used by
Washington as President of the Constitutional
Convention. At the signing of the docu-
ment, Franklin commented that finally he
was certain that the figure symbolized for
America a rising, not a setting, sun.
(Independence National Historical Park.)

Signing of the Constitution of the United States,
by Howard C. Christy, hangs in the U. S. Capitol, in the
House of Representatives. Washington presides, and
Franklin sits in the foreground. His speech of reconciliation
over representation did much to assure the Constitution would
be adopted unanimously. *(Franklin Institute, Philadelphia.)*

The "*Fur Collar*" *Portrait* of Franklin, 1778, by J. S. Duplessis, was copied many times by the artist and other painters and often freely adapted. Franklin said this image of him was as familiar as the moon and as changeable. (*The Metropolitan Museum of Art, Michael Friedsam Collection.*)

BENJAMIN FRANKLIN

Ministre plenipotentiaire a la Cour de France pour la Republique

des Provinces unies de l'Amerique Septentrionale

Diogenes, the ancient Greek philosopher
who in legend searched for a real man, reveals
Franklin as his discovery in this 1780 French print.
(American Philosophical Society.)

Christ Church, Philadelphia, was an early landmark completed in 1744. Inside, a pew is marked with Franklin's name, and he is buried outside in the churchyard. Painting by William Strickland, 1811. *(Courtesy, Christ Church, Philadelphia.)*

Below: "View of Several Public Buildings in Philadelphia, 1790," from the *Columbian Magazine.* From the left are, 1, the Episcopal Academy; 2, Congress Hall; 3, the State House; 4, the American Philosophical Society Hall; 5, Library Company of Philadelphia; 6, Carpenter's Hall. *(Historical Society of Pennsylvania.)*

View of several Public Buildings, in Philadelphia.

Franklin as he is most fondly thought of: reading his own words to the wise from an *Almanack* and sitting beside his stove. *(Courtesy of John Hancock Mutual Life Insurance Company.)*

A finely detailed Franklin medallion, by J. B. Nini, 1777. *(Courtesy, Henry Francis du Pont Winterthur Museum.)*

One of the finest examples of Bristol porcelain used in a portrait plaque is this of Franklin, ca. 1777, which he owned for a time. *(British Museum.)*

en toss off your glasses, and scorn the dull asses,
Who, missing the kernel, still gnaw the shell;
at's love, rule, or riches? Wise Solomon teaches,
They're vanity, vanity, vanity still.
(Chorus) That's true; / He knew;
He'd tried them all through;
Friends and a bottle still bore the bell.
— Poem for L'Abbé de la Rouche.

From the DIALOGUE BETWEEN FRANKLIN AND THE GOUT

Midnight, October 22, 1780.

Franklin. Eh! Oh! Eh! What have I done to merit these cruel sufferings?

Gout. Many things; you have ate and drank too freely, and too much indulged those legs of yours in their indolence.

Franklin. Who is it that accuses me?

Gout. It is I, even I, the Gout.

Franklin. What! my enemy in person?

Gout. No, not your enemy.

Franklin. I repeat it; my enemy; for you would not only torment my body to death, but ruin my good name; you reproach me as a glutton and a tippler; now all the world, that knows me, will allow that I am neither the one nor the other.

Gout. The world may think as it pleases; it is always very complaisant to itself, and sometimes to its friends; but I very well know that the quantity of meat and drink proper for a man, who takes a reasonable degree of exercise, would be too much for another, who never takes any.

. . . If your situation in life is a sedentary one, your amusements, your recreations, at least, should be active. You ought to walk or ride; or, if the weather prevents that, play at billiards. But let us examine your course of life. While the mornings are long, and you have leisure to go abroad, what do you do? Why, instead of gaining an appetite for breakfast, by salutary exercise, you amuse yourself, with books, pamphlets, or newspapers, which commonly are not worth the reading. Yet you eat an inordinate breakfast, four dishes of tea, with cream, and one or two buttered toasts, with slices of hung beef, which I fancy are not things the most easily digested. Immediately afterward you sit down to write at your desk, or converse with persons who apply to you on business. Thus the time passes till one, without any kind of bodily exercise. But all this I could pardon, in regard, as you say, to your sedentary condition. But what is your practice after dinner? Walking in the beautiful gardens of those friends, with whom you have dined, would be the choice of men of sense; yours is to be fixed down to chess, where you are found engaged for two or three hours! . . . What can be expected from such a course of living, but a body replete with stagnant humours, ready to fall a prey to all kinds of dangerous maladies, if I, the Gout, did not occasionally bring you relief by agitating those humours, and so purifying or dissipating them? . . . Fie, then Mr. Franklin! But amidst my instructions, I had almost forgot to administer my wholesome corrections; so take that twinge, — and that.

Franklin. Oh! Eh! Oh! Ohhh! As much instruction as you please, Madam Gout, and as many reproaches; but pray, Madam, a truce with your corrections!

Gout. No, Sir, No, — I will not abate a particle of what is so much for your good. . . .

Do you remember how often you have promised yourself, the following morning, a walk in the grove of Boulogne, in the garden de la Muette, or in your own garden, and have violated your promise, alleging, at one time, it was too cold, at another too warm, too windy, too moist, or what else you pleased; when in truth it was too nothing, but your insuperable love of ease?

Franklin. That I confess may have happened occasionally, probably ten times in a year.

Gout. Your confession is very far short of the truth; the gross amount is one hundred and ninety-nine times.

Franklin. Is it possible?

Gout. So possible, that it is fact; you may rely on the accuracy of my statement. You know M. Brillon's gardens, and what fine walks they contain; you know the handsome flight of an hundred steps, which lead from the terrace above to the lawn below. You have been in the practice of visiting this amiable family twice a week, after dinner, and it is a maxim of your own, that "a man may take as much exercise in walking a mile, up and down stairs, as in ten on level ground." What an opportunity was here for you to have had exercise in both these ways! Did you embrace it, and how often?

Franklin. I cannot immediately answer that question.

Gout. I will do it for you; not once.

Franklin. Not once?

Gout. Even so. During the summer you went there at six o'clock. You found the charming lady, with her lovely children and friends, eager to walk with you, and entertain you with their agreeable conversation; and what has been your choice? Why to sit on the terrace, satisfying yourself with the fine prospect, and passing your eye over the beauties of the garden below, without taking one step to descend and walk about in them. On the contrary, you call for tea and the chess-board; and lo! you are occupied in your seat till nine o'clock, and that besides two hours' play after dinner; and then instead of walking home, which would have bestirred you a little, you step into your carriage. How absurd to suppose that all this carelessness can be reconcilable with health, without my interposition!

Franklin. I am convinced now of the justness of poor Richard's remark, that "Our debts and our sins are always greater than we think for."

Gout. So it is. Your philosophers are sages in your maxims, and fools in your conduct. . . .

Franklin. Ah! how tiresome you are!

Gout. Well, then, to my office; it should not be forgotten that I am your physician. There.

Franklin. Ohhh! what a devil of a physician!

Gout. How ungrateful you are to say so! Is it not I who, in the character of your physician, have saved you from the palsy, dropsy, and apoplexy? one or other of which would have done for you long ago, but for me.

Franklin. I submit, and thank you for the past, but entreat the discontinuance of your visits for the future; for, in my mind, one had better die than be cured so dolefully. . . .

Oh! Oh! — for Heaven's sake leave me! and I promise faithfully never more to play at chess, but to take exercise daily, and live temperately.

Gout. I know you too well. You promise fair; but, after a few months of good health, you will return to your old habits; your fine promises will be forgotten like the forms of last year's clouds. Let us then finish the account, and I will go. But I leave you with an assurance of visiting you again at a proper time and place; for my object is your good, and you are sensible that I am your *real friend.*

"He seized fire from the heavens and sceptor from tyrants" — (Eripuit caelo fulmen sceptrumque tyrannis) — A.R.J. Turgot's famous epigram on Franklin may seem too sublime praise for a man who was altogether down to earth. Yet, to political leaders, scientists and the populace of eighteenth-century Europe, he was America's most eminent scientist and living symbol of democracy. To the newly made American nation, he must have been a stronghold of sensibility and harmony, always available for service or advice. To two of the younger men we now call Founding Fathers, George Washington and Thomas Jefferson, he was always "the good old Doctor." A last letter from Washington is included in this chapter as a kind of tribute to Franklin's generosity of spirit. To modern historians and readers, Franklin is still approachable and certainly more vulnerable than other American leaders of the time.

EPILOGUE

To Philadelphians, he was a well-known figure for over a half century, active in most political events and instigator of social benefits that made the city among the most progressive in America. At his death in 1790, it has been said that no other town burying its great man ever buried more of itself than Philadelphia with Franklin. An estimated twenty thousand people attended his funeral. The House of Representatives, hearing of Franklin's death, unanimously passed James Madison's motion that members wear the badge of mourning for one month.

In Paris, the French National Assembly wore mourning badges for three days, and its President wrote to Congress:

The name of Benjamin Franklin will be immortal in the records of freedom and philosophy; but it is more particularly dear to a country, where, conducted by the most sublime mission, this venerable man knew how very soon to acquire an infinite number of friends and admirers, as well by the simplicity and sweetness of his manners, as by the purity of his principles, the extent of his knowledge, and the charms of his mind.

Eulogies also came from The American Philosophical Society, the President of Yale University, the French Academy of Sciences, a fraternity of Parisian printers and more. The Commune of Paris (the Revolutionary government) ordered a public celebration in his memory.

The codicil to Franklin's last will and testament has been excerpted for this chapter to show his final desire to be useful, even after death. The codicil is his plan for distributing loans from a trust fund, for 200 years, to ambitious and upstanding young apprentices in Boston and Philadelphia.

Perhaps the most moving and fitting piece is from Franklin's own hand: the epitaph he composed in 1728 and often rewrote for friends from memory. It is prophetic, though Franklin hardly anticipated the degree of lettering and gilding the world would bestow on him. It shows that ease and confidence which prevailed throughout the "corrections" meeted out to him in his life.

In America after his death, historians' and popular regard for Franklin fluxuated with the mode. His straightforwardness in gaining material comfort, particularly in viewing political, religious and social conventions, and general tolerance and cheerfulness were often unpopular in the century following his time. His outlook was perhaps too healthy and happy to appeal to Romanticists, somewhat too materialistic or pragmatic to appeal to New England Transcendentalists, and generally too openly liberal and cosmopolitan for Victorian America. In recent decades Franklin has come to be better understood and admired as his life has been studied more carefully. Yet even now he might be mistaken for nothing but a *label*: a moralist, or an irreligious rogue; a penny-pincher, or an opportunist; a sophist, or a sage; a discreet diplomat, or a clever politician; a mechanical wizard, scientist or both; and other generalizations. In his long life and throughout his voluminous writings, one can find indications that Franklin was all these and more, but no one or two can name him. The excerpts in this book show him, we hope, as his eminent biographer Carl Van Doren saw, "a harmonious human multitude."

Le Docteur Franklin Couronne par la Liberte, 1778,
aquatint engraving by J. C. R. de Saint Non, after a
drawing by J. H. Fragonard. In this allegorical work,
Liberty descends with wreaths for the bust of Franklin,
and the scroll covering part of the globe refers to
the Pennsylvania laws, indicating Franklin's service
as legislator as well as liberator. *(Philadelphia Museum of Art.)*

Would to God, my dear sir, that I could congratulate you upon the removal of that excruciating pain under which you labor, and that your existence might close with as much ease to yourself as its continuance has been beneficial to our country and useful to mankind; or, if the united wishes of a free people, joined with the earnest prayers of every friend to science and humanity, could relieve the body from pain or infirmities, that you could claim an exemption on this score. But this cannot be, and you have within yourself the only resource to which we can confidently apply for relief, a philosophic mind.

If to be venerated for benevolence, if to be admired to talents, if to be esteemed for patriotism, if to be beloved for philanthropy, can gratify the human mind, you must have the pleasing consolation to know that you have not lived in vain. And I flatter myself that it will not be ranked among the least grateful occurrences of your life to be assured that, so long as I retain my memory, you will be recollected with respect, veneration, and affection by your sincere friend,

George Washington

FROM THE CODICIL TO FRANKLIN'S LAST WILL AND TESTAMENT

I, Benjamin Franklin, in the foregoing or annexed last will and testament named, having further considered the same, do think proper to make and publish the following codicil or addition thereto.

It having long been a fixed political opinion of mine, that in a democratical state there ought to be no offices of profit, for the reasons I had given in an article of my drawing in our constitution, it was my intention when I accepted the office of President [of Pennsylvania], to devote the appointed salary to some public uses. Accordingly, I had already, before I made my will in July last, given large sums of it to colleges, schools, building of churches, etc....

I was born in Boston, New England, and owe my first instructions in literature to the free grammar-schools established there. I have, therefore, already considered these schools in my will. But I am also under obligations to the State of Massachusetts for having, unasked, appointed me formerly their agent in England, with a handsome salary, which continued some years; and although I accidentally lost in their service, by transmitting Governor Hutchinson's letters, much more than the amount of what they gave me, I do not think that ought in the least to diminish my gratitude.

I have considered that, among artisans, good apprentices are most likely to make good citizens, and, having myself been bred to a manual art, printing, in my native town, and afterwards assisted to set up my business in Philadelphia by kind loans of money from two friends there, which was the foundation of my fortune, and of all the utility in life that may be ascribed to me, I wish to be useful even after my death, if possible, in forming and advancing other young men, that may be serviceable to their country in both these towns. To this end, I devote two thousand pounds sterling, of which I give one thousand thereof to the inhabitants of the town of Boston, in Massachusetts, and the other thousand to the inhabitants of the city of Philadelphia, in trust, to and for the uses, intents, and purposes hereinafter mentioned and declared.

Several decades after Franklin's death and the execution of his will for benefitting his two homes cities, Boston and Philadelphia, Boston was in its prime as a maritime center. Painting by Robert Salmon. *(U. S. Naval Academy Museum.)*

The said sum of one thousand pounds sterling, if accepted by the inhabitants of the town of Boston, shall be managed under the direction of the selectmen, united with the ministers of the oldest Episcopalian, Congregational, and Presbyterian churches in that town, who are to let out the sum upon interest, at five per cent per annum, to such young married artificers, under the age of twenty-five years, as have served an apprenticeship in the said town, and faithfully fulfilled the duties required in their indentures, so as to obtain a good moral character from at least two respectable citizens, who are willing to become their sureties, in a bond with the applicants, for the repayment of the moneys so lent, with interest. . . .

If this plan is executed, and succeeds as projected without interruption for one hundred years, the sum will then be one hundred and thirty-one thousand pounds; of which I would have the managers of the donation to the town of Boston then lay out, at their discretion, one hundred thousand pounds in public works, which may be judged of most general utility to the inhabitants, such as fortifications, bridges, aqueducts, public buildings, baths, pavements, or whatever may make living in the town more convenient to its people, and render it more agreeable to strangers resorting thither for health or a temporary residence. The remaining thirty-one thousand pounds I would have continued to be let out on interest, in the manner above directed, for another hundred years, as I hope it will have been found that the institution has had a good effect on the conduct of youth, and been of service to many worthy characters and useful citizens.

All the directions herein given, respecting the disposition and management of the donation to the inhabitants of Boston, I would have observed respecting that to the inhabitants of Philadelphia. . . .

Considering the accidents to which all human affairs and projects are subject in such a length of time, I have, perhaps, too much flattered myself with a vain fancy that these dispositions, if carried into execution, will be con-

tinued without interruption and have the effects proposed. I hope, however, that if the inhabitants of the two cities should not think fit to undertake the execution, they will, at least, accept the offer of these donations as a mark of my good will, a token of my gratitude, and a testimony of my earnest desire to be useful to them after my departure. . . .

I wish to be buried by the side of my wife, if it may be, and that a marble stone, to be made by Chambers, six feet long, four feet wide, plain, with only a small moulding round the upper edge, and this inscription:

Benjamin
And   Franklin
Deborah
178-

to be placed over us both. My fine crab-tree walking-stick, with a gold head curiously wrought in the form of the cap of liberty, I give to my friend, and the friend of mankind, *General Washington*. If it were a Sceptre, he has merited it, and would become it. . . .

The epitaph Franklin composed in 1728 (version at Yale)

The Body of
B. Franklin,
Printer;
Like the Cover of an old Book,
Its Contents torn out,
And stript of its Lettering and Gilding,
Lies here, Food for Worms.
But the Work shall not be wholly lost;
For it will, as he believed, appear once more,
In a new and more perfect Edition,
Corrected and amended
By the Author.
He was born Jan. 6, 1706.
Died   17-

CHRONOLOGY

Franklin's Life and Events in His Time

FRANKLIN		OTHER EVENTS
Benjamin Franklin born Jan. 17 (Jan.6 Old Style) in Boston to Josiah & Abiah Folger Franklin	1706	
	1713	Treaty of Utrecht, French cede Newfoundland, Acadia & Hudson Bay to British
Attends school for two years	1714	George I of England, reigns 1714-27
	1715	King Louis XIV of France, the "Sun King" dies; Louis XV, reigns 1715-24
Apprenticed to brother James, printer — writes several popular ballads — practices prose writing	1718	New Orleans founded by French — William Penn, founder of Pennsylvania, dies in England
	1721	James Franklin publishes first *New England Courant*
Letters of Silence Dogwood printed in *Courant*	1722	Samuel Adams born in Massachusetts
Runs away to Philadelphia	1723	
Travels to London at instigation of Governor William Keith	1724	
Returns to Philadelphia, keeps Journal of Voyage from London to Philadelphia	1726	Jonathan Edwards & George Whitefield lead Great Awakening in New England, a series of religious revivals, ca. 1725-1770
Forms Junto, club of mutual improvement	1727	George II of England, reigns 1727-60
Starts own printing business with partner	1728	John Bartram establishes first botanical garden in colonies at Philadelphia
Begins publishing *The Pennsylvania Gazette*	1729	
Enters common-law marriage with Deborah Reed Rogers, September 1	1730	
Initiates Library Company of Philadelphia — William Franklin, son, born (?)	1731	
Poor Richard's Almanack published 1732-57 — son, Francis Folger Franklin born — backs establishment of the *South Carolina Gazette*	1732	George Washington born in Virginia — first public almshouse established in the colonies, Philadelphia
	1733	Georgia founded — Molasses Act restricts colonial trade
	1735	John Peter Zenger, tried for libel for publishing criticism of New York government, acquitted — John Adams born in Massachusetts
Son Francis dies — forms Union Fire Company, first company in North America — holds first public office, clerk of General Assembly	1736	Patrick Henry born in Virginia
Appointed deputy postmaster at Philadelphia	1737	Thomas Paine born in Norfolk, England
	1738	Colonial scientist, second to Franklin, John Winthrop begins 41 years of teaching at Harvard — John Singleton Copley, greatest colonial artist, born in Boston
	1740	War of the Austrian Succession, 1740-48
Devises Pennsylvania Fireplace (later called Franklin stove)	1742	
Proposes plan for The American Philosophical Society — daughter Sarah born	1743	Thomas Jefferson born in Virginia — American phase of King George's War (Austrian Succession), 1743-48
	1744	Western movement of Pennsylvanians & Virginians, 1744-54, to Ohio Valley
	1745	John Jay born in New York City
Begins work on electricity	1746	
Proposes Plan for Education of Youth of Pennsylvania (opened as Philadelphia Academy in 1751)	1749	
	1750	Ohio Company sends surveyors to Ohio Valley

FRANKLIN

FRANKLIN		OTHER EVENTS
Assists in founding Pennsylvania Hospital — *Experiments & Observations on Electricity* published	1751	James Madison born in Virginia — John Bartram's *Observations on American Plants* published
Kite experiments	1752	
Appointed joint Deputy Postmaster General of North America with William Hunter	1753	
Proposes Plan of Union at Albany Conference	1754	French & Indian War begins, 1754-63
Assists Braddock with provisions & funds	1755	British General Braddock sent to defend colonial frontiers against French & Indians with Lt. Col. Washington at head of colonial troops; defeated at Fort Duquesne
Leads Philadelphia volunteers to Western frontier of Pennsylvania to build forts — elected to Royal Society of England — receives honorary Master of Arts from William & Mary College	1756	Seven Years' War in Europe involving all major powers, 1756-63
Sent to London by Pennsylvania Assembly to negotiate with proprietors (Penns) and crown — resumes scientific experiments	1757	
Visits ancestral home in Ecton, Northamptonshire — his *Way to Wealth* published	1758	James Monroe born in Virginia
Receives honorary doctorate from University of St. Andrews — journeys in Scotland & England	1759	General Wolfe (British) defeats General Montcalm (French) at Quebec
Obtains Penns' assent to let their estates be taxed — William Temple Franklin, grandson, born	1760	George III of England, reigns 1760-1820 — surrender of Canada to British — 13 colonies' population estimated at 1,600,000
Travels to Holland and Belgium	1761	James Otis, in Massachusetts, argues in court against Writs of Assistance, basing his opposition on English common law
Receives honorary Doctor of Civil Law degree from Oxford University — departs to America	1762	William Franklin appointed Governor of New Jersey
Organizes defense of Philadelphia against Paxton Boys' threat	1763	Pontiac's (Ottawa Indian chief) Rebellion against British westward expansion — Paxton Boys' march — Treaty of Paris ends west European & colonial phases of Seven Years' War
Returns to London as Pennsylvania's agent, with petition to George III for royal rather than proprietary rule	1764	Sugar Act — Currency Act — committee of correspondence formed in Massachusetts against taxation without representation — non-importation by several colonies
Writes satires & essays against Stamp Act for London newspapers	1765	Quartering Act — Stamp Act — ad hoc Sons of Liberty groups springing up in colonies
Examination before House of Commons on Stamp Act — visits Germany	1766	Stamp Act repealed — Lord Chatham Ministry, 1766-67
Visits France, received by Louis XV	1767	Townshend Acts — revival of non-importation — John Dickinson of Pennsylvania writes *Farmer's Letters* against Townshend duties — Grafton Ministry, 1767-70 — Daniel Boone explores Kentucky
Appointed agent (representative to London government) for Georgia	1768	Massachusetts House passes Circular Letter to other colonies denouncing recent acts
Named New Jersey's agent	1769	Members of Virginia House of Burgesses form Virginia Association to ban importation of British goods on which duty is charged — Napoleon born in Corsica
Named agent for Massachusetts — becoming non-official spokesman for all colonies	1770	Boston Massacre — Lord North Ministry, 1770-82 (Whig opposition forms in Parliament)
Tours northwestern England — begins *Autobiography* — visits Ireland and Scotland	1771	
Sends "Hutchinson Letters" to Thomas Cushing in Boston for private use of patriots	1772	
	1773	Samuel Adams reads Hutchinson Letters to the Massachusetts House; it petitions for removal of Governor Hutchinson et al. — Tea Act; Boston Tea Party

FRANKLIN		OTHER EVENTS
Summoned to appear before Lords Committee on Plantation Affairs — dismissed from office in postal service — resigns his agencies — Deborah Franklin dies	1774	Further disorders in Boston over tea — Parliament passes Coercive (Punitive) Acts — first Continental Congress — Louis XVI of France, reigns 1774-92 — war preparations in New England — Thomas Paine comes to America from England, sponsored by Franklin
Secret negotiations with agents of North Ministry on reconciliation — returns to America — elected to second Continental Congress — appointed first Postmaster General, 1775-76	1775	Battles of Lexington, Concord, Bunker Hill — second Continental Congress — Silas Deane secretly sent to seek French alliance — Patrick Henry delivers "Give me liberty or give me death speech" in Virginia — Edmund Burke delivers "Speech on Conciliation with America" in House of Commons — Daniel Boone takes first settlers to Kentucky
Assists in draft of & signs Declaration of Independence — Franklin, Arthur Lee & Silas Deane named commissioners to France — sails for France	1776	Thomas Paine publishes *Common Sense* — British evacuate Boston, then occupy New York City
Received in French court — meets Madame Brillon	1777	Stars & Stripes flag adopted — Articles of Confederation — Battle of Saratoga — winter at Valley Forge — France recognizes U.S. independence
Commissioners secure French alliance in commerce & assistance — John Adams arrives in France to assist in any peace negotiations	1778	English attempt to forestall French-American alliance with reconciliation proposal — John Paul Jones makes raids aboard the *Ranger* — Captain James Cook discovers Sandwich Islands (Hawaii), explores Pacific coast from Oregon northward — French writers & philosophers Jean Jacques Rousseau & Voltaire die
Named Minister Plenipotentiary to French court (Deane & Lee recalled)	1779	Spain enters war against England — Congress begins considering peace terms — John Paul Jones' *Bonhomme Richard* defeats *Serapis* off coast of Scotland — George Rogers Clark conquers Old Northwest with capture of Vincennes
Proposes marriage to Madame Helvetius & is rejected	1780	Russia forms League of Armed Neutrality to protect trade — inflation in America
Submits resignation to Congress, which rejects it & appoints him to peace commission	1781	Pennsylvania troops mutiny — Congress appoints John Jay, Henry Laurens, Thomas Jefferson, to join John Adams as peace commissioners — Pueblo de Los Angeles founded in California
Adams, Jay & Franklin sign preliminary peace treaty with England	1782	British surrender at Yorktown — Rockingham and Shelburne Ministries
Signs final peace treaty with England — France & England sign peace	1783	British evacuate New York City — American army disbands without authority — Congress flees Philadelphia — first hot-air balloon ascensions in France — Noah Webster's *Spelling Book* published
Invents bifocals	1784	Jay named Secretary of Foreign Affairs
Sails for America — chosen President of Pennsylvania	1785	Jefferson appointed minister to France, Adams to England
	1786	Shay's Rebellion in Massachusetts over high cost of justice, tax system & lack of issuance of paper money
Attends Constitutional Convention in Philadelphia — elected honorary member of Medical Society of London	1787	Constitutional Convention — Northwest Ordinance passed by convention for government north of Ohio River — states begin ratifying Constitution
Elected President of Pennsylvania Society for Promoting the Abolition of Slavery	1788	Constitution ratified
	1789	Washington & Adams inaugurated — French Revolution begins with storming of Bastille
Benjamin Franklin dies in Philadelphia April 17	1790	Alexander Hamilton's First Report on the Public Credit — first U.S. census: 3,929,214 — first copyright law enacted — Jefferson becomes Secretary of State